C000147311

Resolving Business Disputes

How to get better outcomes from commercial conflicts

Stephen Bate

Published June 2020

by
Spiramus Press Ltd,
102 Blandford Street
London W1U 8AG
Telephone +44 20 7224 0080
www.spiramus.com

© Stephen Bate, 2020

ISBN
Paperback   9781913507008

Digital   9781913507015

British Library Cataloguing-in-Publication Data.
A catalogue record for this book is available from the British Library.

All rights reserved. No part of this publication may be reproduced in any material form (including photocopying or storing it in any medium by electronic means and whether or not transiently or incidental to some other use of this publication) without the prior written permission of the copyright owner except in accordance with the provisions of the Copyright, Designs and Patents Act 1988 or under the terms of a licence issued by the Copyright Licensing Agency Ltd, 5th Floor, Shackleton House 4 Battle Bridge Lane London SE1 2HX.

The right of Stephen Bate to be identified as the author of this work has been asserted by him in accordance with the Copyright, Designs and Patents Act, 1988.

Disclaimer: This publication is intended to assist you in identifying issues which you should know about and about which you may need to seek specific advice. It is not intended to be relied on as legal advice, nor is it a substitute for seeking specific advice, and it does not contain exhaustive statements of the law.

Printed and bound by Grosvenor Press, Loughton, Essex

'We may try to see things as objectively as we please. None the less we can never see them with any eyes except our own'

Justice Benjamin N. Cardozo, The Nature of the Judicial Process

Preface

Business disputes cost time, money and often endanger commercial relationships, or end them. This book is a guide to resolving those disputes. To get the best outcomes, businesses need to make sound decisions, make the best use of advice from lawyers and see that effective action is taken.

This guide should also be of interest to lawyers and others concerned with dispute resolution, such as litigation funders and insurers. Its roots lie in my experiences and observations in dispute resolution over many years, as a barrister, mediator and arbitrator.

References to relevant law are as at 17 February 2020. There is mention of later legal developments, including changes brought about by Covid-19. The book has been updated in other respects as a result of the pandemic.

The Government's *Guidance on responsible contractual behaviour in the performance and enforcement of contracts* issued on 7 May 2020 has urged parties to engage in 'responsible and fair performance and enforcement of contracts' impacted by Covid-19. Lord Neuberger and Lord Phillips, former heads of the Supreme Court, have been among those arguing for the creation of a legal 'breathing space' to enable viable contracts to continue: see *Breathing Space – a Concept Note on the effect of the pandemic on commercial contracts*, British Institute of International and Comparative Law, 27 April 2020. The law in this area may well develop, but there is a risk of a deluge of claims on the court system, all adding to the outcome uncertainty of disputes resulting from the pandemic.

In the near term at least, the interruption of commercial contracts by Covid-19 will make the search for a negotiated outcome paramount in very many cases. However, some disputes arising from the pandemic will still have to go to court.

I am indebted to several people for their help in this venture. The late Sir Brian Neill, former Appeal Court judge, provided invaluable suggestions, thoughts and also encouragement to write in a style for non-lawyers. The reader will judge whether the book meets that standard.

I thank Marcus Croskell, barrister, for his help in editing parts of the book that deal with litigation and legal costs in particular. I am grateful to Judge Jones of the Insolvency and Companies Court for his thoughts and suggestions on Chapter 2 (rights and remedies). For their thoughts on data analytics in case outcome prediction, thank you to Alexander Oddy, dispute resolution partner at Herbert Smith Freehills and to Edward Bird, Managing Director of Solmonic. For reviewing and commenting on Chapter 4, 'Who will win?', I am grateful to Sir David Foskett, former High Court judge and now mediator and arbitrator. Thank you to Tony Allen, mediator, for reviewing Chapter 7 (negotiation) and to Tony and James South of CEDR for allowing me to use written pieces on mediation.

For their reviews of and suggestions for Chapter 8 (dispute strategy), thank you to Tim Hardy, ex-head of Commercial Litigation at CMS and now mediator and arbitrator and to Zoe Adlam, General Counsel and Company Secretary of XPS Group. Thank you also to Tim and Jonathan Barnes, barrister, for each reviewing Chapter 9 (decision-making) and to Jonathan for his review of some previous chapters too.

I am also grateful to Daniel Priestley, CEO of Dent Global for the idea that I might have a book worth writing. Apparently, that is true of many!

A special thanks to Fiona, my wife and business psychologist, for her patience, encouragement, ideas and reading suggestions in the field of psychology.

I am grateful to Carl Upsall at Spiramus Press for his help and flexibility in getting this book published at a time when the Covid-19 virus has upended the lives of so many.

The pandemic has highlighted the often under-estimated importance of decision-making. I hope that this book will shed further light on how to make decisions to resolve business disputes and also help readers to obtain better dispute outcomes for their businesses and clients.

Stephen Bate, 15 May 2020

Preface v

INTRODUCTION 1

1.   BUSINESS DISPUTES – THE PROBLEM EXPLAINED 5

2.   THE LAW: RIGHTS AND REMEDIES 11
   2.1.   Rights 11
      2.1.1.   Sources of rights and duties 12
      2.1.2.   Contract disputes (1) 16
      2.1.3.   Contract disputes (2) – the pandemic 20
   2.2.   Remedies 21
      2.2.1.   Order for the payment of money 21
      2.2.2.   Injunction 22
      2.2.3.   Declaration 23
      2.2.4.   Remedies: further questions 23

3.   BINDING DECISIONS 24
   3.1.   Introduction 24
   3.2.   Litigation: court proceedings 24
   3.3.   Non-payment; is there a dispute at all? 31
      3.3.1.   Insolvency 31
      3.3.2.   The debtor who knows payment is due but refuses to pay 33
   3.4.   Other types of binding decision 33
      3.4.1.   Introduction 33
      3.4.2.   Arbitration 34
      3.4.3.   Expert determination 36
      3.4.4.   Adjudication 37
      3.4.5.   Financial Ombudsman 37
   3.5.   Litigation, arbitration and expert determination compared 38

4.   WHO WILL WIN? 40
   4.1.   Introduction 40
   4.2.   Finding the facts 40
      4.2.1.   The factual dispute: the problem of two worlds 41
      4.2.2.   Witnesses: perception, bias and memory 43
   4.3.   Forecasting: advice on the litigation outcome 51
      4.3.1.   What is an advice on the merits? 51
      4.3.2.   Key aspects of an advice on the merits 52
      4.3.3.   Probability of success 54
      4.3.4.   Underlying assumptions and information 56
      4.3.5.   Decision trees 59
      4.3.6.   Outcome prediction software 61
      4.3.7.   Bias and litigation forecasting 62

CONTENTS

4.3.8. *Limitations on outcome predictions; some data and further* *considerations* 64

4.3.9. *Best use of forecasting* 67

4.3.10. *Covid-19 and further outcome uncertainties* 69

4.4. The Trial: Judicial Decision-Making and the Trial Outcome 70

4.4.1. *The jigsaw of facts* 70

4.4.2. *Legal principle, the overall merits and 'dirty dogs'* 72

4.5. Conclusion 76

5. **LAWYERS, THEIR FEES AND LEGAL COSTS** 77

5.1. Introduction 77

5.2. Funding your own costs 77

5.2.1. *Payment on the usual basis* 78

5.2.2. *Conditional Fee Agreements (CFAs)* 81

5.2.3. *Third party funding (TPF)* 83

5.2.4. *Damages-based agreements (DBAs)* 84

5.2.5. *Insurance* 85

5.2.6. *Settlement offers under CFA, TPF and ATE arrangements* 85

5.3. Costs-shifting orders 86

5.3.1. *When is a cost-shifting order made; and for how much?* 86

5.3.2. *Further considerations* 89

5.4. 'Insuring' legal costs exposure through court processes 91

5.4.1. *Introduction* 91

5.4.2. *Part 36 Offers* 91

5.4.3. *Security for costs* 94

5.5. Comparison with arbitration and expert determination 95

6. **SETTLEMENT** 97

6.1. Introduction 97

6.2. What disputes and claims are being settled? 97

6.3. Further legal requirements 98

6.4. Settlement and broader commercial terms 99

6.5. Payment terms 100

6.6. Confidentiality and agreed statements 100

6.7. Dispute resolution procedures 101

6.8. International elements 101

6.9. Settlement during legal action 102

6.10. Rights under the settlement agreement 102

6.11. Settlement and uncertainty 103

6.12. Routes to settlement 104

6.12.1. *Introduction* 104

6.12.2. *Dispute resolution clauses* 104

6.12.3.   Part 36 Offers and Calderbank Offers 104
6.12.4.   Negotiation...105
6.12.5.   Mediation 106
6.12.6.   Early neutral evaluation 109
6.12.7.   Financial Dispute Resolution 111
6.12.8.   Dispute Boards 111
6.12.9.   Mediation-Arbitration (Med-Arb)...........................111

7.   NEGOTIATIONS 113
7.1.   Introduction 113
7.2.   The Negotiations 113
7.2.1.   Preparation..114
7.2.2.   Conduct of negotiations 120
7.2.3.   The end of negotiations?..131
7.3.   Mediation: advantages 132
7.4.   Conduct of the mediation 133
7.5.   Conclusion 135

8.   OBJECTIVES AND STRATEGY 136
8.1.   Objectives..136
8.2.   Dispute strategy 137
8.2.1.   The commercial strategy 137
8.2.2.   The legal strategy..144
8.3.   The role of lawyers...151
8.4.   Covid-19 – Considerations 152

9.   MAKING THE DECISION 155
9.1.   Uncertainties...155
9.2.   Identifying and balancing the considerations 157
9.3.   Decision frames, biases and other behaviours 158
9.4.   Making the decision 161
9.5.   Conclusion...162

Appendix 1 – LITIGATION 163
1.   Introduction and pre-litigation procedures....................163
2.   The start of litigation and up to trial 165
Statements of case...166
An early end to the case?..167
Interim remedies..169
Case allocation..171
Disclosure of documents 172
Case management directions...173
Court support for ADR..173

CONTENTS

Witness statements..174
Expert evidence 176
The lead-up to trial...177
3.   Trial 177
4.   Appeals, enforcement and assessment of costs.....................181
Enforcement 182
Costs assessment...182
Appeals...182
5.   Other courts and trial schemes...184
The Shorter and Flexible Trials Schemes..................................184
Intellectual Property Enterprise Court 185
6.   The without prejudice rule and other forms of privilege........185

APPENDIX 2 – COMPARISONS: LITIGATION, ARBITRATION AND EXPERT DETERMINATION **187**
1.   Litigation and arbitration compared.....................................187
2.   Litigation and arbitration compared to expert determination 192

Reading list **195**

Index..**200**

RESOLVING BUSINESS DISPUTES

INTRODUCTION

This book is a guide to help those in trade and commerce to make better choices about resolving business disputes. Those choices are are often many, complex and change over time. The book also explains how to get the best outcome from a business dispute. The disputes it covers are mainly those between businesses, and not consumer disputes.

The aim is to provide the reader with a broad overview of the landscape of a commercial dispute, to explain the more important considerations at play and how to make the best decisions for the business to resolve it, in consultation with lawyers. This guide is also designed to assist awyers, litigation funders and insurers, particularly those parts of it concerned with outcome forecasting, strategy, negotiation and decision-making. The book is not intended as a manual for a business to "go it alone" in litigation or other dispute resolution processes.

In view of the profound implications of Covid-19 for business dispute resolution, an introduction to particular issues raised by the pandemic has been added at various stages in the book. This mainly relates to disputes over contracts.

Chapter 1 considers the unique challenges of commercial disputes. They rarely have an upside, creating risk that has to be managed. This opening chapter explains the more important challenges and introduces the issues for effective decision-making both to contain and resolve the dispute.

The next two chapters give a summary overview of aspects of English law relating to business disputes. Core features of the legal landscape are explained.

INTRODUCTION

Chapter 2 explains the main types of legal rights, such as contractual and property rights.[1] It also addresses 'remedies', such as court orders for the payment of money. The chapter makes particular reference to the law of contract that underlies so many disputes. Chapter 3 deals with the basic steps in taking a case to court and an overview of the process of litigation. It explains how that resembles boarding a train stopping at various stations before the terminus, the various steps in the litigation culminating in a court trial. How there are various branch lines that can bring the case to an early end or require a return to the main line, e.g. after an application for an interim injunction; and other stages, such as appeals and enforcement.

Litigation is not the only pathway to a binding decision. The chapter also looks at arbitration and expert determination in particular. All three methods are compared and contrasted. For ease, more details are placed in two Appendices at the end of the book.

Every litigant wants to know whether they are likely to win or lose their case. Chapter 4 is entitled 'Who will win?' It looks at how judicial decisions are made. It considers the key role of 'fact-finding' by judges (i.e. their decision as between the rival versions of the events in a dispute), how a judge decides which version prevails, and the importance of the 'optics' of a dispute, i.e. the broad justice of the case and its relevance to the outcome. The chapter also examines the value and limitations of legal advice on the merits of a case. It discusses the challenges for lawyers in assessing the strength of a case – why the perceptions of parties and their lawyers may be wrong or require re-thinking. These include various biases. This chapter considers the different ways in which lawyers express advice on the merits of a case and the importance of the

---

[1] Public law disputes (between a state or public body and a commercial entity) are outside the scope of the book. But parts of the book are relevant to those disputes, particularly in Chapters 7-9.

assumptions and information behind the advice. In addition, there is often a difference in the usefulness of advice before and after legal proceedings have begun. Further information from the other side's documents and evidence will become available as the case progresses.

Legal costs are a key consideration. Lawyers will generally have to be paid if engaged. If a case is fought to the end, the loser usually has to pay most of the winner's legal costs ('costs-shifting'). The train passenger may want to stop the litigation and get off the train before trial. But, if so, the litigant must generally pay most of the other side's legal costs, unless a deal is done with them. Litigation can resemble a game of poker. Each player has to keep betting money to stay in the game as the case progresses, with lawyers' bills to be paid regularly, until the final outcome is known at trial when the judge makes a decision.

Therefore, Chapter 5 looks at the various ways of funding legal costs and the basics of costs-shifting. Funding includes arrangements where litigation risk associated with legal costs is taken on by the lawyers or third-party funders. The chapter also considers how parties using a legal process can secure a degree of protection in relation to legal costs through court procedures (e.g. 'Part 36 Offers' and 'security for costs').

The next two chapters look at ending the dispute by negotiation ('settlement'). This may be without legal proceedings or once they have begun. So, Chapter 6 looks at settlement in more detail. How do you settle a dispute and what does that mean in law? The chapter considers the various ways of obtaining a settlement, particularly by negotiation and mediation.

To have the best chance of a good settlement deal, you must negotiate effectively. Many people believe they are good negotiators, because they are tough. As we have seen with Brexit, making a series of demands does not get you very far. So, Chapter 7 examines effective negotiation for getting the best settlement.

By this stage of the book, the reader has been informed of the various ways in which a business dispute can be resolved. He or she now has an understanding of the advantages, disadvantages and opportunities that may be available. This leads to the need for a strategy to secure the best outcome. Chapter 8 looks at dispute strategy and the objectives on which the strategy is based. It also examines how a strategy should be structured, with regular reviews as a legal case proceeds.

Finally, Chapter 9 draws together the threads from previous chapters so that decision-makers can make the best choices for resolving the dispute: factors to be kept in mind when deciding whether to fight, or to continue to fight, the dispute or to settle it, and how to weigh and balance these considerations to deliver the best outcome.

1. BUSINESS DISPUTES – THE PROBLEM EXPLAINED

Business disputes take many forms. They all create uncertainty and risk. Nearly all are about money in one way or another. A trader may be owed for goods sold or services rendered. A customer may be disappointed because the goods or services supplied were not as agreed. Renewal of a commercial lease may be in issue. An ex-employee may be working with a competitor of his former employer, despite a clause in the contract that forbids this. Or a contract may not be fulfilled due to supply chain issues caused by the pandemic.

Whatever the details, a business dispute sets unique challenges for decision-makers. Unless the dispute is settled quickly, they must decide whether to pursue or defend a legal claim; whether to make further attempts at a negotiated way-out, and if so, on what terms.

The risks presented by the dispute must be identified and managed. There is potential financial exposure from the transaction that has gone wrong. A contract that has not been performed by the counterparty requires an analysis of the available courses of action to minimise losses and manage risk, e.g. continuing with a contract or terminating it. Ultimately, should the business take on the cost of bringing a case to court but also the risk of losing it?

The difficulties may be more than financial. Pursuit of the claim may endanger customer relationships, the reputation of the business or both. If there are other similar contracts, there may be a temptation to take the case to court so other contracting partners do not think you are a 'soft touch'. There may be other implications; having staff tied up dealing with the legal case, so they are less available for other work. Or the dispute may be part of a long-term contract. There may be a risk of the dispute spilling over and endangering vital relationships, with damage to the project itself.

Businesses are constantly called on to place a likely value on commercial opportunities and to decide whether or not to exploit them, e.g. by buying products for re-sale, spending money on marketing or entering into a contract at a particular price. These are transactions with a potential commercial upside, where the price is worth paying to improve the business.

But what price is worth paying to resolve a business dispute? If a business is owed money, there is usually no incentive to settle for much below what is owed. As for going to court, even if the case were won, there will have been delay, irrecoverable legal costs and a waste of resources in dealing with the case. All in all, commercial disputes rarely have an upside.

Likewise, if a business considers that money is not due, there is little reason to volunteer payment of anything near what is claimed if the contract work has not been carried out to the required standard. But the prospect of a legal claim means that the business will either waste money if payment is made or be left with a liability hanging over it that may result in an adverse court judgment and a hefty bill for legal costs.

The loser in a typical legal case generally has to bear its own legal costs and pay around two-thirds of the other side's costs. That is because of 'costs-shifting' rules. These are generally a key consideration in the process of dispute resolution.

So what to do? Some disputes can be sorted out promptly by a phone call, an exchange of emails or the like. Others may result in some give-and-take, extending delivery dates under a contract or even changing some of the other terms of the contract. But in more difficult disputes, it is often necessary to grasp the practical implications of using the law to end a dispute.

If there is no real dispute, but the debtor is withholding payment for tactical reasons or because it has no money, that may dictate one set of legal procedures (see Chapter 3).

Genuine disputes, however, are usually driven by rival versions of events. One side says the facts of the dispute were 'x' and the other that they were 'y'. These competing 'stories' would be played out in court by the evidence given for each party. Generally, they determine the trial outcome, the judge preferring one side's version of events on the important parts of the case. That side usually wins the case, as explained later in the book.

The brew is made more toxic because financial interests are at stake. One side says that it is being kept out of its money, but the other side disagrees. Each considers the other to be in the wrong. In stark terms, 'Why should I pay you when you have not done what you promised?' Or, 'The work has been done and you must pay for it.' It has been said that parties in dispute have four needs when the dispute occurs: vindication, revenge, humiliation and retribution.[1]

If lawyers are instructed, letters are drafted that widen the gap between the parties, reinforcing each side's story and adding legal argument to it. Law is cited to show that either the case will plainly succeed or fail in court, as may be. Even if attempts are made to settle the dispute at this stage, as often happens, the climate for a negotiated outcome may be unfavourable; a party not wishing to settle when the dispute is so raw. A settlement offer may be made and rejected. But a deal might have been done, had there been a greater objectivity and understanding of the commercial realities of the dispute.

Legal advice may be given about the chances of winning the case. But how useful is the advice at the early stages of a dispute when all the facts and evidence are not available? How much more information is required and what will that cost?

If the business has a disputed claim for £1 million say, what is the value of the claim? It is probably less than £1 million. How much

---

[1] Randolph (2015).

less? Various factors must be borne in mind. These include the chances of success in court and the effect of legal costs, but there are generally other considerations too. From the debtor's viewpoint, how should this potential liability be calculated, with the added implications of legal costs and other downsides of the legal process?

Decisions have to be taken, whether to start or to defend legal proceedings or other forms of process. Once taken, decisions have to be reviewed. The decision-makers must also decide whether or not to negotiate and if so, how, and what terms to offer. If negotiations would be premature, when should they start?

Settlement of disputes now has a central importance in the landscape of civil litigation. The legal process requires parties to go to court as a last resort. The legal process is not just akin to a train journey, but it can seem like a runaway train. And the train may have to be boarded to get the other side to listen and engage with you. If one side has boarded, the other may think it has no choice but to get on as well, to avoid a court judgment.

Legal action may fail to produce a satisfactory outcome. A case is lost or the result is a draw or some other messy outcome neither side wants. If the case is won, success may be at an unsatisfactory price. The winner has had to bear the costs of using lawyers and limits on costs-shifting in a typical case mean that around one third of those legal costs are not recoverable from the loser.

If a settlement is reached after a legal case has started but before trial, the result may be a negative for both sides. The deal may be bad for both, but the outcome potentially even worse for them, had they gone all the way to trial. Legal costs can also make it impossible to settle the dispute. By the time real dialogue happens, each side has incurred substantial costs and one side does not want to bear its own costs, the other side's costs and pay money to settle the actual dispute as well. In the past few years, there have been many judicial comments about the often disproportionate cost of litigation.

The advantages of a negotiated settlement on the right terms are obvious: money is recovered or the exposure to claims is limited to an acceptable level. Time and money are saved. Control of the dispute is given back to the parties and the risk is contained. Most disputes are resolved by agreement during or before the process of litigation, sometimes involving mediation with a neutral. The best strategy to resolve a dispute is often a combination of fighting the claim or case and attempting to settle it at the *appropriate point in time*. Even that is not a risk-free strategy. The other side may not want to settle on your terms. What other steps can be taken to control the risk?

The virtues of settlement are many, yet there are cases where commercial interests are best served by going to court. Settlement terms offered may be inadequate or a point of principle may have to be established.

In summary, the advantages of litigation may include:
- resolution of the dispute by an independent and impartial third party, the court;
- the court's decision is binding on the other party, subject to appeal;
- for the winner, obtaining a court order that the other side pays most of its legal costs;
- a public judgment may vindicate the winner, establish property rights (e.g. a patent) or an important contractual precedent;
- a claimant may obtain a judgment for a sum of money higher than that achievable by negotiation;
- a defendant may establish that it is not liable at all or that its liability and exposure to legal costs is less than any settlement figure achievable by negotiation.

The disadvantages of litigation may include some or many of the following:

- losing the case; if a claimant, not getting what you claimed (e.g. money) and being ordered to pay the winner's legal costs; if a defendant, having to pay what you disputed plus most of the winner's legal costs and bearing your own legal costs;
- if you lose – having forfeited whatever settlement offer was or might have been on the table, plus legal costs (your own and most of the winner's);
- if the winner, time and money diverted to the court process and ending up with a net loss because court rules prevent recovery of 100% of the legal costs incurred;
- possibility of a messy draw and no-one wins;
- risk of reputational damage from documents filed at court, evidence given in open court or a public judgment if you lose and sometimes if you win;
- in the case of property rights or contractual precedents, the adverse effects of a public judgment if you lose;
- win or lose, the opportunity cost of directors/employees being tied up in the case;
- funding the litigation up to trial with possible implications for cashflow (unless alternative funding arrangements have been made);
- if the winner, having to enforce the judgment against the other side's assets, assuming they are still solvent;
- if the winner, the risk of losing on appeal.

But the crucial question is: to fight the dispute or to do a deal? To understand the implications of that question, a basic understanding is required of using court and other processes to obtain a legally binding decision and the implications of doing so. The next two chapters address this, and Chapter 5.

2.   THE LAW: RIGHTS AND REMEDIES

2.1.   Rights

The English civil law operates by recognising certain rights and also duties enforceable by legal action. Apart from EU laws,[1] these come from statute and subsidiary legislation and also non-statutory principles at common law and in 'equity'.[2] A commercial transaction may involve a system of law other than English law. The discussion in this chapter does not address other laws.

The English law concerning rights and duties has been developed through cases decided by judges over many years. The body of case law constitutes 'precedent'. The basic rule is that the principles in the case law are binding on decision-making courts. The rules of precedent lie outside this book.

Rights and duties are enforceable by 'causes of action'. Civil rights in the commercial field take many forms. The main areas relate to contracts, property (particularly land and intellectual property), trusts, statutory rights and a range of civil wrongs or 'torts' such as negligence.

To establish a claim, a litigant must establish various facts. The basic position is well explained in **A Handbook for Litigants in Person:**[3]

> 6.1 To bring proceedings in a civil court, the claimant must have a claim against the defendant that is recognised as being enforceable

---

[1] In view of Brexit, references to EU laws have largely been omitted. However, where applicable, they will be relevant during the transition period at least, currently projected to 31 December 2020.

[2] Equity is a parallel jurisdiction that grew up beside the common law. See Jowitt (2019).

[3] Bailey (2013), p.23.

in law. To be successful in the proceedings the claimant must have a good 'cause of action' against the defendant.

The cause of action is the entire set of facts that gives rise to an enforceable claim.

6.2 .... [T]here must be a claim that is recognised as being enforceable in law. English law recognises a wide variety of claims, but not everything which causes injury, loss or annoyance to another will constitute a valid claim. ...

6.3 The second element is the factual basis of the claim. To take two examples. Where a person breaks an agreement he has with another he may have to pay compensation (damages) to that other person (the innocent party). Or where a person who is under a duty to act with due care fails to do so with the result that another person suffers harm, a claim may be made by the victim of the harm. It is for the claimant to establish all the essential facts that go to make up that valid claim.

In litigation, the party pursuing a claim is known as 'the claimant' and the party against whom it is made, 'the defendant'.[4]

2.1.1. Sources of rights and duties
The following is a summary of the main sources of rights and duties.

Contracts
Contracts are the main source of business disputes, examined in more detail later in the chapter. Even in areas that are legally distinct (see 'Property rights' and following, below), the disputes are often contract-based. Examples are in the areas of companies (articles of association, shareholder agreements), partnerships (partnership agreements) and property (terms of leases and licences). 'Smart contracts' are capable of being legally enforceable. As in the case of

---

[4] In arbitration proceedings, the defendant is known as 'the respondent'.

other contracts, a smart contract will be binding if the legal rules on the formation of contracts are met in any particular case.[5]

Property rights

There are commercial disputes over property. Property capable of legal ownership is not confined to physical things, such as land, buildings or articles of commerce. It includes things that have no physical existence.[6] Examples are goodwill, intellectual property or 'IP', an option to purchase land, a sum in a bank account or a debt.[7] In principle, crypto-assets are property under English law.[8] Where the property is land (and buildings), it is not the property itself that is owned in strict legal terms, but an 'estate' or 'interest' in it, such as a freehold or leasehold. The legal framework for property rights is based on statute, common law and equity.

In the case of physical goods, ownership and possession often go together. But not always. In a contract for the sale of goods, rules regulate when property in the goods passes from buyer to seller.[9] Property may pass to a buyer before the contractual date for delivery. This has practical consequences, not only for insurance but also the rights that may be in dispute.

In addition to ownership, property rights include the right to sell or transfer that ownership, and also the right to chop up ownership into lesser interests and rights. These have particular application in the case of land and IP. Examples are leases of land and licences of IP rights. The terms of the bargain are set out in the lease or licence. There may be disputes over those terms, e.g. about repairing or

---

[5] See Vos & others (2019) [18].
[6] The law divides property rights (note not 'property') into real property and personal property. This distinction is not useful for present purposes.
[7] The right to recover money owed by legal action is itself a type of intangible property, e.g. a debt or damages for breach of contract.
[8] See fn.5, at [15].
[9] Sale of Goods Act 1979, ss 16-26. There are further details for the 'passing of risk'; see e.g. s 20.

insuring covenants in a lease or concerning a licensee's obligation to exploit the licensed IP. There may also be arguments about the terms for a new lease or licence; e.g. the rent or royalties to be paid.

Property ownership generally means that third parties may not use or exploit the property without the licence or consent of the owner. This explains how the owner of a patent, for example, can secure exclusivity over exploitation of an invention. Thus, there are disputes between IP rights owners and those whom they say are infringers.

Trusts

A trust is a legally binding arrangement where property (money, land, etc) is held by one or more persons (the trustee/s) for the benefit of one or more other persons (the beneficiary/ies). In law the trustee must act in the interests of the beneficiaries and according to the terms of the trust. Beneficiaries have rights that are enforceable against trustees. The terms of the trust are usually found in a trust 'deed' or other document. The obligations of a trustee are to be understood from that document, statute law and elsewhere.[10] Trusts have many uses in commerce, including:

- enabling the holding of money as security to protect from an insolvency;
- pension funds;
- collective investment arrangements;
- escrow structures.

Disputes between beneficiaries and trustees may concern how the trust is run or administered, e.g. investment decisions, the upkeep of property or the payment of money. There may be arguments over ownership and distribution of trust property.

---

[10] Trustees owe fiduciary duties to beneficiaries in respect of obligations of their office that are fiduciary in nature.

Statutory rights

Many aspects of commerce are regulated by statutory rights and duties, contained in Acts of Parliament or regulations, rules or other secondary legislation made under statute.[11] Statute law governs the following areas of commerce, for example:

- Companies – the 'Companies Acts', in particular the Companies Act 2006;
- Partnerships – Partnership Act 1890, Limited Liability Partnerships Act 2000;
- Insolvency – Insolvency Act 2006;
- Employment – Employment Rights Act 1996 as amended (unfair dismissal and redundancy).[12]

In areas such as employment, both statutory and common law rights exist. Statutes also affect contracts. For example, the Unfair Contract Terms Act 1977 regulates some clauses that exclude or restrict liability for breach of contract. Statutes are the derivation of most IP rights, e.g. the Patents Act 1977.

Torts and other civil wrongs

The law of tort creates legal duties owed by one person to another. In the commercial sphere, the main examples are claims in negligence for breach of a duty of care. Duties are owed by auditors, surveyors, engineers, architects, lawyers and other professionals. The right of action (where it exists) creates a duty owed not only to the client but also to third parties with whom no contract exists in some (often limited) circumstances. So, it has been decided that auditors of a company owe a duty of care to any person whom they

---

[11] See fn. 1.

[12] Other statutes regulate different employment rights, e.g. those based on discrimination.

ought reasonably have foreseen would rely on them, for example in seeking to take over a company.[13]

Other examples are the wrong of inducing or procuring breach of a contract; for example, a trade competitor poaching staff from a rival business. Misuse of confidential information is another area of disputes.

2.1.2. Contract disputes (1)

There is a contract in English law when two or more parties have reached an agreement, intending to create a legal relationship by doing so, and have each given something of benefit.[14]

Sometimes, there is a dispute about whether a contract exists at all. A contract is made by what lawyers call 'offer and acceptance', i.e. an offer by one party to contract on certain terms, which is accepted by another party. A contract does not have to be written and may be 'oral'.

A contract contains a set of promises or 'obligations' of each contractor. The 'express terms' of the contract are to be found from the actual words used in the agreement. A term may also be 'implied' if not contrary to the express terms of the contract and if further conditions are satisfied. One situation is where the implication is obvious, necessary or both to make the contract work due to a gap in the wording.[15] Another is a duty of good faith, which will be implied into a 'relational contract' (some long-term contracts), again if not contrary to the language of the contract. That duty contains a number of aspects, including transparency and co-

---

[13] *See* Charlesworth & Percy (2018) [10-36] citing *JEB Fasteners Ltd v Marc Bloom & Co* [1981] 3 All ER 289 and further commentary.

[14] See Vos & others (2019) [18].

[15] *Marks and Spencer plc v BNP Paribas Securities Services Trust CO (Jersey) Ltd* [2015] UKSC 72.

operation, and may include detailed consequential duties under the contract.[16]

Disputes over contracts generally concern whether one party has done what it promised to do under the contract. The claim is for a 'breach of contract.'

There are many disputes over the meaning of a contract. These are usually a proxy for arguments about whether the other party has done what it promised to do. The claiming party says that the contract meant that the other was obliged to do X and the other party will say, "No, it did not."

The interpretation of a contract and its terms is based on a fiction: the meaning the words used would convey to a reasonable person. A judgment in a leading case stated: [17]

> The language used by the parties will often have more than one potential meaning.... [T]he exercise of construction [i.e. interpretation] is essentially one unitary exercise in which the court must consider the language used and ascertain what a reasonable person, that is a person who has all the background knowledge which would reasonably have been available to the parties in the situation in which they were at the time of the contract, would have understood the parties to have meant. In doing so, the court must have regard to all the relevant surrounding circumstances. If there are two possible constructions, the court is entitled to prefer the construction which is consistent with business common sense and to reject the other. ... Where the parties have used unambiguous language, the court must apply it.

Evidence of subjective intention is not relevant and previous negotiations are generally to be ignored.[18]

---

[16] *Alan Bates & Ors v Post Office* [2019] EWHC 606 (QB) at [725] – [727], [737], [738] and [746].
[17] *Rainy Sky SA & Ors s v Kookmin Bank* [2011] UKSC 50 at [21] and [23], Lord Clarke.

In addition to disputes about interpretation, arguments over contracts usually concern claims that the other party has breached the terms of the contract, by not paying money or by not doing something it promised to do, or both. In a genuine dispute, the facts relied on to support the claim are generally contested. If the claimant does not establish the necessary facts, the claim will fail.

There are particular 'defences' to a claim for breach of contract. For example, a misrepresentation may release a party from the contract where the deal was entered into as a result of an untrue pre-contract statement. Or a defending party might even establish that there was no contract at all: the negotiations did not result in an arrangement sufficiently complete or clear to amount to a contract, or the terms agreed were expressed to be 'subject to contract'.

As indicated, most contractual disputes are about whether one side has done what it promised to do. The seller might say that the goods delivered complied with the contract and the price is due. The buyer might disagree and respond that he rejected the goods and should pay nothing. He might say that he is entitled to financial compensation or 'damages' for the seller's failure to deliver compliant goods.

A contract for services may generate a dispute about how well or badly the job was done. Should the contractor be paid the contract price? Is the contractor liable to pay damages for breach of contract to the employer because the employer says that the job was not done or done badly?

A defendant might say that the contract was changed, a 'variation' of the contract. A contracting party may have 'waived' compliance, or it might be unfair to require strict compliance because of

---

[18] See generally on interpretation, Chitty (2019) Vol. 1 [13-041] – [13-105], 1st Supplement and cases referred to.

statements made by the other party about what it expected to be done under the contract – creating an 'estoppel'.

Variation of a contract may not be a source of dispute, but an opportunity to resolve it. Where parties are arguing about performance of a contract, the most productive exit is often a negotiated variation to the deal (see generally Chapters 6 and 7).

'Limitation' is another common defence in contract cases. Contract claims must be brought within a specified period of time and some contracts also provide for a contractual time bar. If the claim is brought too late,[19] the defendant can rely on limitation as a complete defence.

A party to a contract may have a choice it is called on to make by law. What to do in response to an actual or threatened breach of contract: whether to continue to perform the contract or to terminate it.[20] But not every breach or threatened breach of contract entitles the innocent party to terminate the contract, and under what is sometimes termed 'the general law', most breaches do not.

Some contracts contain clauses that specify circumstances in which a contract may be terminated in response to a breach. These often entitle a party to terminate in a wider range of situations. But they may require the innocent party to take certain steps before doing so, in particular giving the party in breach an opportunity of remedying the breach (if remediable) following a notice procedure identifying the breach alleged.

Termination brings the contract to an end. The basic rule is that each party is released from their future obligations under it, except that the party that has broken the contract may be liable to pay damages

---

[19] There are technical rules for when a claim is brought. Limitation and similar defences may be raised against other 'late' claims.

[20] Effective termination in law has other requirements, particularly as to its communication to the party in breach.

to the innocent party. But wrongful termination in the face of a breach of contract puts the 'innocent' party at risk of a claim of damages.

2.1.3. Contract disputes (2) – the pandemic

Many contracts for the supply of goods and services have been adversely affected by the effects of Covid-19. Other commercial deals have been hit too. As supply chains have broken down and businesses have run out of money, legal disputes concern defaults on both supply and payment obligations as well as the recovery of money paid (including deposits) under affected contracts.

From those disputes, various legal rights will come into play.[21] The following is an introduction to just some of the areas of likely contention.

A principle of 'frustration' of contracts relates to unforeseen events:[22]

> Frustration of a contract takes place where there supervenes an event (without default of either party and for which the contract makes no sufficient provision) which so significantly changes the nature (not merely the expense or onerousness) of the outstanding contractual rights and/or obligations from what the parties could reasonably have contemplated at the time of its execution that it would be unjust to hold them to the literal sense of its stipulations in the new circumstances: in such case, the law declares both parties to be discharged from further performance.

Money paid under a frustrated contract will be recoverable in law in certain circumstances.[23]

---

[21] The Government's *Guidance on responsible contractual behaviour in the performance and enforcement of contracts* 7 May 2020 urges flexibility in response to impaired performance of contracts affected by Covid-19. Detailed recommendations are given. The note is non-statutory guidance.

[22] *National Carriers Ltd v. Panalpina (Northern) Ltd* [1981] 1 AC 675 at 700, Lord Simon.

Some contracts contain a so-called force majeure clause. This may allow the suspension of obligations or even complete discharge of the contract. A party's actual rights under the clause will depend both on its wording, other obligations under the contract, any requirements of the clause (e.g. compliance with notice provisions) and the particular facts of the case. Other contracts may contain a 'material adverse change' clause or similar provision, found in financial and corporate deals. Again, the terms of the contract will be decisive.

Disputes over pandemic-affected contracts may centre on whether the innocent party was entitled to terminate it. The answer will probably depend on several matters. Among these would be any arguments over frustration, any contractual force majeure or like clause, the effect of any implied terms and if the contract is relational, the particular rights under such a contract, the seriousness of any breach (if the default was a breach) and the operation of any provisions of the contract that address termination (see **2.1.2** above).

There may well be further development of the law in the area of contract interruption due to the pandemic.[24]

2.2. Remedies

If a claimant can establish that the defendant has breached one or more of its obligations under the contract, the next question is what, if any, 'remedy' will be granted by the court?

2.2.1. Order for the payment of money

An obligation to pay a sum of money under a contract, if broken, creates a right to obtain a court judgment for the debt.

---

[23] Law Reform (Frustrated Contracts) Act 1943 s 1(2).

[24] See BIICL (2020).

If a contracting party breaches the other's rights under the contract, he will be liable to pay damages to that innocent party for the foreseeable loss caused by the breach. The basic principle is that contract damages are compensation for that loss.

An innocent party who validly terminates a contract in response to the wrongful conduct of the other contractor may claim damages for the breach(es) of contract and recover any money that was due under the contract, before termination. The innocent party may also claim damages for being deprived of the benefit of the other party's future obligations in the contract.

There are other money remedies for breach of contract, particularly 'restitution'. A typical case is where money has been paid under a contract, but the paying party is regarded in law as having received nothing in return. If a party obtains a money judgment from the court, it may be awarded pre- and post-judgment interest.

2.2.2. Injunction

The court may order a party to a contract to do or to stop doing something. This is called an injunction. In a contract dispute, the court is enforcing by an order what one party has contractually promised to do or not do.

Where the court orders a party to do what it promised to do by contract, that is often referred to as 'specific performance.' Often the court does not grant that remedy, even where there has been a clear failure to perform. Instead, it awards damages. But sometimes, damages are not an adequate remedy and the court will make the mandatory order.

An order prohibiting a party from doing something is generally easier to obtain from the court. An example is an order enforcing a valid restrictive covenant in a contract of employment; the ex-employee may be required not to contact certain clients of the ex-employer for a period of time.

Failure to comply with an injunction may be a 'contempt of court', resulting in a fine, imprisonment or other adverse consequences.

2.2.3. Declaration

The other main remedy is the declaration. The dispute may be about whether certain rights or obligations exist at all. It may be vital to know whether the contract continues or not, e.g. so that a fresh contract may be made with a third party. Where a party terminates the contract, the right to terminate may be disputed and a court ruling necessary to determine whether the termination was valid.

2.2.4. Remedies: further questions

If a party succeeds in establishing that its rights have been breached, it does not always follow that remedy x or remedy y will be granted as claimed.

Take claims for damages. There may be a dispute about what is called 'causation': did the breach of contract cause the loss claimed? Did the claimant act unreasonably in failing to 'mitigate', i.e. prevent or reduce, the loss claimed? Was the loss excluded or limited by a term in the contract; if so is that clause enforceable? These are some of the more important considerations. That said, in most disputes at least some compensation is payable for a breach of contract.

There are also questions of amount or what lawyers call 'quantum'. The defendant may say that even if his breach of contract caused a loss, it was less than claimed. There are principles for calculating damages in particular cases, e.g. where the claim is for 'loss of a chance' such as for lost sales.

The injunction and declaration are 'discretionary' remedies. Judicial discretion is to be exercised according to largely settled principles, though these do give the court leeway in balancing the various factors relevant to exercise of the discretion. This sometimes results in the order being refused and a different remedy granted, e.g. damages instead of an injunction.

3. BINDING DECISIONS

3.1. Introduction

This chapter is intended to give the reader a broad understanding of the different ways of obtaining a legally binding decision to resolve a dispute, or defending a case that has been brought. Legal proceedings by action ('litigation') in the courts of England and Wales[1] are discussed. The alternatives are also explained and contrasted, with particular emphasis on arbitration and expert determination. Further details are in Appendix 1 and Appendix 2.

If there is a dispute, any right to litigate is not necessarily in the English courts, as opposed to another set of courts.[2] For example, contracts often contain a 'choice of jurisdiction' clause that identifies the jurisdiction for court proceedings. More generally, in disputes that engage the laws of one or more other countries, states or territories, litigation may have to be in those courts under different procedural rules, or a choice may exist between litigating there or in the English courts.

3.2. Litigation: court proceedings

The court procedures for business disputes are contained in the rules and practice directions of the Civil Procedure Rules (CPR) and associated rules.[3] Court proceedings consist of a set of procedures leading to a trial almost always before a judge alone (i.e. no jury), who issues a binding decision called a judgment and a resulting order or orders of the court. The general rule is that a trial is held in open court i.e. in public, which means that the press may also attend. As a result of the Covid-19 outbreak, for as long as necessary the courts may conduct remote hearings by conferencing facilities,

---

[1] Scotland and Northern Ireland have their own courts, under different civil justice systems.

[2] See **3.4.2** below as to arbitration clauses.

[3] www.justice.gov.uk/courts/procedure-rules/civil/rules.

as opposed to in-person hearings. Remote hearings will, so far as possible, still be public hearings; e.g. the judge sitting in a public court room and making the hearing audible in that room or by other methods.[4]

Generally, certain documents filed in the litigation are open to public inspection and the court may grant access to further documents referred to or used in court.[5]

At trial, each side has an opportunity to present its evidence and the judge will give judgment after hearing representations (generally from advocates) for the parties. As we have seen in Chapter 1, the loser will generally be ordered to pay a proportion of the winner's legal costs ('costs-shifting'), generally around two-thirds of those costs.

Pre-pandemic, it was usually taking over a year from the start of a case to the trial and obtaining a court judgment (see **4.3.10** below). In weightier disputes, this could have been two years at least. In all but the most urgent of cases you must add the time before the start of the case to instruct lawyers, obtain legal advice and attempt to engage with the other side. Expect around a further three months in the general run of cases. A fee is payable to start litigation[6] and there are some additional fees[7] if a case proceeds to trial.

---

[4] See CPR 39.2(3)(g), PDs 51Y and 51ZA; Courts Act 2003, s 85A inserted by Coronavirus Act 2020 Schedule 25 and Protocol Regarding Remote Hearings 26 March 2020. If what should be a public hearing has to proceed in private, a recording will be made if practicable, accessible on request in a court building, subject to the court's agreement.

[5] CPR 5 and 39 and *Cape v Dring* [2019] UKSC 38.

[6] Commencement fees for claims of more than £200,000, a fee of £10,000, for claims of more than £100,000 and up to £200,000, a fee equal to 5% of the claim value. For claims of more than £10,000 and up to £100,000, a fee equal to 5% of the claim value but 4.5% if the claim is made online.

[7] Additional fees: final hearing fees for claims up to £10,000 a maximum of £335, for more than £10,000 and up to £25,000 the sum of £545 and all other

The CPR procedures are much like a train line with different stations, with the trial as the terminus. There are also several branch lines off the main line, which may bring the proceedings to an end before trial or that are travelled before getting back on to the main line. The different stations are the various stages in the progress of a case to trial. These are considered in outline summary below.[8]

To pursue the analogy of the train journey, getting off before the terminus may be expensive. Once started, the proceedings will continue until ended. If one side stops the case before trial without a settlement of the dispute, it must generally pay most of the other side's legal costs in addition to their own. A defendant must 'submit to judgment' and a claimant must 'discontinue' the claim. Only in rare cases can proceedings be put into abeyance or 'stayed' for any length of time.

Before starting proceedings, the court will generally expect the parties to have exchanged sufficient information to try to settle the issues without proceedings. Litigation should be a last resort and parties should consider whether negotiation or some other form of Alternative Dispute Resolution or 'ADR' (see below) might enable them to settle their dispute without proceedings.[9] There are exceptions to this principle (see e.g. those in Appendix 1, page 164). Parties that skip this stage do so at their peril and may be penalised later in legal costs, even if they win.

The CPR sets down the procedure for a claim to go to trial. In summary, the main stages are these:

---

claims above this claim value, £1,090. For applications to court, a fee of £225 for each application is payable.

[8] There are several books on civil procedure for those interested in a more detailed picture. The leading practitioners' textbook is called 'Civil Procedure'. It is in two volumes and is known as 'The White Book'.

[9] Practice Direction – Pre-Action Conduct and Protocols.

- start of proceedings by the formal issue and service of the 'claim form' and 'particulars of claim'[10];
- period for any challenge to the court's jurisdiction;
- filing of defence and any counterclaim by defendant (with subsequent filing of responsive case statements by the parties as appropriate);
- allocation of case to appropriate court 'track';
- case management conference including costs management for claims over £25,000;
- disclosure of documents;[11]
- exchange of witness statements;
- exchange of experts' reports, if appropriate;
- trial;
- judgment on the claim; e.g. loser to pay winner (i) £X plus interest at £Y and continuing interest at a daily rate of £Z until paid and (ii) winner's legal costs generally 'on the standard basis' if not agreed;[12]
- order for an interim payment on account of costs, if appropriate;
- procedure for assessment of winner's legal costs if amount not agreed;
- enforcement of judgment if loser does not pay.

This summary excludes any applications for urgent and non-urgent orders from the court before trial; e.g. for an interim injunction pending trial.

---

[10] A 'Disclosure Pilot' scheme for documents was introduced in the Business and Property Courts for a period of two years from 1 January 2019. For qualifying cases (most), it requires 'Initial Disclosure' of key documents with case statements which includes the particulars of claim and the defence: see Appendix 1 p 167.
[11] See fn 10. The pilot provides for Extended Disclosure in certain circumstances: see Appendix 1 p 172.
[12] Costs are often agreed because of the expense of having them assessed.

At least some 'disclosure' of documents is generally required in litigation. Disclosure concerns documents in the possession or control of a party that assist its case or are adverse to its case. The basic rule is that parties may not use copies of documents disclosed to them for purposes other than the litigation.[13] However, documents may be read out or referred to in open court, at any interim hearing and trial.

Not all disclosable documents have to be shown to the other side. Documents attracting 'litigation privilege' or 'legal advice privilege' do not have to be produced. This allows litigants to seek legal advice and to prepare their cases without showing their hand to the other side (see Appendix 1, section 6). In limited circumstances, privilege can be waived or otherwise lost.

The analogy of the train journey is not total. Proceedings can continue beyond the terminus, to an appeal or appeals, to a formal assessment of legal costs and enforcement of the court's judgment if the loser does not comply with the court's orders. The winner who obtains a money judgment and a costs-shifting order in its favour may have to use enforcement procedures to get paid if the loser does not pay.

The fact that a court makes an order for payment of money (including a costs-shifting order) does not mean that the money will be paid by the loser. There are various court procedures for enforcement (e.g. charging orders and orders for sale on property), alternatively insolvency proceedings may be appropriate, through bankruptcy of an individual party or the winding up of a company. In some cases, enforcement is overseas if that is where the loser's

---

[13] By CPR 31.22(1),(2), a document disclosed in litigation may not be used by the party to whom it is disclosed for another purpose unless, a) it is referred to in court or read to or by the court in a hearing held in public subject to any contrary order, b) the court gives permission, or c) the party who disclosed the document and the person to whom the document belongs agree. See also *Cape v Dring* referred to at footnote 5 above.

assets are located. Further steps may have to be taken or hurdles overcome before the judgment can be enforced abroad (see Appendix 1, section 4). Despite these possible measures, judgment debts are sometimes not paid or satisfied.

An appeal from the trial judge may take time to pursue to a higher court. Permission to appeal may first be obtained from the trial judge (this is rarely granted), or alternatively, it must be sought from the appellate court. Permission is difficult to obtain, as appeals succeed only in limited types of situation. The hearing of an appeal is generally much shorter than trial, as oral witness evidence is not usually allowed.

Again, there is a 'loser pays' costs regime for appeals (often referred to as 'costs follow the event'). If the appeal is successful and overturns an adverse judgment in its entirety, the appellant will expect to be awarded the costs of the appeal. If the appellate court sets aside the result of the court below and replaces it with its own decision, the appellant will also seek its costs of that original trial, i.e. a reversal of the costs order made by the trial judge. However, the appeal court may set aside the decision but then remit the case to the lower court for a re-trial, i.e. the trial starts all over again. The appellant risks a further set of costs (his own and his opponent's) to add to the two sets of costs to and including trial, should the appeal fail. Having said that, appeal costs may be much lower than the trial costs and very much lower than the overall costs of the proceedings.

Litigation procedures allow parties to progress the case, but to negotiate at the same time, or to pause the litigation for a short period to do so. Rules prevent the trial judge from knowing what offers have been made, at least before judgment. There are also court procedures for making settlement offers by a claimant and a defendant. These 'Part 36 Offers' (i.e. CPR Part 36) result in the end of the main litigation if an offer is accepted. They also provide costs protection if the recipient does not accept the offer and fails to get a better result at trial. Tactically, a Part 36 Offer is a useful tool to put pressure on opponents. See further, **5.4.2** below.

Mediation is a structured process by which a neutral known as a 'mediator' facilitates negotiations between the parties that are aimed at resolving or 'settling' the dispute. Mediation may take place at any stage of a dispute, particularly before litigation. Once litigation has started, the court has powers to incentivise, though not force, a party reluctant to engage in mediation. A party who refuses to mediate may be penalised in costs.[14] There is also a Court of Appeal mediation scheme (see Appendix 1, page 183).

Most cases do not go to appeal. If there is an appeal, the steps after judgment may be these:

- applications for permission to appeal, for a 'stay' of the judgment[15] and of any interim costs order pending appeal (granted / refused); application(s) may be renewed to the appeal court if refused by trial judge – interim costs orders rarely stayed;
- appeal hearing; winner at trial wins again, loses or there is some form of 'draw', with resulting costs orders of the appeal and of the proceedings 'below' if applicable;
- procedure for assessment of legal costs if costs not agreed;
- enforcement of judgment if loser does not pay.

It is also possible to have 'costs only' proceedings. The procedure can be used if the parties have reached an agreement (made or confirmed in writing) on all issues on the claim, including which party should pay the costs, but cannot agree how much those costs should be.[16]

---

[14] See Chapter 5 fn 36.
[15] Here a stay is a court order that payment of the judgment sum is not required pending outcome of the appeal.
[16] CPR 8.1 and 46.14.

3.3.   Non-payment; is there a dispute at all?

3.3.1.   Insolvency

Sometimes payment is not made, because the other party is insolvent. But the debtor may have some assets. A creditor may apply to the court for a bankruptcy order in the case of an individual or partnership or to put an insolvent company or limited liability partnership (LLP) into liquidation. In each case, the creditor starts what are separate court proceedings.

The court may wind up a registered[17] company or LLP if it is unable to pay its debts.[18] There are several ways to show that, including:[19]

- non-payment of a sum exceeding £750 then due, after proper service of a 'statutory demand' in the required form where the debtor has 'neglected' to pay within three weeks of the demand;
- inability to pay debts as they fall due; and
- the value of the organisation's assets is less than the amount of its liabilities, taking into account contingent and prospective liabilities.

There is no 'neglect' if the debt is disputed on substantial grounds; i.e. there is a fair and reasonable probability that the company has a *bona fide* defence.[20] The company may also rely on a cross-claim which exceeds the petition debt or leaves a debt of less than the £750 statutory minimum, if its claim is substantial and genuine.

---

[17] i.e. registered in England and Wales; see the further requirements in EC Regulation on Insolvency Proceedings (EC) No 1346/2000; gen. Gore-Browne (2020) 55[3].

[18] Insolvency Act (IA) 1986 s 122 (1)(f). On 28 March 2020 the Government announced its intention to legislate to create a short moratorium for companies from creditor action while seeking restructuring or rescue and to allow companies to continue to access supplies, with other measures.

[19] IA 1986 s 123.

[20] Halsbury (2017) Vol.16 [356] fn 9 and cases cited.

A similar regime applies to bankruptcy proceedings. The debtor must have the requisite connection with England and Wales.[21] The debt(s) must:

- exceed a designated amount currently £5,000;
- be for a 'liquidated sum'[22] payable either immediately or at some certain, future time, and be unsecured (i.e. unsupported by any mortgage or charge); and
- the debt is one which the debtor appears either to be unable to pay or to have no reasonable prospect of being able to pay.[23]

A bankruptcy 'petition' may be set aside if the debt is disputed on substantial grounds or the debtor appears to have a claim against the creditor that is at least equal to the debt.[24]

Sometimes a judgment must be made, whether or not to try to recover money by insolvency proceedings. In the case of a company, a search can be made of its latest filed accounts (though these may be out-of-date) and to see if it has secured creditors. If the business were to start insolvency proceedings, some creditors (e.g. HMRC) have preferential or secured claims that would rank in priority to a debt or one based on a court judgment. This often leaves little or nothing for such 'unsecured' creditors. In contrast, a creditor may always later make a claim or 'prove' in a bankruptcy or in the liquidation of a company, once the debtor has been made bankrupt or 'wound up' on the application of another creditor, even though the priorities would still apply.

---

[21] IA 1986 s 265.

[22] What amounts to a 'liquidated sum' has been decided by various cases; e.g. it excludes a right to damages until quantified by an order or judgment of the court and even then, a judgment may not be sufficient: Halsbury (2017) Vol. 5 [136].

[23] IA 1986 s 267.

[24] Insolvency Rules 1986 SI 1986/1925 r 6.5(4).

Use of insolvency proceedings to obtain payment of a genuinely disputed debt is not appropriate and likely to be expensive. The risk is having to pay two sets of legal costs; one's own costs and the other side's because the procedure was not justified. In addition, there are the legal costs of the main dispute, yet to be litigated. The right course is to litigate and apply promptly for summary judgment, there being no real defence to the claim (see Appendix 1, page 168).

3.3.2. The debtor who knows payment is due but refuses to pay

What of the debtor who has no defence to the debt claim but refuses to pay? The debtor may not be insolvent, just bloody-minded or want further time that the creditor is not prepared to give. Again, legal proceedings followed by an application for summary judgment may be the best course. If a court judgment is obtained and the debtor does not pay, the judgment may be enforced against the debtor's assets or insolvency proceedings may be appropriate if that does not work.

Sometimes the debtor will try to hide assets, move them out of the jurisdiction or dissipate them in some other way in order to render a claim pointless. The creditor may litigate the main claim and apply to court for an asset freezing order to prohibit the removal of assets (see Appendix 1, page 170).

3.4. Other types of binding decision

3.4.1. Introduction

ADR is a shorthand for various techniques of dispute resolution, which are alternatives to litigation. ADR was born out of the shortcomings of litigation in resolving many disputes. The CPR (Glossary) defines it as, *"Collective description of methods of resolving disputes otherwise than through the normal trial process."* Its advantages include cost-effectiveness, speed of outcome and confidentiality. ADR is now so mainstream that the word 'alternative' is no longer apt.

ADR is a catch-all for non-litigation processes that provide either a binding outcome through the decision of a neutral or a party-agreed settlement by negotiation. Arbitration, expert determination and adjudication are examples of binding decisions and are examined here. Negotiations can take a number of forms, including simple negotiations and mediation. The main alternatives are explored in more detail in Chapter 6.

3.4.2. Arbitration

Arbitration is a process for a binding decision by a neutral tribunal (a single arbitrator or panel of usually three arbitrators) after each party to the arbitration has had an opportunity to have its case considered by the tribunal. Arbitration is private and confidential.[25] It usually derives from an agreement to refer the dispute to arbitration. An arbitration clause in a contract (or one for expert determination – see below) that covers the dispute will generally displace a party's right to litigate. Some statutes require arbitration of disputes.

An agreement to refer a dispute to arbitration is made before a dispute occurs by a contractual arbitration clause, or once it has arisen.

The Arbitration Act 1996 ('the 1996 Act') applies to many UK arbitrations. It gives powers to arbitrators similar (though not always equivalent) to those of a court.[26] The process results in a decision called an 'award', enforceable by court action if necessary.

The 1996 Act requires the arbitral tribunal to act fairly and impartially, giving each party a reasonable opportunity of putting its own case and dealing with that of their opponent; and to adopt procedures appropriate to the particular case, avoiding unnecessary

---

[25] There are practical and legal limits to this (see Appendix 2, section 1).
[26] Parts of the statute may be excluded by agreement, though some fundamental ones may not be: AA 1996 s 4(1), Schedule 1.

delay and expense.[27] This creates a flexibility for tailoring cost-effective procedures for a prompt disposal of the dispute.

The full apparatus of court-like procedures does not apply. There is usually an exchange of case statements and production of documents. Similar rules on privilege apply to those in litigation. Often there are witness statements. Arbitration can be conducted with or without an oral hearing, depending on the circumstances. If there is no oral hearing, parties can expect to be able to make written representations to the arbitrator. The likely effect of the Covid-19 virus on in-person hearings will be to increase the number of remote hearings by video-conferencing.[28]

Used efficiently, arbitration can deliver a speedy, reasoned and enforceable decision. The 1996 Act contains default powers, so once a dispute has been referred to arbitration, the tribunal can issue an award despite a party's non-engagement.[29] A 'loser pays' principle generally applies to legal costs, unless the parties agree otherwise.[30] The parties pay the arbitrator(s)' fees and expenses and those of any arbitral institution and the loser will generally be ordered to bear the tribunal's recoverable fees and expenses.

Arbitration also allows the selection of an arbitrator experienced in a particular trade or industry and is used in claims of all values, low and high. For example, the Chartered Institute of Arbitrators ('CIArb') operates one scheme for claims from £5,000 - £100,000 and another for those not exceeding £2 million;[31] respectively the 'Business Arbitration Scheme' and the Cost-controlled Expedited

---

[27] AA 1996 s 33.

[28] See e.g. *Guidance Note on Remote Dispute Resolution Proceedings*, Chartered Institute of Arbitrators (2020).

[29] AA 1996 s 41.

[30] AA 1996 s 61(2).

[31] The parties can agree that the CCEAR apply regardless of the amount in dispute.

Arbitration Rules ('CCEAR'). Both provide for a speedy decision and also control legal costs: see further below.

Arbitration is also regularly used for high value claims. These include multi-million pound/dollar disputes, particularly in international arbitration. Established arbitral institutions include the London Court of International Arbitration (LCIA), the International Chamber of Commerce (ICC), CIArb, Dubai International Arbitration Centre (DIAC) and the Singapore International Arbitration Centre (SIAC). Arbitration also allows parties to run their cases while negotiating, in such a way that the arbitral tribunal is unaware of the details of the negotiations (see **5.5**, **6.12.3** and **6.12.4** below).

3.4.3. Expert determination

Expert determination is apt for disputes about the value of an asset. The expert is appointed as a valuer, e.g. a surveyor to assess a market rent on a rent review or an accountant to value company shares. It has been said that, *"The whole point of instructing a valuer to act as an expert (and not as an arbitrator) is to* [achieve] *certainty by a quick and inexpensive process."*[32]

Expert determination is also used to decide other types of business dispute. The expert appointed may be a lawyer tasked to decide issues more often associated with litigation or arbitration, e.g. commercial contract disputes.

The contract will often set out the procedure for expert determination before a dispute has arisen, e.g. in a partnership deed. Parties may also agree to expert determination after a dispute has arisen.

---

[32] *Morgan Sindell plc v Sawston Farms (Cambs) Ltd* [1989] 1 EGLR 93, CA Robert Walker LJ.

3.4.4. Adjudication

Adjudication is a procedure which has some similarities to arbitration. In non-consumer commercial disputes, adjudication is a procedure that applies by statute to disputes over most categories of 'construction contract.' A tight timetable applies and any decision is enforceable through the courts, or may be challenged there, but on limited grounds.[33] Dispute Adjudication Boards and similar bodies may rule on disputes, typically those arising from long-term contracts. Their powers derive from the contract between the parties and the 'Dispute Board' rules chosen by them. Those rules specify the circumstances in which those decisions may be binding: see Dispute Boards at **6.12.8** below.

3.4.5. Financial Ombudsman

The Financial Ombudsman Service for Small Businesses has the power to award compensation up to £355,000[34] for claims made by qualifying small and medium sized businesses about financial products.[35] These include banking, credit and insurance. The award may include interest and, occasionally, costs. Directions may also be given to the financial business, e.g. that a credit file be amended.

If the financial business has not resolved a complaint made to it, the complainant may ask the ombudsman to investigate. The ombudsman gives an opinion after the financial business has been given the opportunity to respond. If either side disagrees with the opinion of the investigator (often a problem-solving solution), it can ask an ombudsman for a final decision. A decision is based on what is 'fair and reasonable' and it is binding on the financial business if the complainant accepts it. The complainant does not have to accept

---

[33] See Keating (2019), Chapter 18 and Supplement.

[34] For claims made on or after 1 April 2020 about acts or omissions by firms on or after 1 April 2019. Lower limits apply to other dates.

[35] See financial-ombudsman.org.uk. The ombudsman's powers derive from Part XVI and Schedule 17 of the Financial Services and Markets Act 2000.

the decision, and may enforce their legal rights and go to court. The legal principles applied by the courts differ to those of the ombudsman. Claims must be brought within certain time limits.

The ombudsman's powers interact with those of the Financial Conduct Authority (FCA) for SMEs. The FCA's response to Covid-19 has included action over business interruption insurance claims.[36]

3.5. Litigation, arbitration and expert determination compared

The basic differences between arbitration and litigation are these:

- arbitration is private and confidential, a trial is generally held in public;
- the arbitrator must be paid but the parties may be able to select the arbitrator;
- arbitration allows the parties to have their dispute decided by a more flexible and potentially cheaper and faster procedure, in many cases;
- in the absence of agreement, it is not possible to add parties to an arbitration or to 'consolidate' the hearing of two or more arbitrations, whereas the court may order these steps;
- rights of appeal are more limited in arbitration than in litigation;
- enforcement of an arbitral award abroad may be easier than foreign enforcement of a court judgment.

See Appendix 2 for more information.

The following is a summary of the main differences between expert determination and arbitration/litigation:

- the expert process may be speedier and cheaper;
- litigation and arbitration generally have clearer safeguards for procedural fairness;

---

[36] The response includes legal proceedings (see **8.4** below).

- litigation and arbitration have greater reservoirs of useful procedures;
- if the parties are unable to agree on the expert, the process will not work unless there is an appointing power in the contract;
- no obligation to disclose documents unless the contract says so;
- expert need not be independent (unless contract says so) but must be impartial;
- oral hearing with witnesses unlikely;
- no right of appeal and very limited right to challenge enforcement;
- the expert may be liable in negligence if the determination is wrong - difficult and expensive to prove;
- but, greater finality;
- no costs-shifting unless the contract says so;
- limitation 'clock' does not stop in the expert process unless contractual arrangements so provide.

See Appendix 2, section 2 for more information.

4.   WHO WILL WIN?

4.1.   Introduction

Businesses involved in a commercial dispute want to know whether they will win the litigation. This chapter explains how the decision 'on the facts' of the case is key to the outcome in court. It examines the forecasting of litigation outcomes, the type of legal advice that may be given, its benefits and limitations.

It looks at some of the reasons why disputants generally have very different perceptions of the facts in dispute. And how witnesses, parties and legal advisers have perceptions and views that are selective and biased. An important aspect of this chapter is to help parties not to be 'prisoners' of their own story, drawn into over-optimistic assumptions about the strength of their own case. The chapter concludes by explaining how judges make decisions; the decision-making processes that result in their findings of fact and law that determine the outcome of the case.

4.2.   Finding the facts

In deciding the outcome of a civil trial, the judge is not simply applying legal principle to the case. There is the crucial intermediate step of 'finding the facts'. A court does not establish historical truth. A judge's findings of fact are an assessment of probabilities based on the evidence placed before the court by the parties. The outcome of most cases usually turns on the facts found by the judge.

In his essay, *The Judge as Juror: The Judicial Determination of Factual Issues,*[1] the distinguished judge Tom Bingham (later Lord Bingham of Cornhill) wrote:

> To the civil litigant.., whose case will almost always be tried by a judge sitting alone without a jury, findings of fact are likely to be crucial. This is because, first, most cases turn largely, if not entirely,

---

[1] Bingham (1985).

on the facts. ..... And secondly, it is so because factual findings ... are very hard to dislodge on appeal.. .... Of the litigants who each year tramp out of the law courts muttering darkly of a bad day for ... justice, I strongly suspect that a large majority have been outraged not by a decision against them on the law but by a factual decision which they know or believe or claim to be wrong.

A court in civil disputes decides disputed issues of fact on 'the balance of probabilities' from the evidence. This means: what is more likely than not to have occurred in the circumstances? In percentage terms a fact will be taken as proved if there is more than a 50% chance that it was true. This is called the 'standard of proof'. The party who has to meet it is the person who bears the 'burden of proof'. So, a claimant is required to prove its case. The general principle is that the burden of proof rests on the party alleging a particular fact.[2]

4.2.1.   The factual dispute: the problem of two worlds

Each side's version of events cannot be true; and yet in most cases each litigant will believe its own story to be broadly accurate. They can't both be right. Discussing this topic with me, the late Sir Brian Neill (former judge in the Court of Appeal) described how when he was a trial judge it struck him that when hearing the witness evidence the two sides appeared to be living in different worlds. That parties in dispute put forward radically different versions of the same transaction is a puzzle. In this section I will suggest some reasons why this happens.

In genuine business disputes, contradictory versions of the key events drive the litigation. The factual case presented to the court by each party is essentially a story, told by its witnesses and taken from the documents it relies on. Sometimes the stories of each side are

---

[2] The burden of proof will remain on that party, though in some cases the 'evidential burden' may move to the other side on a particular issue of fact, if certain facts are established.

contradictory because witnesses are lying. But in most disputes, judges are dealing with what witnesses genuinely believe to be accurate recollections; i.e. honest witnesses.

Chapter 1 described how a breakdown in commercial trust is often the cause of a business dispute and drives it. One side will say that the other has broken the contract, for example. If there is no pre-existing relationship between the parties, one side may say that its rights have been invaded (e.g. an intellectual property right). In both cases the defending party will deny that it has acted wrongfully.

Whatever the dispute,[3] each side presents its factual (and legal) case to the court in its story or 'case'. The basic story will have driven the dispute. 'You broke the contract', 'you infringed my rights', etc. Usually the story has a second part, such as 'You now owe me money and/or compensation.'

At trial, the witness evidence is where the rival versions of events are laid out. There are many studies that look at the fallibility of witness evidence. There is also much literature in the field of psychology about the unreliability of human perception and recollection. I have set out below some of the reasons, collected from that literature and legal case law, explaining why perceptions and recollections may differ and why parties may present opposing cases, convinced that they are true. Those reasons are not a summary of the workings of perception and memory as applied to witness evidence. They are intended to give insights to help decision-makers to make an informed understanding of their dispute.

---

[3] A minority of cases concern arguments of law, where the facts are not disputed.

4.2.2. Witnesses: perception, bias and memory

In his article *Why eyewitnesses fail,*[4] the psychologist and neuroscientist Thomas D. Albright referred to the fact that approximately 70% of the convictions overturned by DNA evidence in the USA are cases where eye-witness identification contributed significantly to the conviction. He stated:

> Without awareness, we regularly encode information in a prejudiced manner and later forget, reconstruct, update and distort the things we believe to be true.

In varying ways, the textbooks on psychology explain how our vision of the world is a construct. The neuroscientist Beau Lotto says that an accurate picture of reality is neither possible nor suited to our wellbeing and survival. The brain is habituated to detect differences. Imagine dense jungle in which you know that a large cat predator may be concealed. Detection of the predator requires extreme speed. The key is to spot what is different, i.e. what is not trees or undergrowth. If you don't do that fast, you are dead. Survival and other reasons (e.g. the need to adapt) mean that we are not wired to take in reality as it is.[5] 'Who cares about accuracy when what is at stake is survival?!'[6]

A mere 10% of the information the brain uses comes from the eyes. The other 90% comes from other parts of the brain and its sophisticated network that makes sense of all the incoming information. Thus, *'perception is just your brain's construction of past utility.'*[7]

If I put on a pair of glasses with pink lenses, the world looks pink. After a few hours, the pink disappears and the world looks normal again, in the colours we would expect to see. Take the glasses off,

---

[4] Albright (2017) (30): 7758-7764.
[5] Lotto (2017), pp 66-106.
[6] Lotto (2017), p 105.
[7] Lotto (2017), pp 2, 110-111.

the colour of the world will change again and look wrong, before settling back into what you would expect to see. The disappearance of pink and taking off the pink glasses each show that in key respects our vision is a construct of what the brain expects to see.

We may accept that our perceptions of an event are incomplete. We have not quite heard what someone said, or quite seen what happened. There may have been background noise or our view was partly obscured, or we were not paying close attention. But generally we are confident that we heard or saw what actually occurred.

But often that is not true. Perception is selective and not objective. In 1951 a game of American football was played between Princeton and Dartmouth universities. It was rough, violent and very controversial. Studies were carried out by a social psychologist and survey researcher, published in a now famous article, *They Saw a Game: A Case Study*, by Albert Hastorf and Hadley Cantril (1954).[8]

In the first part of the study, students from each college were asked questions about which team started the rough play, and whether the game was clean and fair, rough and fair or rough and dirty. The results showed wide discrepancies of perception, comparing one set of students against the other. In a further part of the study, Hastorf and Cantril asked students from the two universities to watch a film of the game and to say which team had committed the greater number of fouls. Students from one university saw the other team making more than twice as many fouls as their own team. Students from the other university thought that the number of fouls was about even. The authors came to this striking conclusion:

> It seems clear that the 'game' actually was many different games ...
> It is inaccurate and misleading to say that different people have

---

[8] Plous (1993), pp 18-20.

different 'attitudes' about the same 'thing'. For the 'thing' simply is *not* the same for different people ...

The problem of faulty testimony is not confined to recollections of visual events. Consider this example of flawed recollections that followed a meeting of the Cambridge Psychological Society, recorded in Ian Hunter's book, *Memory*. Two weeks later, each of the participants was asked to recall what had been said in a discussion after the meeting. Their recollections were compared against a recording of the discussion. The participants forgot over 90% of the points discussed. They were wrong about nearly half of the points that they did recall. They recalled comments that had not been made and 'converted implicit meanings into explicit comments.'[9]

A few years ago, I was listening to a radio programme on the law broadcast by BBC Radio 5. A list of about 20 everyday objects, such as windows, doors, etc, was read out to members of a studio audience. Once the list had been read out, each was then requested to respond 'yes' or 'no' to questions that asked whether a particular object had been mentioned. Some of the objects read out had been on the list, and others not. Many of the answers were wrong.

The number of the mistakes made by the programme participants included things in the same category but not on the list that was read out. Research has shown a tendency to false memories where subjects recall words from a list of words, particularly where these have associations with a non-listed word.[10]

Academic psychologists have explained that: [11]

> ... what gets *encoded* into memory is determined by what a person attends to, what they already have stored in memory, their expectations, needs and emotional state. This information is

---

[9] Plous (1993), p 37; Kiser (2010), pp 99 and 100.
[10] Roediger & McDermott (1995), 803.
[11] Howe and Knott (2015) at pp 651-3; referred to in *Blue v Ashley* [2107] EWHC 1928 (Comm) at [68].

subsequently integrated (consolidated) with other information that has already been stored in a person's long-term, autobiographical memory. What gets *retrieved* later from that memory is determined by that same multitude of factors that contributed to encoding as well as what drives the recollection of the event. Specifically, what gets retold about an experience depends on whom one is talking to and what the purpose is of remembering that particular event (e.g., telling a friend, relaying an experience to a therapist, telling the police about an event). Moreover, what gets remembered is reconstructed from the remnants of what was originally stored; that is, what we remember is constructed from whatever remains in memory following any forgetting or interference from new experiences that may have occurred across the interval between storing and retrieving a particular experience. Because the contents of our memories for experiences involve the active manipulation (during encoding), integration with pre-existing information (during consolidation), and reconstruction (during retrieval) of that information, memory is, by definition, fallible at best and unreliable at worst.

The literature on the fallibility of memory contains numerous striking examples of its shortcomings. Memory is 'malleable' because information stored at the time of perception is subject to alteration. Consider this example:[12]

Bartlett (1932) provided one of the earliest demonstrations of the malleability of memory. He asked a group of British students to read a Native North American story, and then recall it. As people attempted to recall the story, errors crept into their reports. But the most striking finding was the pattern of errors that people produced: they distorted details of the story in line with their own knowledge and experience. They reworked elements of the story to be more familiar, misremembering a canoe rather than a rowboat, and a fishing trip instead of a seal hunt. In describing this demonstration, Bartlett emphasised the reconstructive nature of

---

[12] Newman & Garry (2014), p 110.

memory, proposing that people weren't simply playing back what they had read, but reconstructing details from the story. He suggested that people remember details as being more typical and familiar than they really are because people craft what they remember so it fits with how they made sense of the story in the first place.

A perception of accuracy leads to a feeling of confidence. The 'illusion of validity' has been described in these terms:[13]

> Subjective confidence in a judgment is not a reasoned evaluation of the probability that this judgment is correct. Confidence is a feeling, which reflects the coherence of the information and the cognitive ease of processing it. ... [D]eclarations of high confidence mainly tell you that an individual has constructed a coherent story in his mind, not necessarily that the story is true.

Tom Bingham described three factors relied on by judges when rejecting the evidence of *honest* witnesses.[14] First, the inherent unreliability of a witness who attempts to recall the detail of an event taking place over a short period of time, such as an accident. He considered that most people are in the position of the television viewer, who sees a goal scored in a football match but would be hard pressed to recall the passes that led up to it. 'It all happened so quickly' would be the response of most spectators, unable to recall the detail of the passes.

Second, what he described as 'misinformation', where a witness is exposed to post-event information which alters the actual recollection of a witness, sometimes permanently. His third factor was the inevitable fading of memory when a witness is called on to recall events some years later when giving evidence.

As for the second factor, Tom Bingham referred to work done by psychologists on the workings of memory, and a paper given by the

---

[13] Kahneman (2012), p 212.
[14] Bingham (2000).

cognitive psychologist Elizabeth Loftus, *'The Misfortunes of Memory'* at a meeting of the Royal Society in January 1983, which contained the following passage:

> ... in one study, subjects who had just watched a film of an automobile accident were asked: 'How fast was the white sports car going when it passed the barn while travelling along the country road?' ... [N]o barn existed. The subjects were substantially more likely to 'recall' having seen the non-existent barn than were subjects who had not been asked the misleading questions.

The literature shows that exposure to 'post-event information' can contaminate or even dictate the content of evidence, in some cases dramatically so.[15] Talking about an event with another is a classic case of the contamination of evidence. Two people who were present at a meeting can actually change each other's recollection of what took place by talking about the events of the meeting. Suggestibility is but one of the fallibilities of recollection.

In *Gestmin SGPS S.A. v Credit Suisse (UK) Limited & Anr* the trial judge stated:[16]

> [20] ... A witness is asked to make a statement, often ... when a long time has already elapsed since the relevant events. The statement is usually drafted for the witness by a lawyer who is inevitably conscious of the significance for the issues in the case of what the witness does nor does not say. The statement is made after the witness's memory has been "refreshed" by reading documents. The documents considered often include statements of case and other argumentative material as well as documents which the witness did not see at the time or which came into existence after the events which he or she is being asked to recall. The statement may go

---

[15] See e.g. Teversky and Marsh (2000).

[16] [2013] EWHC 3560. Leggatt J, now Lord Leggatt. At [22] he stated that the best approach for a judge to adopt in the trial of a commercial case is to place little if any reliance on witnesses' recollections of what was said in meetings and conversations, and to base factual findings on inferences drawn from the documentary evidence and known or probable facts.

through several iterations before it is finalised. Then, usually months later, the witness will be asked to re-read his or her statement and review documents again before giving evidence in court. The effect of this process is to establish in the mind of the witness the matters recorded in his or her own statement and other written material, whether they be true or false, and to cause the witness's memory of events to be based increasingly on this material and later interpretations of it rather than on the original experience of the events.

[21] It is not uncommon... for witnesses to be asked in cross-examination if they understand the difference between recollection and reconstruction or whether their evidence is a genuine recollection or a reconstruction of events. Such questions are misguided in at least two ways. First, they erroneously presuppose that there is a clear distinction between recollection and reconstruction, when all remembering of distant events involves reconstructive processes. Second, such questions disregard the fact that such processes are largely unconscious and that the strength, vividness and apparent authenticity of memories is not a reliable measure of their truth.

We also draw conclusions from what we see and hear, i.e. attribute meaning. Below are two drawings made by my daughter. The dots represent pieces of information. The lines represent the alternative pictures made by joining up the same dots. The pictures are quite different.[17]

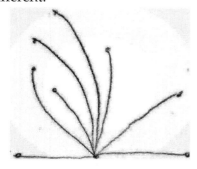 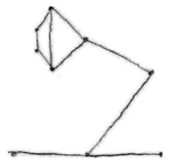

Harriet Bate

---

[17] See Furlong (2006), pp 32-33.

The rival approaches of each side to the documentary evidence before the court are an example of this. Particularly significant in trial outcomes is the contemporaneous evidence at or around the time of the transaction. The contents of the documents are the data points. Each side will usually differ in their *interpretation* of those documents, or the inferences that can be drawn from them.

Perceptions and interpretations also lead us to make assumptions, particularly about the motivations of others. We operate under a number of biases, including 'self-serving bias'. That has been defined as '*any cognitive or perceptual process that is distorted by the need to maintain and enhance self-esteem, or the tendency to perceive oneself in any overly favourable manner.*'[18]

This bias is the belief that individuals tend to ascribe success to their own abilities and efforts, but put failure down to external factors.[19] For example, if something goes wrong in a transaction, the employee(s) responsible for its success and/or their employing business may wrongly look for reasons to blame the counterparty or to absolve themselves of blame in some other way.

There is also a powerful tendency for people to remember past events about themselves in a self-enhancing light. Numerous experiments have also shown that when new information is encoded which is related to the self, subsequent memory for that information is improved compared with the encoding of other information.[20]

In conclusion, -

- Your story *may* be true.
- There is also a fair chance that it is not an accurate picture of the key events, or all of them.

---

[18] Myers (2014).
[19] Campbell, Keith, Sedikides & Constantine (1999).
[20] *Blue v Ashley* [2107] EWHC 1928 (Comm) at [69] and sources there referred to.

- Each side's story is likely to be internally logical, but generally only one of them will be reasonably accurate.
- That it is your side of the story only adds to its seeming persuasiveness.

4.3. Forecasting: advice on the litigation outcome

Any business facing the prospect of legal action, whether as claimant or defendant, should usually seek legal advice. Lawyers are routinely asked for advice on the legal merits of a dispute. So, an 'advice on the merits' is usually an essential tool for informed decision-making. This section considers the nature, value and limitations of such advice.

4.3.1. What is an advice on the merits?

The instructions to the lawyer should make clear that the client requires legal advice on the merits of its case. A client should not assume that they have a good or even arguable case because the lawyer has said nothing, i.e. given no advice on its merits. Sometimes, lawyers represent clients in a dispute and run their litigation without advising on the merits of the case or express a reluctance to do so. It is essential that legal advice on the merits is insisted on (see Chapter 8).

Legal advice on the merits may state that the client is likely to win, likely to lose, has a reasonable case or prospect of success or has a particular percentage chance of success. That view is based on the information provided to the lawyer on which the advice is based. This includes statements to the lawyer as to the material events, accompanied by documents, such as the contract and correspondence, etc. generated at or around the time of the transaction. As the dispute unfolds, further documents become available through the litigation process from the opposing party or parties.

What can a litigant expect of their lawyer's advice or forecast? Importantly, the lawyer's duty to their client in law is to exercise reasonable skill and care in making the forecast. It is not a duty to provide an accurate forecast.

We have seen the importance of the facts to the outcome of most cases. Competent legal advice will not assume the truth of the instructions given to the lawyer. A lawyer will consider all the available information, including information from the other side.

The advice is likely to be hedged about with 'ifs', 'buts', 'possibilities' and the like, but its core is likely to be an indication of the client's prospects of success. Competent litigation lawyers are attuned to how judges make decisions. A competent litigator will weigh the cases of each side to the dispute in the light of the contemporaneous documents available, the facts that do not appear to be in dispute, the inherent probabilities of the case and other matters that are likely to weigh with the court. Having done so, they will apply the relevant law and make a call on what the outcome is likely to be. This is basis of an 'advice on the merits.'

The lawyer giving the advice should be – but is not always - removed from the partisanship that affects witnesses and parties. The lawyer can piece together the evidence, like the judge will do at trial. The barrister or solicitor giving this advice is engaged in technical work based on their training and qualifications. Essentially, it requires a judgment from all the available information as to which version of events is more credible and so more likely to be accepted by a judge. In making that judgment, the lawyer may bear in mind the 'overall merits' of the case (see **4.4.2** below).

4.3.2. Key aspects of an advice on the merits

The most useful type of advice is one that gives a percentage chance of success, even if approximate, or a percentage band, say 60-70%. The advice should contain the essential reasoning so the reader can understand the underlying logic.

It is surprising how unclear advice on the merits can be. Litigants may be advised that they have a 'good' case, or even a 'reasonable' one; or some other description. None of these are of much use. They are imprecise and mean different things to different people. For example, 'good' might indicate slightly better than 50% or a case that is much stronger, or a little stronger. As bad, if not worse is, 'You should win.'

Worse still is where no advice is given and the client believes that they have good prospects because they have been advised that they 'have a case', or because they have not been advised that they have a bad case.

The advice should make clear the outcome(s) to which the percentage assessment relates. If the claim is to recover a single debt of £1 million, the advice would be, there is a x% chance of a judgment for £1 million. If the claim is for three debts totalling £1 million, the advice should be clear whether the same percentage applies to each of the three debts. If the facts for each are different and disputed, the percentage chances of obtaining a judgment for each debt will differ. In this example, the overall percentage chance of getting a court judgment for £1 million may be less than the percentage chance of a judgment for one of them (see **4.3.3** below).

If the claim is for damages of £1 million, the assessment should make clear what percentage applies to the recovery of damages of £1 million. If there are issues about the amount of the damages, the advice should give a percentage assessment to any lower figure. So that advice might read, 'There is a 70% chance of a judgment for damages of £500,000 and a 60% chance of a judgment for £1 million.' If the claim includes other elements, such as an injunction, a percentage assessment of succeeding on that issue should be given too, and an overall percentage assessment of succeeding on all the claims.

The advice should also make clear both the information and assumptions on which it is based (see **4.3.4** below).

The advice on the merits updated should be reviewed regularly during the litigation or other legal process (see Chapter 8). Again, the client should require those reviews.

4.3.3. Probability of success

In simple cases an assessment may be looking at a single issue; e.g. was there an oral agreement, was the machinery defective, or was the cause of an admitted defect something for which the other party was responsible in law? Here, a percentage assessment of the merits depends on the chances of one side being proved right on a single issue.

In most cases, success depends on more than one issue. Take a claim against a supplier who has delivered goods to the customer who says that they are not fit for purpose and that he lost money as a result. Here there are four potential issues, whether (1) the goods were not fit for the purpose, (2) the contract required that the goods be fit for that purpose, (3) the customer lost money and (4) the loss was caused as a result of the breach of contract.

Many, if not most, cases involve a number of issues and the prospects of success will depend on each. The ultimate chances of success may depend on the outcome of the various probabilities. The inclination is to multiply these together to create an overall probability of success (the multiplication rule); e.g. 70% x 80% x 90%.

But we all know that events are not always unrelated. The multiplication rule depends on the events being independent, as in a succession of coin tosses. The probability of drawing the king of clubs twice in a row from a full deck of cards (assuming the card is put back into the pack) appears to be 1/52 x 1/52 i.e. 1/2704 according to the multiplication rule. But that depends on how the card is put back into the pack and the multiplication rule will not apply unless the cards are shuffled properly for the second pick. [21] Again, to assume that a second plane crash is unlikely to happen soon after one has occurred because plane crashes are very rare is to overlook possible connected causes. [22]

Therefore, in assessing the overall probability of success, the multiplication rule is a useful but not invariable guide. Where a claimant has suffered a financial loss and the defendant has acted in breach of contract, the multiplication rule may not be apt in a particular case, because the likelihood of a connection between the two appears very likely or certain in the absence of some other possible explanation of the loss.

Bear in mind too that judges tend to look at the overall merits of the case in their decision-making (see **4.4.2** below). So, if a judge considers that a party broke a contract, they are likely to be *inclined to* award a remedy to the innocent party if it claims to have suffered loss as a result. The remedy might not be everything that the claimant seeks, but still something significant. [23] When identifying separate issues of breach of contract, causation and loss and ascribing probabilities to each, one must be careful not to lose sight of the whole picture.

There are cases, particularly in the field of professional negligence, where a breach of duty does not result in a remedy. For example, a solicitor's failure to advise competently may not have caused the claimant to lose his business, because it would have failed anyway. Here, the overall merits are, 'Yes, your solicitor ought to have advised you properly, but you cannot blame him for the way you ran your business.'

---

[21] Levitin (2014), p. 225.
[22] Levitin (2014), p 226.
[23] There are exceptions; e.g. 'no loss' cases.

Issues that require success on disputed facts tend to have lower probabilities than issues which are of pure law or legal principle. Thus, an issue in the chain of probability may be relatively straightforward. For example, case law might establish a 95% chance of success on that issue.

In some cases, particular care has to be taken in calculating the probabilities. For example, 'representativeness bias' may generate errors due to the following:

> ... a tendency to treat the probability of a hypothesis given the evidence (for example, the probability that a defendant was negligent given that a plaintiff was injured) as the same as, or close to, the probability of the evidence given the hypothesis (for example, the probability that the plaintiff would be injured if the defendant were negligent).[24]

4.3.4. Underlying assumptions and information

It is important that the legal advice identifies the information that has been used and any underlying assumptions. The assumptions should be made explicit. For example, a 70% chance of success might be based on an assumption that the court accepts your factual case. That is very different from an overall chance of success of 70%, to include the probabilities of the judge accepting that factual case.

Assume that advice has been given that there is a 60% chance of success of making out your factual and legal case. That assessment is made on the information that is *available*. As the dispute goes

---

[24] Guthrie, Rachlinski, Wistrich (2001) at 807. The facts from *Byrne v Boadle* (1863) 159 ER. 299 concerned a plaintiff who was hit by a barrel of flour as he passed by the defendant's property. There were a number of issues in the case, that depended on probabilities that were given numbers for a study. A number of US federal magistrates were given those probabilities and asked how likely it was that the accident had been caused by the defendant's negligence. More than 40% of the magistrates got the answer correct: 8.3%. However, 40% answered that the percentage likelihood was more than 75%; *Ibid* at p.808.

through the litigation process, increasing amounts of information are generated that may be used to update the legal advice.

Advice given before proceedings have started may assume the basic factual picture painted by the information provided by the client, unless there is reason to disbelieve it; e.g. it is inherently improbable or contradicted by the contemporaneous documents.

The person who has provided that information on behalf of the business, e.g. in-house lawyer or the responsible officer or employee, may not know whether the facts are true or not. Staff involved in a transaction that has escalated into a dispute may wish to put themselves in a good light. They may give a varnished account of the truth. Of course, that is not to say that they will do that. But they may be both motivated to present themselves in a good light, and also biased however honest their version of events (see above). Equally, the information may be incomplete or otherwise deficient.

Advice given before legal proceedings is best informed by the other side's position and arguments. These should be in the responsive Pre-action Protocol letter. Typically, there will be a challenge to the essential facts advanced in the letter of claim, often with reference to legal principles that justify that side's position. There may be a clash as to the facts argued for by the claiming party and also an assertion that additional facts are relevant, which the claiming party may or may not be aware of and which may or may not be true.

Once this exchange of correspondence has taken place with an exchange of the basic documents relied on by each side, it may be clear that one side's case will fail. For example, essential factual points may be flatly contradicted by contemporaneous documents. Or even if the facts alleged by the other side were assumed to be true, legal principle may mean that its case would fail.

An advice on the merits at this stage, before proceedings, will be able to take into account the facts that appear not to be in issue, the inherent probabilities and the degree of consistency of each side's case with the available contemporaneous documents. The advice may be – you are likely to win, 60/40 on the available information, or it is a 50/50 case, it depends on who the court believes; or the advice may be a 70-80% case if what you have told the lawyers were accepted as true by the court. It is a key time to get an advice on the merits, particularly if you are a claimant. Once started, legal proceedings are expensive to stop for a claimant, and potentially both difficult and even more expensive to end for a defendant (see Chapters 3 and 5).

At pre-action stage, it is unlikely that you will have seen much of the other side's evidence – as opposed to their assertions in correspondence. It is all too easy to assume that one's own story is more persuasive. It is likely to be internally logical or mostly so, as stories often are (see above).

The evidence for the other side's version of events is generally not available until well after the case has started. The separate processes of disclosure and exchange of witness statements will generate more information to update the advice on the merits.[25] But by then, the rules of the game will have changed. As we have seen, once litigation starts the legal costs and financial risks for each side generally go up. The stages of disclosure and witness statements are particularly expensive in most cases.

After the exchange of witness statements, the client's lawyer will be able to give a more informed advice on the merits once they have seen all the documents from disclosure and the witness statements.

Even at this stage, further information may become available as the case moves towards trial. Expert evidence may be necessary. For example, in a defective goods case, this might be expert opinion on

---

[25] See Chapter 3 and Appendix 1 pp 167 and 172 in connection with disclosure of documents.

the degree and significance of the defects. The legal advice may need to be updated to include the reports of the experts for both sides.

But assuming that no expert evidence is necessary or that stage in the litigation has been passed and the legal advice updated, what next? In a minority of cases, there are 'unknown unknowns'. The other side may apply to the court to change or 'amend' its case at trial in a way that could not have been predicted. If the application is successful, this may change the odds. Or a piece of late but crucial evidence is produced by the other side. There may be a dispute as to whether that evidence should be 'allowed in'. That may skew the probabilities; e.g. with a 75% chance that the court will allow the late evidence to be called.

But how will your witnesses perform in court? A witness may give evidence well, acceptably or badly. So, will X make a good witness? The same applies to expert witnesses. The weight of an expert opinion is likely to be influenced by how the expert gives evidence. The performance of the advocates can also make a difference to a judge's perception of the case.

The limitations and best use of litigation forecasting is examined in more detail at **4.3.9** below.

4.3.5. Decision trees

As we have seen, litigation of any substance often involves several issues for the court to decide. Used properly, 'decision trees' setting out the various issues and percentage assessments can be a valuable tool to provide a framework for an informed understanding of the prospects of success.[26] This form of decision analysis discourages the type of intuitive, in this context sloppy, thinking which might lead a lawyer to advise that their client has a 'good' case or give advice

---

[26] See e.g. Jones and Clark (2015), pp 317-324.

based on percentages without considering the need to succeed on all the issues.

There are other advantages of decision trees, e.g. to focus evidence-gathering on a particular issue. Or to make a settlement offer, e.g. one based on the percentage likelihood of a particular outcome.

Decision trees can be dynamic, with the inputted probabilities changing over time as more information becomes available during the litigation. Sensitivity analysis also allows the decision tree to show probabilities of success if the probabilities on a particular issue are changed. If the evidence of one witness is key, for example, varying percentages can be inputted to the model to see what difference is made to the overall prediction.

But bear in mind that decision analytics give an impression of scientific accuracy. In substance, a decision tree is no more than an aggregate of forecasts, albeit a potentially useful one.

The greater the number of issues on which success depends, the lower the overall percentage probability of success appears to be. But we have seen that the multiplication rule on which this approach depends should be a guide and not a rule and that many judges bear in mind the broad justice of a case in deciding the outcome. So, simply multiplying probabilities on the different issues *may* underestimate the overall chances of success.

There appears to be no reason why decision analytics cannot be modelled to estimate the probabilities of issues being decided in a claimant's favour *on the assumption* that the claimant established a breach of contract or other breach of duty. This would overcome some, but not necessarily all the possible difficulties caused by the multiplication rule in any particular case.

Some law firms offer decision analysis as part of their offering to clients. Herbert Smith Freehills uses decision analysis tools incorporating decision trees coupled with related analytics.[27] Its website includes examples of how the tool has been deployed. In one case there were apparently 20,000 possible outcomes and the tools were used to help the client decide to reject initial settlement offers and gain a much higher offer that was accepted.

4.3.6. Outcome prediction software

There has been a growth in studies, processes and computer software providing data analytics to predict the outcome of cases. Two sets of analytics provide forecasts for the outcomes in cases before the European Court of Human Rights and the US Supreme Court. The success rates of prediction have been 79% and 70% respectively. However, the facts in dispute had already been decided by a court before the case went to the higher court.

Of more relevance to this book are analytics that have been produced for domestic civil cases. There is a set of litigation analytics called 'Solmonic'.[28] The data is based on cases decided in the Commercial Court and Chancery Division of the High Court of England and Wales over the past six years and beyond. Analytics deal with different types of claim; e.g. the construction (meaning) of contracts, frustration of contracts[29] and negligence, but exclude cases where there is no dispute such as insolvency matters. The results show different percentages of success for each type of claim. The analytics have also assembled the body of cases decided by each judge, with resulting information.

The analytics do not identify all claims issued in these courts and the data relates to case outcomes. Generally, the analytics are not predictive of an individual case but may be useful as part of an overall assessment of the merits of a case.

---

[27] See at herbertsmithfreehills.com.
[28] See solmonic.co.uk.
[29] See **2.1.3** above.

4.3.7. Bias and litigation forecasting

As described earlier in this chapter, the legal adviser tries to put themselves in the place of the trial judge and make an objective judgment on how likely it is that the client's case will be accepted by the court.

Bias is an everyday feature of thinking and decision-making. Witness bias has already been discussed. Party bias is the view of the dispute taken by those directly involved in it for a party, as well as the party's decision-maker(s) responsible for conduct of the litigation. The decision-maker may or may not be a participant in the dispute, and a potential witness.

Legal advisers are also susceptible to bias. They are called on to give objective advice. But they are also advocates of their client's cause. An indication of the biases at play is apparent from a series of studies that examined the effects of the same information on different parties in litigation. In one study, a group of law students were given the same set of facts and divided into two groups, one acting as lawyers for the claimant and the second group, for the defendant. The groups interpreted the facts in favour of the party they were representing.[30]

The following is a list of some of the biases that may affect parties and their legal advisers.[31] Examples of each are given:

- **Blind spot bias** – to see oneself as less biased than others. 'People's conviction that their perceptions directly represent reality.'[32] Example: a party believes itself to be objective in its

---

[30] Korobkin and Ulen (2000); see articles by Lowenstein, Babcock and others footnoted on p 1093.

[31] For readers interested in the above list and fuller lists, see Cuthbert (2016); Goodman (2018), p 31. A number of the descriptions in the text differ from those sources.

[32] Pronin (2007).

decision-making about the dispute or litigation; or more objective than the other side;

- **Confirmation bias** – the tendency to interpret contradictory evidence as supporting evidence or as not inconsistent with an existing viewpoint. Example: new evidence received in the litigation process undermines the case, but is downplayed or fitted in;

- **Self-serving bias** – any cognitive or perceptual process that is distorted by the need to maintain and enhance self-esteem, or the tendency to perceive oneself in any overly favourable manner.[33]

- **Empathy gap** – 'the tendency to underestimate the influence of our emotional state and overestimate the intellectual influence on our decisions.'[34] Example: treating the dispute as purely 'commercial', uninfluenced by emotion (e.g. anger);

- **Endowment effect** – when we overvalue something we own. Example: for a claimant to believe its legal claim is more valuable, i.e. a better case, than it is;

- **Halo effect** – a tendency to allow particular characteristics of a person to influence our judgments about them. Example: giving excessive weight to the fact that the complaint originates from one of your colleagues or staff, so making it credible;

- **Focusing effect** – to over-emphasise the significance of part of an event. Example: that the counterparty has broken the contract and underplaying the complexities of assessing any resulting loss;

- **Groupthink** – 'mode of thinking in which individual members of small cohesive groups tend to accept a viewpoint or conclusion that represents a perceived group consensus ...'[35] Examples: (1) business colleagues uncritically accepting a point

---

[33] See Furlong (2006), pp 32-33.
[34] See Kahneman (2012), p 212.
[35] britannica.com.

of view or version of events put forward by one of their number, (2) client and lawyer mutually reinforcing each other's biases;

- **Primacy effect** – 'information considered early in the judgement process tends to be overweighted in the final judgment ... biases the nature of additional information sought'.[36] Example: your side's version of events is the first to come to the attention of the business decision-maker(s) and their lawyer;

- **Optimism bias** – tendency to be excessively optimistic about an outcome. Example: a legal adviser having an undue confidence in their prediction of the trial outcome; and

- **Sunk cost bias** – the tendency to maintain a position because of the money and/or time spent or invested in it. Example: a party believing the litigation to be more worthwhile than it is, because of the investment in it.

4.3.8. Limitations on outcome predictions; some data and further considerations

There are numerous studies in the USA about errors in outcome forecasting of legal disputes. Three are of particular interest.

In *Let's Not Make a Deal: An Empirical Study of Decision-Making in Unsuccessful Settlement Negotiations*, Kiser *et al* [37] examined decision error in lawyer / client decision-making by comparing unaccepted settlement offers with case outcomes. The yardstick used was an outcome in the litigation or arbitration that was the same as or worse than the offer. The cases were all claims for money.

The authors studied 2,054 civil litigation cases resolved through the courts or by arbitration in California between November 2002 and December 2005 in which each side was represented by lawyers and

---

[36] Hastie, Reid and Dawes (2001) at pp 100 and 102; see Kiser (2010), pp 119 and 311; particularly where the source of the information is the person 'who caused [the conflict] or could not resolve it.'
[37] Kiser, Asher and McShane (2008). The authors' expertise included law, statistics and economics.

settlement offers had not been accepted.[38] They found decision error in 61.2% of cases in the case of plaintiffs and 24.3% in the case of defendants. However, the defendants' mean cost of error was much greater, by approximately ten times.[39]

The authors pointed out that the vast majority of cases of the type they considered would conclude by voluntary settlement or 'pre-trial proceedings.' The sample excluded settled cases and the authors acknowledged the resulting selection bias.

The breakdown of the headline figures is interesting. In contract cases plaintiff and defendant error rates were approximately 44% each. In all the cases sampled (contract, medical malpractice, etc), there were differences between the error rates for jury verdicts as opposed to judge-alone trials and arbitrations. Jury verdicts accounted for around 90% of the decisions. The error rates were, for plaintiffs 64% (jury) versus 42.6% (judge-alone) and 28.9% for arbitration cases. Interestingly, for defendants the error rates were for 22.1% (jury) versus 42.6% (judge-alone) and 45.4% for arbitration cases. (In the USA, juries are still used in the trial of civil cases.)

The authors considered the striking discrepancy in the mean cost of error between plaintiffs and defendants to be consistent with other research that people tend to make risk-averse choices when

---

[38] About 4,600 cases in tort, contract and real property (i.e. land) disputes were reported in *Verdict Search California* during the 38-month study period. 29% of those cases were excluded from the study because they reported pretrial settlements and thus did not proceed to an adjudicated outcome, and 26% were excluded because the amount of settlement demands or offers was omitted or disputed, non-monetary relief was sought, the parties were not represented by counsel, the trial was bifurcated and only the liability outcome was reported, or the case did not otherwise meet the authors' selection criteria.

[39] The study was updated (2002-2007 cases) and its implications for outcome prediction discussed with those of other studies in Kiser (2010), ch.3. The mean cost of defendant decision error found was 19 times plaintiff decision error; p 42. Error rates were similar, plaintiffs 60%, defendants 25%.

choosing between gains but risk-seeking to avoid a loss. This reflects what in behavioural economics has been called 'prospect theory', advanced by Kahneman and Tversky.[40]

The study in *Let's Not Make a Deal* was carried out under the civil litigation rules of California that provided for no costs-shifting, except for 998 Offers (similar to Part 36 Offers).[41] One of the earlier studies it referred to considered medical malpractice claims in the courts of Florida before and after introduction of 'loser pays' costs rules, and after their repeal.[42] The author of that earlier study considered the effects of prospect theory on 'loser-pays' and 'conventional' (not loser-pays) costs rules. One conclusion was this:

> Increasing the risks associated with litigation increases the attractiveness of wasteful litigation to risk-seeking defendants. It is significant that the same parties [who] wanted a loser-pays system in Florida [insurers] also wanted the system repealed.

In *Insightful or Wishful: Lawyers' Ability to Predict Case Outcomes*[43] the authors (a psychologist and a legal academic) brought together previous research and conducted surveys into the accuracy of advice given by trial lawyers across a broad national sample in the USA in 144 criminal cases and 337 civil cases; specifically, the success in predicting chances of achieving declared goals measured against case outcomes at trial, settlement or other resolution.

Introducing their study, the authors pointed to overconfidence and other biases in many fields of predictive decision-making, stating:

> Previous research revealed that expert predictions of the likelihood of events were influenced by the person on whose behalf they were working and that overconfidence was more prevalent when the

---

[40] Kahneman (2012), Chapter 26.
[41] See **5.4.2** below. The results of the Kiser study did include 998 Offers and separated out the error rates for those cases.
[42] Rachlinski (1996), p 70.
[43] Goodman-Delahunty, Loftus, Hartwig and Granhag (2010) pp 133-157.

expert had some degree of commitment to, and emotional investment in, the outcome (Rehm & Gadenne, 1990). More generally, lawyers may engage in wishful thinking: They might believe a certain outcome is probable simply because of a desire to reach it (Babad, Hills, & O'Driscoll, 1992; Kunda, 1990).

Other factors included commitment over time to a goal and studies suggested that where an event is perceived as controllable, overconfidence results.

The participants in the study were litigators from the total of 481 cases, both newly qualified and experienced lawyers. These were the active participants from a larger sample. The others did not participate for various reasons, e.g. did not reply, did not follow up, refused to participate, did not do trial work, could not recall outcomes.

Those chosen were asked about cases due to go to trial within the following 6-12 months. Participants were asked to identify their minimum goal in the case. The majority of participants gave chances of success for the minimum outcome that exceeded 50%. In 56% of the cases the outcomes matched or bettered the outcome targets, but 44% of the outcomes were worse than predicted (the percentages for criminal cases and civil cases were about the same, i.e. 44%).

The results did not show greater accuracy by experienced litigators. But women seemed to do better than men! As settlement involves client decision-making, it is not possible to exclude client decisions from those cases that settled at figures lower than the minimum outcome. The authors considered that overconfidence was an important factor in the error-making and concluded that the results showed 'clear evidence of unrealistic litigation goals.'

4.3.9. Best use of forecasting

It is critical to bear in mind the nature of a forecast. There is a common confusion between two things: the accuracy of a forecast and its reasonableness. In *Superforecasting* Philip Tetlock and Dan Gardner stated:[44]

> If a meteorologist says there is a 70% chance of rain and it doesn't rain, is she wrong? Not necessarily. Implicitly, her forecast also says there is a 30% chance it will *not* rain. So, if it doesn't rain, her forecast may have been off, or she may have been exactly right. It's not possible to judge with only that one forecast in hand.

After the Iraq war, there was an investigation into how the US intelligence services came to predict that Saddam Hussein had weapons of mass destruction, when in fact he did not. The investigation has been regarded as balanced. Its conclusion was that the prediction was both sincere and reasonable.[45] The authors of *Superforecasting* pick up the story, stating:[46]

> "But the conclusion wasn't reasonable", you may think. "It was wrong!" That reaction is totally understandable – but it too is wrong. Remember, the question is not, "Was the ... judgment correct?" It is "Was the ... judgment reasonable?" Answering that question requires putting ourselves in the position of the people making the judgment at the time, which means looking at only the information available then ....

These two passages from *Superforecasting* illuminate what a forecast is, and what it is not. It is essential to keep in mind the exact nature of a forecast to derive benefit from it.

Good litigation forecasting 'requires a relentless search for contrary evidence.'[47] It is essential in order to make the initial forecast. It is also required when reviewing the advice as the case progresses, to mitigate against confirmation bias as new information becomes available to the lawyer from the parties to the litigation.

---

[44] Tetlock and Gardner (2016), p 57.
[45] Tetlock and Gardner (2016), pp 81-83.
[46] Tetlock and Gardner (2016), p 83.
[47] Kiser (2010) p 332.

It is true that the greater the amount of information, the more informed the forecast is likely to be. But sufficient information is often available at a reasonably early stage of the case, once Statements of Case have been exchanged and disclosure is complete or near complete.

A selection of literature on forecasting in other fields has been brought together in Randall Kiser's, *Beyond Right and Wrong: The Power of Effective Decision Making for Attorneys and Clients* (see in particular section 9.3.6). The key point made is to focus on what you do know and not to fuss over the comparatively small amount of information that you do not know. If you know 75% or 80%, that should be enough. Otherwise, you are left with diminishing returns.

The key is the client's appetite for risk. Lawyers tend to want to take risk out of advice. However, clients are used to making important business decisions with information missing; whether in R&D, the selection of products or the choice of employees.[48]

As we shall see in Chapters 8 and 9, forecasting is only one element in the mix of factors that have to be weighed in pursuit of a litigation strategy.

4.3.10. Covid-19 and further outcome uncertainties

There have been warnings about the risk of a deluge of claims for breach of contract due to defaults caused by the pandemic, which would place great strain on the system of international dispute resolution: see *Breathing space – a Concept Note on the effect of the pandemic on commercial contracts*, British Institute of International and Comparative Law, 27 April 2020. Any business contemplating binding dispute resolution should consider that this may leave a dispute (and also a dispute unrelated to the pandemic) unresolved

---

[48] Mnookin (2004), p 230, citing the observations of Richard Weise, former General Counsel of Motorola.

for a longer period of time, unless it is referred to arbitration and disposed of within a reasonable timeframe.

Additionally, the law may undergo some development in the area of contract interruption (see **2.1.3** above), with additional outcome uncertainty were this to happen.

4.4. The Trial: Judicial Decision-Making and the Trial Outcome

Almost all civil cases are tried by judge alone, without a jury. An appeal court is reluctant to interfere with a trial judge's findings of fact and will only do that if something has gone seriously wrong (see Appendix 1, section 4). Therefore, the trial judge has a high degree of autonomy. The judge does not conduct an investigation but makes a decision based on the evidence presented by each party at trial.

Having heard the evidence, the judge gives a reasoned judgment that decides the issues in the case. The judgement contains 'findings of fact' and of law,[49] with the outcome of the case.

In most disputes, the law will be uncontroversial and settled. Accepted principles are applied by the trial judge to the facts found. In relatively few cases will the law be uncertain, e.g. because the legal principles are developing.

In making findings of law, the judge applies the facts found to precedents from the case law and, if relevant, to the words of a statute or other legislation. The meaning of legislative sources of law may also be found in case law.

4.4.1. The jigsaw of facts

A litigant will probably win the case if its case on the facts is accepted by the trial judge (see **4.1** above). Findings of fact are made

---

[49] Some findings are of 'mixed fact and law'; but these are not important for present purposes.

from a consideration of all the evidence, both written and oral. In fact-finding, the judge is building a jigsaw. It is built from facts not in dispute, the inherent probabilities, the contemporaneous documentary evidence, the recollections of witnesses and the judge's assessment of the witnesses' credibility.

Contemporaneous documents are given particular weight by the judge in decision-making. These are the documents created at, before or shortly after, the time of the transaction in dispute. They give the context for the disputed oral evidence of the witnesses. What is or is not in those documents carries considerable weight from an evidential viewpoint. What the parties said or did at the time when there was no dispute on matters subsequently in dispute, is often the critical indicator of where the truth lies. In that sense, the contemporaneous documents do not lie.

However, if the truth behind factual disputes could be solved by reference to those documents, you might think that it would be simple to predict which side would win on those aspects of the dispute. But that is rarely so. If a case can be resolved by reference to the documents, it will generally have been possible to obtain summary judgment without the need of a full trial. Sometimes, the documents favour one side's case over the other's, but not decisively. In other cases, the documents may be silent on the crucial issue(s), though favouring one side's case on the surrounding facts. So, the oral evidence may be decisive and the credibility of a witness may be crucial.[50]

In *Onassis v Vergottis* Lord Pearce said about witness credibility:[51]

> 'Credibility' involves wider problems than mere 'demeanour' which is mostly concerned with whether the witness appears to be telling the truth as he now believes it to be. Credibility covers the following

---

[50] But see the reservations expressed by Lord Leggatt, at fn 16.

[51] [1968] 2 Lloyds Rep. 403, at 431; referred to in Bingham (2000).

problems. First, is the witness a truthful or untruthful person? Secondly, is he, though a truthful person, telling something less than the truth on this issue, or though an untruthful person, telling the truth on this issue? Thirdly, though he is a truthful person telling the truth as he sees it, did he register the intentions of the conversation correctly and, if so, has his memory correctly retained them? Also has his recollection been subsequently altered by unconscious bias or wishful thinking or by overmuch discussion of it with others? .... And lastly, although the honest witness believes he saw or heard this or that, is it so improbable that it is on balance likely that he was mistaken? ... And motive is one aspect of probability. All these problems compendiously are entailed when a Judge assesses the credibility of a witness; they are all part of one judicial process. And in the process contemporary documents and admitted or incontrovertible facts and probabilities must play their proper part.

4.4.2. Legal principle, the overall merits and 'dirty dogs'

How does the law achieve justice in a case, or a just result? The case is tried by a judge who is required to be independent and impartial.[52] Like the rest of us, judges are susceptible to bias, though they are encouraged to be aware of bias and put it to one side.[53] A number of those biases are the same as those referred to earlier in this chapter.

Turning now to the judge's decision. The principles established by case precedent developed over many years create a framework of legal consequences that apply to particular sets of facts. These principles are derived from the 'common law' and the law of 'equity'.[54] They operate as principles of abstract justice and public policy that apply to particular factual situations. These principles are supplemented by statute and related legislation.

---

[52] For the meaning of those words, see Bingham (2010), p 93.
[53] See Stafford (2017); and Cuthbert (2016).
[54] See Chapter 2.

In a contract case, common law principles define the circumstances when a contract comes into existence. Other case law shows that a party to a contract is generally required to keep its contractual promises and is liable in law to compensate the innocent contracting party who suffers loss as a result of their broken contractual promise. These principles tend to deliver a just outcome if the facts fit within them. Equally, if the defendant did not break its contractual promise, it is just that their defence should succeed.

A defendant might allege that it is not bound by the contract, because he was induced to enter into the contract by the claimant's false misrepresentation. The Misrepresentation Act 1967 and principles from common law and equity may operate to free a party from a contract where the misrepresentation induced that party to enter into the contract. The statute and those principles are indicative of a just result when the facts are fitted to them.

The question of how the law achieves a result is quite different from whether it actually does so in a particular case, or even whether the trial judge is concerned with achieving justice, as opposed to applying the law to the facts as the judge finds them from the evidence.

The reader would be forgiven for thinking that the judge will read the case papers, hear the evidence and submissions for the parties with a totally open mind and then sit back, deliberate and give a judgment. The late judge Sir John Donaldson MR said this in a lecture:[55]

> It was always said of Lord Denning[56] that he claimed to decide intuitively what should be the outcome of a case and then go on to analyse the law in such a way as to justify his intuitive decision. Of

---

[55] *Judicial Techniques in Arbitration and Litigation*, December 1988.
[56] A highly respected and outstanding judge, some of whose judgments were controversial in making the law correspond to the justice of the case.

course he was wrong to say that. Quite Wrong. Most of us do exactly that, but we would not dream of saying so.

Lord Browne-Wilkinson said this in a lecture he gave on the domestic human rights legislation:[57]

> When I was first made a judge, a wily old judge advised me – 'just remember Nick, dirty dogs don't win.' That is a principle which lies at the heart of the common law. It is the basis on which the overwhelming majority of cases are decided. The judge looks for what are called 'the merits' and having found them seeks to reach a result, consistent with legal reasoning, whereby the deserving win and the undeserving lose.

> Unfortunately, this judicial method is seldom reflected in judicial behaviour or in the reasons given by judges for their decisions ... When we get to the judgment, we very seldom find any reference to 'the merits'. The articulated reasoning purports to be based on a process of compelling legal argument leading inexorably to the result achieved ...

> In the case of statutory interpretation, the courts have acted in much the same way ...

So, the wider picture often matters too. The broader merits and demerits of each side's overall position are found in the evidence, be it background, contextual or entering the arena through cross-examination,[58] and the court may be swayed by this wider picture.

There is not a 'dirty dog' in every case, or if there is one it does not mean that the judge will necessarily take that into account. However, many judges do bear firmly in mind the broad justice of the case. Sometimes that is not confined to the facts that are in

---

[57] See Zander (2015), p 320.
[58] The evidence is 'admissible'; i.e. may be received by the court, as sufficiently connected to the issues or, if not, relevant to an assessment of witness credibility, known as 'credit.'

dispute, i.e. what the case is supposed to be about – but extends to other aspects of the facts presented in evidence.

Some years ago, I represented at trial a company that granted licences of the TV game show, *Who Wants to be a Millionaire?* The dispute was with the licensee for Indonesia, which was entitled to a new licence if it had complied with its expiring licence. The licensee was refused a renewal. The licensor's case was that the licensee had sub-licensed production of the show to the broadcaster, in breach of a term in the contract not to sub-licence production of the show.

The case was technically concerned with that one issue and with closely related issues. However, the court heard evidence that the licensee had invested huge sums of money in the licence, its CEO had been required to fly half way across the world to the licensor's London offices to be given what it considered to be the briefest of opportunities to rebut allegations (of sub-licensing) that the licensee argued had not been put to it properly before the meeting, how the licensor then refused to grant a new licence and then re-licensed the show to a third party for more money than it would have been paid by the licensee under a new licence. And there was nothing wrong with the quality of the show as produced for Indonesian TV.

The judge accepted the licensee's evidence, rejected the licensor's and decided that the licensee had not sub-licensed the production and was entitled to a new licence. However, the wider points are likely to have played a part in the outcome, even though the judgment was largely silent on them.[59]

This example is in some ways typical of many civil disputes, where the broader merits of a dispute are taken into account by the parties in presenting the case and by a judge, in deciding it.

---

[59] *Arief Productions Inc. v Celador International Ltd.* [2004] EWHC 1277 (Ch). There was some discussion of the re-licensing fee in the judge's assessment of the credibility of Celador's witnesses: see at [77] onwards.

4.5.   Conclusion

The discussion in this chapter should give the reader information to:

- better understand the value and limitations of forecasting advice on the trial outcome;
- be aware of the reasons why both parties in dispute can honestly believe that they are right;
- gain an insight into how judges decide cases; and as a result,
- make better decisions from the forecasting advice that they do receive from their lawyer.

5. LAWYERS, THEIR FEES AND LEGAL COSTS

5.1. Introduction

A party who uses lawyers in a dispute resolution process must generally make funding arrangements for its legal costs. If a party wins the legal case, it usually obtains an order that the loser pays for a substantial amount of its legal costs. But if a party loses the case, it must generally pay a large part of the other side's legal costs. This chapter considers the basic implications of different funding arrangements and their interplay with these costs-shifting rules.

5.2. Funding your own costs

How does a business fund its own legal costs? Generally, a solicitor is instructed to advise and represent the client in the litigation.[1] The representation at trial may be by a barrister or solicitor advocate. There are broadly four main ways in which litigation is funded and each has important commercial implications for a dispute resolution strategy. In limited cases, free or *'pro bono'* legal representation may be available from a solicitor or barrister.[2] Legal Aid is generally not available for business disputes.

Whichever method of funding is used, it is essential that the client understands all the commercial and practical implications of the arrangement. The available sources of litigation funding and costs insurance, the implications of each and the terms attached to them should all be explained and understood by the client.[3] The following is an overview.

---

[1] See further, Chapter 8.

[2] See e.g. lawsociety.org.uk and barcouncil.org.uk.

[3] The Legal Ombudsman has published a helpful guide, 'Ten Questions to ask your Lawyer about Costs':
https://www.legalombudsman.org.uk/downloads/documents/publications/Consumer-Guide-Costs-BW.pdf.

5.2.1. Payment on the usual basis

In most cases, the client is liable to pay the fees of their lawyer, whether or not they win the case in court. Where a solicitor is engaged by a client, the contract between them is known as a 'retainer'.[4] Terms of acting will be set out in a 'client care letter' with terms and conditions, which should explain clearly on what basis the firm proposes to charge for its services; e.g. fixed fee, hourly rate or some other basis.[5]

Solicitors are obliged to ensure that, 'clients receive the best possible information about how their matter will be priced and, both at the time of engagement and when appropriate as their matter progresses, about the likely overall cost of the matter and any costs incurred.'[6]

Although lawyers tend not to offer fixed fee arrangements to run litigation to trial, the stages of the litigation may be split up for fee purposes, with fixed fees for one or more of those stages and estimates given for others.

A solicitor's bill of costs must contain sufficient detail to allow the client to consider the fairness of the charges.[7] There is a right to ask the court to assess, review and alter the charges in certain cases, subject to time limits in applying to the court.[8]

---

[4] The Solicitors Regulatory Authority (SRA) is the regulator of the solicitors' profession. Solicitors' professional obligations are set out in the SRA's Standards and Regulations. They tend not to offer fixed fees for business disputes due to the nature of litigation work.

[5] A solicitor may lawfully require a client to pay a reasonable sum of money on account of costs to be incurred for 'contentious business' and may terminate the retainer if payment is not made within a reasonable time and following reasonable notice of termination: Solicitors Act 1974 s 65(2).

[6] *Code of Conduct for Solicitors*, [8.7].

[7] *Cordery* (1996), Vol. 1 [1171].

[8] See Solicitors Act 1974 ss 59-61 and 70.

Solicitors and barristers

Where a solicitor and barrister have been engaged, it is the solicitor who contracts with the barrister, whose fees are treated as a disbursement for which the solicitor is paid by the client. Those fees are covered by the barrister's written contract terms. These may be based on an hourly rate, a fixed fee or a combination of both.[9]

A barrister's charges for a trial are based on a 'brief fee' (a fee for reading the trial papers, preparing written arguments and the first day in court), followed by daily fees for appearing in court, known as 'refreshers.' The brief fee may be payable in stages and sometimes it is agreed that if the case settles before one or more stages are payable, no further fee is due (save for any fee already incurred).

There are two situations where a client may instruct a barrister directly, without going to a solicitor. These are under 'public access' and 'licensed access' arrangements.

Barristers may provide services directly to a client where the business is a 'licensed access client'. The Bar Standards Board (BSB) as the barristers' regulator may licence the business entity, e.g. a company. That is where the business is considered to have the ability and understanding to instruct barristers directly.

The second situation is where the barrister has been authorised by the BSB to engage in 'public access' work. This method of engaging lawyers has increasingly been used by individuals and companies to save costs in obtaining advice and representation, as and when required.

However, a barrister must not accept public access instructions or continue to act for the client, if it would be in the client's best

---

[9] See the Bar Council website: www.barcouncil.org.uk. The Bar Council represents barristers in England and Wales and discharges its regulatory functions through the Bar Standards Board (BSB). The regulatory obligations of a barrister are set out in a Code of Conduct called the 'BSB Handbook.'

interests to instruct a solicitor or in the interests of justice to do so.[10] Similar rules apply in licensed access cases.[11] Barristers generally do two things; give advice and represent clients in court. They do not conduct the litigation and are generally not allowed to do so. The conduct of litigation is doing the technical things necessary for the litigation to run.[12]

In litigation, it is generally not in the client's best interests for a barrister to act on a public access basis, because the client will not have the knowledge and experience necessary to run litigation. The same may well apply to litigation where licensed access arrangements are in place.

A good use of these direct access arrangements (public and licensed access) may be to engage a barrister for the initial correspondence with the other side and obtain an initial advice on the merits of the case. After that, it is likely to be in the client's best interests to engage a solicitor to conduct any litigation, using the barrister's services as and when required. The basis of charging for the barrister's legal services in direct access cases is to be set out clearly in a 'client care letter' and any written 'terms and conditions.'[13] In contrast to solicitors, there are restrictions on barristers holding client money. Advance payment of a fee is not holding client money if certain requirements are met.

Client remains liable to pay fees if it 'wins' the case

If the client wins the case in court, it should obtain a cost-shifting order in its favour.[14] Around one-third of the lawyer-client costs are

---

[10] *BSB Handbook*, C122, C123.

[11] *BSB Handbook*, C135, C138.

[12] For example, to issue proceedings or act as an address for service of documents in litigation.

[13] *BSB Handbook*, C125, C126 for public access.

[14] The amount of costs recovered depends on several factors; see also the contrary effects of a qualifying offer to settle the case that is not accepted; see **5.4.2** below.

generally irrecoverable under a usual costs-shifting order: see further below.

However, the client remains liable to pay the fees it has agreed to pay to its lawyers. Where money is paid by the loser under a costs-shifting order, the winner can apply that money towards the costs it has paid to its lawyers or those it has yet to pay. If, for some reason, all or part of that money is not recovered (e.g. the loser becomes insolvent), the client will be unable to recoup any legal fees paid to its lawyers and will be liable to pay their lawyer any unpaid fees.

5.2.2. Conditional Fee Agreements (CFAs)

A conditional fee agreement (CFA) is one of the main types of alternative funding. Lawyers in business disputes do not routinely offer CFA arrangements but some do so if they consider that the case has a very good chance of success. If a CFA is used with the solicitor, the CFA is part of the retainer.

Main type of CFA

The basic arrangement is that if the case is lost the lawyer is paid nothing, but if the case is successful the client agrees to pay the lawyer a basic fee, plus a success fee being a percentage uplift of the basic fee. The basic fee is generally based on what the solicitor would charge on the usual basis (see above). Disbursements must generally be funded by the client. The barrister may agree to act on a CFA, in which case the barrister's fees would be covered by that arrangement (see below).

The definition of 'success' in the agreement is very important. In a claimant's CFA, this may include a court judgment for the payment of money and a settlement where the defendant party agrees to pay money. In a defendant CFA, 'success' may be defined to include a settlement below a certain sum of money. The effect of Part 36 Offers (see below) on the CFA should also be considered, particularly where the opposing party makes an offer that the CFA-funded party fails to better at trial. Note that in a claimant CFA, 'success' would often not require the money under a judgment or settlement to be actually received by the client. So, the success fee would be due whether or not recovery was made.

To be valid or 'enforceable' a CFA for most business disputes need only satisfy certain basic requirements; e.g. the CFA must be in writing and the success fee must be set out in the agreement and be no more than an uplift of 100%.[15] The percentage uplift represents the lawyer's assessment of the degree of risk attached to the case.

The success fee is no longer recoverable from the losing party under a costs-shifting order.[16] So, a claimant must generally recoup the success fee from the damages or other money payable and paid by the defendant. A successful defendant will be unable to recoup its success fee from the claimant.

The basic fee and disbursements, i.e. the non-success element (to the extent of about two-thirds), may be recovered under the usual costs-shifting order. But if the loser does not pay, the client cannot recoup its legal costs to that extent. In addition, it would remain liable to pay the success fee.

CFAs generally have an 'escape clause.' In particular, the lawyer's right to withdraw from the case if their assessment is that the prospects of winning have materially changed or if significant information was not disclosed at the outset. In those circumstances, the CFA may impose a payment obligation on the client, at least for basic fees and disbursements to the date of termination. The upshot would be that legal proceedings may have started and the client

---

[15] Courts and Legal Services Act 1990, s 58. There are additional requirements for some other CFAs: s 58A, s 4A and 4B. Personal injury claims are outside this book and hence the different percentage limit that applies.

[16] Except in very limited circumstances. Generally limited to pre-1 April 2013 CFAs and limited classes of post-1 April 2013 CFAs, such as publication and privacy matters: s 58.

would have to find alternative legal representation or itself conduct the litigation. Refusal of a settlement offer may give the lawyer a right to end the CFA (see below).

Other CFA arrangements

There is a CFA 'lite' where the client's obligation to pay costs is restricted to what costs are recovered from the other party in the litigation. Other CFAs may limit the liability to what is awarded on the costs assessment when the court makes a costs-shifting order. Again, the client would be liable to pay those costs if they are not recovered from the 'loser'.

Another variant is where the lawyer may be paid a fee less than the normal fee whatever the outcome of the litigation, plus a success fee if the litigation is won, i.e. a hybrid CFA. There are other variants.[17]

There may be two CFAs, one between the client and the solicitor and one between the solicitor and the barrister; or the solicitor may act on a CFA but the barrister not, or on a hybrid CFA. A barrister may act on a CFA in a public access case.[18]

5.2.3.   Third party funding (TPF)

There has been a growth in third party funding or TPF, by which a commercial organisation funds the litigation in return for a share of the money recovered in litigation or arbitration. If the case is lost, the funder loses its money and the client pays nothing.

In practice, this funding is generally only available to claimants and for claims with good prospects of success in claims of high value (e.g. £10 million or more). However, litigation funding is a rapidly developing market and funding may be opening up to claims of lower value.

---

[17] See the Bar Council's 'Guidance for Barristers and Clerks on Privately Funded Litigation', which is important for anyone considering this type of funding arrangement (with a barrister).
[18] See Bar Council (2018).

TPF is self-regulated through the Association of Litigation Funders. The member funders have agreed to operate under a Code of Conduct.[19] The code contains various requirements, such as capital adequacy and appropriate procedures for termination of funding and approval of settlements. The contract of funding is known as a Litigation Funding Agreement. There are likely to be important terms of the contract that affect the funding; such as a right for the funder to terminate it e.g. if the prospects of success change materially. Some other considerations for use of TPF arrangements are set out in a useful guide.[20]

5.2.4. Damages-based agreements (DBAs)

A contingency fee agreement or 'damages-based agreement' (DBA) is a contract by which the litigant agrees to pay a percentage of the winnings in the event of the actual recovery of damages by court judgment or settlement, but no fee if not. Again, high prospects of success will generally be required. Due to technical reasons the current regulations on DBAs may need to be changed to be more worthwhile in commercial cases and reservations have also been expressed about their legal workability.[21]

DBAs are likely to be worth consideration in appropriate cases, particularly once the legal uncertainties have been cleared up. The current rules are set out in the Damages Based Agreement Regulations 2013. These include rules for 'first instance' proceedings (i.e. before appeals) limiting what fees and disbursements are payable by the client and specifying that these must be no more than 50% of the sums ultimately recovered.[22] There are further implications of a DBA, e.g. whether the client is liable to pay the

---

[19] see www.associationoflitigationfunders.com.
[20] *Litigation funding*, Ashurst LLP, ashurst.com.
[21] See e.g. *Litigation funding,* and Bar Council (2018). [27],
[22] Reg. 4.

solicitor if the damages are not recovered from the loser, the effect of settlement offers, etc.

5.2.5. Insurance

After-the-event insurance ('ATE') is an arrangement where the litigant takes out insurance against the risk of losing the case. ATE is expensive, though deferred and (the more expensive) contingent premiums are offered by some insurers.[23] Before-the-event ('BTE') insurance is generally cheaper than ATE, because the event has not occurred whereas in ATE it has. The client must be satisfied that the insurer is of financial substance, so able to pay out under the insurance. ATE arrangements can keep litigation off the balance sheet.

ATE is available in the market for use with legal fee arrangements on the usual basis. CFAs and ATE are sometimes combined. TPF arrangements are usually accompanied by ATE. That is because the funder is likely to insist on insurance in view of the likelihood of its exposure to a costs-shifting order if the case is lost (see below).

Premiums for ATE insurance are no longer recoverable under a costs-shifting order, except in very limited types of case.[24] Once again, the client will look to be reimbursed for the premiums from any damages or other money if recovered from the opposing party to the litigation.

5.2.6. Settlement offers under CFA, TPF and ATE arrangements

CFA arrangements are likely to contain terms about termination of representation. In particular, if the client rejects advice to accept a settlement offer or Part 36 Offer (see below), the CFA may give the lawyer a right to terminate the CFA. If that happens, the client may

---

[23] For contingent premiums, the premium is payable if the case is won but not if lost.

[24] Courts and Legal Services Act 1990 s 58C. The exceptions include publication and privacy proceedings.

be liable to pay the lawyer at least some fees and disbursements to the date of termination and/or other monies.

Under a TPF, there may be terms that the funder has a role in settlement, even though it has no right to control the litigation or settlement negotiations. The ALF Code contains a dispute resolution clause for a binding opinion of a QC if there is a dispute between funder and litigant about settlement.

ATE insurance terms may also have practical effects on settlement and continuation of cover. For instance, it may prevent a litigant from taking significant risks such as rejecting offers that it would otherwise refuse.

5.3. Costs-shifting orders

A successful litigant is generally entitled to 'costs order' from the court. That order requires the other party or parties to make a payment of an amount equal to some but not all of those costs. However, a costs order will not relieve the litigant from the obligation to pay for the legal services provided by its lawyers, unless the funding arrangements so state. The costs payable by a party to its lawyers will generally exceed the amount a court will order another party to pay.

5.3.1. When is a cost-shifting order made; and for how much?

The CPR sets out principles for making a costs order, i.e. a court order that the other or another party to the litigation pay the first party's costs. The actual recovery of costs depends on a number of things. First, the court must make an 'order for costs.' Second, there are limits to the amount recoverable under an order for costs. Third, the order must be capable of being enforced and also turned into money.

Although the court has a discretion as to whether costs are to be payable by one party to another,[25] the general rule is that the unsuccessful party will be ordered to pay the costs of the successful party, though the court may make a different order.[26] In deciding what order (if any) to make about costs, the court will take into account all the circumstances. These include the conduct of the parties, whether a party has succeeded on part of its case even though it was not wholly successful, and certain settlement offers.[27] A different order may be made where the claimant, though successful, has failed to 'beat' a Part 36 Offer (see below).

Conduct includes conduct before the case was started, including the extent to which a party has complied with the Pre-Action Protocol, whether it was reasonable to raise, pursue or contest a particular allegation or issue, whether a successful claimant exaggerated its claim and the manner in which a party pursued or defended its case or a particular allegation or issue.[28]

For example, if C wins the case, it may suffer a reduction in the costs awarded if it raised or contested and lost on issues that took up significant court time. This may result in a 'percentage costs order' (e.g. that D pay 65% of C's costs) or an 'issued-based' order i.e. that C be deprived of its costs of that issue or even that it pay D's costs of it. A percentage order is not a percentage of 100% of the costs, but of the 'assessed costs' (see next paragraph).

A successful party is not entitled to a 100% recovery of its legal costs. The court determines the 'basis of assessment'. This is either 'the standard basis' or the higher and much less frequent 'indemnity basis'. In broad terms, the standard basis usually represents about two thirds of costs incurred and the indemnity basis about 90%.

---

[25] CPR 42. 2(1)(a).
[26] CPR 44. 2(2).
[27] CPR 44. 2(4).
[28] CPR 44. 2(5).

The standard basis applies to the general run of cases.[29] Indemnity costs will only be ordered if the circumstances took the case outside the ordinary and reasonable conduct of litigation, e.g. a dishonest claim or some other misconduct of the paying party (including their representatives).[30]

In multi-track cases under £10 million, there is a costs management regime.[31] The parties each provide a costs budget from which the court usually makes a 'costs management order' (CMO) for the future costs of the litigation (but not for those already incurred).[32] A CMO is made at an early stage in proceedings so as to incentivise the parties to limit their own costs.

However, this does not prevent parties incurring in appropriate cases large costs in initial preparation of their case as long as they are reasonably incurred and are proportionate. In assessing costs at the end of the claim on the standard basis where a CMO has been made, the court will not depart from the approved or agreed budget except for good reason.[33] Pre-CMO costs will be subject to the general tests of reasonableness and proportionality. A costs-shifting

---

[29] An assessment on the standard basis will identify whether each item of costs has been necessary and if so, whether the amount was reasonably incurred. The figure for reasonable costs is subjected to a test of proportionality. Costs may be disallowed even where they were reasonably or necessarily incurred. Only proportionate costs will be allowed and the costs must bear a reasonable relationship to issues in the litigation (not limited to the sums in dispute) (CPR 44.3). That does not mean that the costs must be equal to or less than the money claimed.

[30] *Excelsior Commercial and Industrial Holdings Ltd v Salisbury Hammer etc (a firm)* [2002] EWCA Civ 879; *Esure Services Ltd v Quarcoo* [2009] EWCA Civ 595. See too p 89 under *'Unreasonable refusal to mediate, etc.'*

[31] CPR 3.12(1) and see Appendix 1.

[32] CPR 3.13-15.

[33] CPR 3.18(b). As an alternative, the court may make a 'costs capping order' limiting recovery of future costs (CPR 3.19-21). This is rare, however.

order may include costs incurred before the proceedings if incidental to them.[34]

There is a procedure for assessment of costs if the amount cannot be agreed. Unless the claim is of high value, there is usually agreement between the parties on the figure. The costs of the actual assessment are generally disproportionate to any dispute over the amount of the costs payable.

5.3.2. Further considerations

Costs-shifting orders may be affected by further factors. Some of the more important are as follows.

Who was the winner?

Sometimes, it is not clear who won the litigation. The costs orders then made by the court may leave both parties dissatisfied. A prime example are some cases where both claim and counterclaim succeed.

The basic rule is that each party obtains a costs order for any claim it won. However, the complexities have led the courts to develop rules to which exceptions have been made to achieve a just outcome; for example, in one case the court made no costs order and in another D was ordered to pay 60% of C's costs.[35] Such orders are often difficult to challenge on appeal.

Unreasonable refusal to mediate, etc

An unreasonable refusal to engage in ADR (particularly mediation) may result in a successful party being deprived of some or all of its costs or a loser having to pay a winner's costs on an indemnity basis.[36]

---

[34] See e.g. *Re Gibson's Settlement Trusts* [1981] Ch 179.

[35] See *Medway Oil and Storage Co. Ltd. v Continental Contractors Ltd* [1929] AC 88, HL, *Burchell v Bullard* [2005] EWCA Civ 358 and *The Square Mile Partnership Ltd v Fitzmaurice McCall Ltd* [2006] EWHC 236 (Ch).

[36] *Halsey v Milton Keynes General NHS Trust* [2004] 1 W.L.R. 3002, C.A; *DSN v Blackpool Football Club Ltd* [2020] EWHC 670 (QB).

Cases for recovery of fixed costs only

A trial pilot scheme has been introduced for certain cases where the claim value is £250,000 or less, where the winner's costs to be paid by the loser are generally limited to £80,000 at most (divided into maximum amounts for each stage of the case) plus court fees.[37] Fixed costs may be rolled out for all claims to that value and possibly beyond. In intellectual property cases brought in the Intellectual Property Enterprise Court, there is a fixed or 'scale' costs regime.[38]

Pre-trial costs

The court may make orders for costs at hearings before trial. However, these generally relate to applications to court, where one party has succeeded and the other failed; e.g. for further disclosure of documents or summary judgment. These are generally a small part of the overall costs. There are exceptions, where substantial costs are generated, e.g. interim injunction hearing(s). The time for payment of those costs may be at the end of the case but not necessarily so.

Non-parties

In certain cases, a costs order may be made against a 'non-party'. One example is where the litigating party is financially insecure and its costs are funded by a third party; e.g. a director or shareholder of a struggling company. Even then, it does not follow that a costs order would be made against the funder.[39] A 'non-party' costs order is likely against a commercial funder where the case is lost, as the funder stood to make a commercial benefit from the litigation. The

---

[37] CPR PD 51W. There are tight controls on the conduct of cases within the pilot; e.g. generally no more than two witnesses per party and parties to rely on core documents only with no obligation of disclosure.

[38] CPR 45.31; inapplicable to intellectual property claims not brought in the IPEC.

[39] See the commentary and cases referred to in *Civil Procedure*, Vol. 1 [46.2.2] and [46.2.3].

amount will not necessarily be capped at the level of funding provided.[40] A costs order may be made against an insurer.

Effect on CFAs and other funding arrangements

What are the consequences of litigating *against* a party using a particular form of funding in view of the principle that the 'loser pays'? The fact that a party has a CFA or DBA for its own costs does not protect it from an adverse costs order. If the loser has ATE insurance, the insurance will cover that exposure if the insurer accepts liability under the policy. As indicated (see **5.2** above), a litigant with CFA funding can no longer recover its success fee from the losing party. The same is true of a party's ATE premiums.

5.4. 'Insuring' legal costs exposure through court processes

5.4.1. Introduction

This section examines how a litigant can take steps to protect its exposure to legal costs in litigation. There are court procedures that give significant protection against an opponent who unreasonably refuses to end the case.

5.4.2. Part 36 Offers

Introduction

Part 36 refers to CPR Part 36. It is a self-contained set of rules both for settlement and protection against the costs of the litigation. A Part 36 Offer is in substance an offer that, if accepted, ends the litigation.

When might a litigant wish to make a Part 36 Offer? The ultimate outcome is often not 'all or nothing'. C may not be entitled to the £200,000 it claims, but to some lower amount. A *qualifying* offer to settle allows the defendant to make an offer that will either settle the case if accepted but give it real protection on costs if not accepted. If

---

[40] *Civil Procedure*, Vol. 1 [46.2.4], 3rd Supplement, *Arkin v Borchard Lines Ltd & Ors* [2005] EWCA Civ 655 and *Davey v Money & Anr* [2020] EWCA Civ 246.

the offeree fails to achieve a result at trial better than the offer, the offeree will generally be penalised in costs and, if the offeror is the claimant, both in costs and in additional money terms. In other words, the Part 36 Offer operates as a form of insurance policy, though it does not address the risk of non-recovery, e.g. from insolvency.

A Part 36 Offer may be made at any time, including before the start of proceedings.[41] The offer may not be seen by the trial judge until the case has been decided, or if the offer has been made in appeal proceedings, before the appeal has been decided. This allows the party making the offer to advance its case without the court knowing about the offer. The court only becomes aware of it when hearing argument about what costs orders should be made at the end of the hearing, after judgment on the main issues.

Use of the Part 36 procedures is generally of much less value where a party wishes to make a 'commercial offer' to end the litigation. That is because the offer is not designed to reflect a predicted outcome if the case were to go to court.

There are technical rules as to when and in what form a Part 36 Offer is to be made and accepted, and various qualifications and exceptions to the basic explanations that follow.

Defendant's Part 36 Offer
If a defendant has made a Part 36 - compliant offer and the claimant accepts it within the relevant period,[42] the claimant is entitled to the remedy or relief offered. The basic rule is that the claimant is also entitled to its costs to the date of acceptance on the standard basis.[43]

---

[41] CPR 36.7(1).
[42] The period is 21 days, subject to exceptions: CPR 36.3(g).
[43] CPR 36.5 – 13.

If a claimant does not accept a Part 36 Offer but does not better the offer at trial, it will generally be ordered to pay the defendant's costs from the date on which the period for acceptance expired.[44]

The claimant's costs before that date would generally be payable by the defendant under a costs-shifting order. The two sets of costs could be set off against each other.

If a Part 36 Offer is not accepted within the prescribed time (usually within 21 days of the offer being made), it can be accepted all the way up to trial but after that, only with the court's permission.[45] There is case law and further rules on 'late acceptance' after the expiry of the prescribed time period and the costs consequences of that.

Claimant's Part 36 Offer

The scheme in Part 36 allows a claimant to offer to accept less than the amount claimed. If the defendant does not accept the offer and judgment against the defendant is at least advantageous to the claimant as the proposals made in a claimant's Part 36 Offer, the court must, unless it is unjust to do so, order that the claimant is entitled to:

- interest at a rate up to and including 10% above base rate on the whole or part of any judgment sum (excluding interest) from the date when the relevant period[46] expired;
- costs on the indemnity basis from the date on which that period expired;
- interest on those costs at a rate not exceeding 10% above base rate;

---

[44] CPR 36.17(3)(a).
[45] Subject to certain exceptions set out in CPR 36.11(3).
[46] 21 days, subject to exceptions: CPR 36.3(g).

- a further sum equal to a prescribed percentage of the judgment sum or if there is no judgment sum, the amount of costs awarded to the claimant, subject to a maximum of £75,000.[47]

Part 36 Offers: conclusion

Therefore, a Part 36 Offer has the merit that if refused and the successful party does not beat it at trial, the refusal has real adverse consequences in costs for the refusing party. That is why recipients of Part 36 Offers do not like them.

Open offers

Another way of seeking some protection on legal costs is to make what is called an 'open offer', typically where a party admits a part of the other side's case. An open offer is one which does not have to be kept from the trial judge. Tactically, it may suit a party to make an open offer; e.g. to appear reasonable and keep costs down particularly if there is no realistic prospect of defending part of the claim. A 'without prejudice' offer does not have this effect, because the trial judge is not allowed to know about the offer at all (see **6.12.4** below).

5.4.3. Security for costs

In some circumstances, the court will order that financial measures be put in place to protect a party against a risk that, if successful at trial, it will not recover costs from the opposing party. This is called a 'security for costs order'. If the order is not complied with, the proceedings may not progress further. Security for costs is only available to a defendant to a claim or a defendant to a counterclaim.

A typical case is where the claimant is a limited company (not an individual person) and there is reason to believe that it would be unable to pay the defendant's costs, if ordered to do so at trial. This may be clear from the claimant company's filed accounts at

---

[47] CPR 36.17(1)(b), (2), (4), (5)-(8). Where interest is awarded on the judgment sum under other powers, the total rate must not exceed 10% above base rate: CPR 36.17(6).

Companies House, showing for instance no net assets on the balance sheet or that the company is loss-making. The court will make an order if it is just. Orders may be made against some non-resident persons, or where the claiming party has taken steps to frustrate any adverse order for costs.[48] There are commercial funders who may offer bond or other arrangements for security for costs.

5.5.   Comparison with arbitration and expert determination

The fee structures for engaging lawyers in arbitration and expert determination procedures are similar to litigation, although the amounts may differ. The arrangements will depend on whether a solicitor and/or barrister are engaged. The fees payable may differ from what they would be in litigation. For expert determination in particular, the fees should be lower in many cases. An enforceable CFA may be made for dispute resolution through arbitration or expert determination.[49] It also appears that the 'success' element of a CFA would not be recoverable in arbitration.[50]

In arbitration, there is also a general principle that 'the loser pays'. In expert determination, there is no costs-shifting unless the contractual arrangements allow the expert to award costs (see Chapter 3).

As we have seen, costs control in litigation is generally exercised by costs budgeting and costs management orders in the majority of cases. In arbitrations under the Arbitration Act 1996, costs may be capped by the arbitral tribunal in advance of being incurred. This limits what 'costs of the arbitration' may be recovered by one party

---

[48] CPR 25.13 (1), (2). See CPR 25.14 as to the liability of third-party funders and others to provide security for costs.

[49] An enforceable CFA under Courts and Legal Services Act 1990 s 58, may apply to 'any sort of proceedings for resolving disputes (and not just proceedings in a court), whether commenced or contemplated': s 58A (4).

[50] See *Merkin & Flannery* (2019) [63.4.2]. For DBAs see [63.4.3].

from the other at the end of the arbitration.[51] Costs may also be capped by the scheme or rules that apply to the arbitration.

Costs capping has so far been rare in litigation. It has been directed at a different problem: where a fair trial would be put at risk as a result of a financial imbalance between the parties. Exceptional circumstances are generally required for a costs-capping order.[52]

However, the move towards reducing litigation costs has resulted in much discussion about the capping of costs: see e.g. the trial pilot scheme for fixed costs referred to above.

There is no machinery for a Part 36 Offer in the Arbitration Act 1996. But similar costs protection or 'insurance' may be available in arbitration by an offer stated to be made 'without prejudice except as to costs', known as a 'Calderbank Offer'.

In arbitration, security for costs may be available against claiming parties unless the parties have agreed otherwise.[53] Arbitration rules adopted by the parties may also provide for security for costs.

---

[51] Section 65; subject to any contrary agreement.
[52] CPR PD3F [1.1].
[53] AA 1996 s 38(3).

6.   SETTLEMENT

6.1.   Introduction

What is a settlement? It is a binding, i.e. legally enforceable, agreement which disposes of the dispute on agreed terms. Although a verbal (oral) settlement agreement is generally binding, most settlement agreements are written. This reflects commercial practice and occasionally is required to make the agreement valid. It is also wise to have the arrangement set out in writing so there is a clear record of the agreed terms.[1]

The essential features of a settlement agreement are two. First, there is an agreement to settle or compromise the dispute and the claims arising from it. Second, there are the other terms of the settlement. At its simplest, these could be that A will pay B £x within y days.

As settlements are contracts, the parties have freedom to choose the deal terms. In rare cases 'public policy' would make the settlement or a term of it invalid; e.g. where the settlement is entered into with the purpose of doing an unlawful act.

6.2.   What disputes and claims are being settled?

The terms of the settlement are very important. Exactly what dispute is being settled? Are there other disputes between the parties and if so, are these being settled? Sometimes, the parties are not aware of all the facts or implications of their dispute or dealings but may wish to settle all and any *claims* arising out of those, whether known or unknown – to give finality. So, the agreement may be drafted to cover not only all legal claims made in the

---

[1] The Centre for Effective Dispute Resolution (CEDR) publishes Model Documents, including a specimen draft settlement agreement: see www.cedr.com and the accompanying guidance notes.

dispute, but any that might be advanced in connection with the facts or subject-matter of the dispute.[2]

A company may wish to ensure that personal claims against its directors or employees are also included.[3] The dispute may not have included those claims to date. So, the identity of the parties to the settlement as well as settlement of potential claims against them, are important considerations.

6.3. Further legal requirements

There are other requirements for any valid settlement agreement. Most relevant are these:

- generally, there must be 'consideration';
- the agreement must be complete and certain; and
- in certain cases, formalities must be present.

Consideration is based on the idea that "something of value in the eye of the law" must be given for a promise to make it binding as a contract.[4] In a settlement, that generally comes from a promise by one party not to pursue a legal claim in return for some act by the other party; e.g. the payment of money. Ordinarily, the court will not concern itself about the adequacy of the consideration, though it must be real.

An agreement must be sufficiently complete and certain. It must not be too vague and all the material terms must be agreed. It is generally better to place the terms in one document that is signed by or for each party, each party having been identified at the start of the written agreement. Although an agreement can be created in an exchange of emails or other written communications, it is sometimes

---

[2] Foskett (2019), [2-08].

[3] Those individuals should be parties to the agreement and sign it; parties should also be aware of the Contracts (Rights of Third Parties Act) 1999.

[4] See Chapter 2 and the references to the making of contracts and 'benefit' at **2.1.2** above.

difficult to see if each side has agreed to what the other has proposed. The result may be an invalid settlement agreement. If it is intended to affect other parties, an exchange of correspondence might not work either.

Sometimes, a document is signed by the parties which states that a more detailed document is to be drawn up and signed. The wording of the first document generally dictates whether or not there is a binding settlement at that first stage.[5]

If there are formalities, these generally require the terms of the agreement be made or evidenced in writing, with related requirements. Examples include the sale or other disposition of most interests in land (e.g. landlord and tenant actions and boundary disputes) and also contracts of guarantee.

6.4. Settlement and broader commercial terms

Parties wishing to settle a dispute have considerable freedom to enter into wider commercial arrangements that facilitate the deal. In simple cases, the settlement may be an agreed change or set of changes to an existing contract. More complex disputes can also be resolved in this way.

Or the parties might agree to end the contract on certain terms and also agree a new deal. Take the example of a dispute over performance of a distribution agreement. The dispute may have concerned payment for goods supplied, the distributor withholding payment due to defects in products supplied and terminating the agreement. The supplier might have claimed that the products complied with the contract, that payment was due and there was no right to terminate.

Settlement discussions might result in the supplier agreeing to forego payment for all the money claimed on one line of products, in

---

[5] *Von Hatzfeldt-Wildenburg v Alexander* [1912] 1 Ch. 284 at 288-289 and Foskett (2019) [3-56] and cases cited.

return for the distributor agreeing to take other lines of products and entering into a new distribution agreement, with the parties agreeing to terminate the agreement in dispute. The settlement arrangements would reflect these terms.

6.5.   Payment terms

The payment terms will identify the necessary details and time for payment. If there is more than one defending party, the liability to pay is often agreed to be 'joint and several'. This means that the payee can look to any of those parties for the full amount of the payment.

Any agreed stage payments may be underpinned by a provision that the entire balance becomes due on default of payment of an instalment. There are variants to this type of clause and interest may be added to unpaid amounts.

6.6.   Confidentiality and agreed statements

Settlement agreements often contain a term that states the settlement is confidential. A defendant may want to keep secret that it has agreed to pay money in response to a claim. There are many other reasons why commercial interests make it in the interests of one party or both that the terms of the deal remain confidential. There are legal limits to confidentiality.

Sometimes, the parties need to be able to say something to others about their settlement. That is generally addressed by an agreed statement, which forms part of the settlement agreement. The parties agree that the only communication either side will make about ending their dispute is what is in the agreed statement.

There are also practical limits to the effectiveness of legal obligations of confidentiality. Once a settlement has been revealed to third parties, there may be no practical remedy. Money does not provide appropriate compensation. Sometimes, terms are included in the settlement agreement to dissuade a party from breaking the confidentiality clause. They may not be effective. An obligation to pay damages may be an unenforceable 'penalty' in law.

In some cases, the parties will agree a statement because one party wants the statement to show to third parties, typically some acknowledgement by the defendant that it has invaded the claimant's rights or breached its obligations. These statements tend to be closely negotiated, particularly due to the legal and practical implications of a defendant making an acknowledgement that would become public.

6.7. Dispute resolution procedures

Dispute resolution procedures are often worth including to cover any dispute over the settlement agreement itself. In simple deals, there is no point in this. But it may be prudent where the settlement deal is more intricate.

6.8. International elements

Any international element to a settlement agreement will require checking, e.g. as to the enforceability of the agreement, the law that governs it and which courts are to have jurisdiction over any dispute.

There is a new multi-lateral agreement for the enforcement of settlements. It is the United Nations Convention on International Settlement Agreements Resulting from Mediation ('the Singapore Convention'). At its opening on 7 August 2019, it was signed by 46 countries includling crucially the United States, China and India. It enters into force on 12 September 2020. The EU supports the Singapore Convention but has been caught in an internal legal debate as to whether it can sign on behalf of member states or whether each needs to sign in its own right. The UK has not signed since it left the EU but it is likely to do so in 2020. The Convention will bring increased certainty to the enforceability of international mediated settlement agreements.

6.9. Settlement during legal action

When a settlement is reached during legal proceedings, the settlement must address what is to be done with the legal action. A 'Tomlin Order' is often used. The order stops or 'stays' the litigation but each party is given permission to apply to the court to enforce the settlement agreement if necessary. The settlement agreement itself is set out in a schedule to the court order and signed by the parties.

The parties may wish the terms of the settlement to be confidential, and not form part of the court record open to public inspection. One course is to identify the document by a sufficient description in the schedule to the order and so keep it off the court file.[6]

An agreed award may be used to stay an arbitration, like a Tomlin Order. The parties may wish to be given permission to apply to the court rather than to the arbitrator for enforcement purposes.

Note that the settlement may only be binding once the order of the court or agreed award has been made, and not before.

6.10. Rights under the settlement agreement

If a party does not perform the terms of a settlement agreement, the remedy for the innocent party is to enforce that agreement. The rights that were the subject of the earlier dispute are not revived, because of the settlement. The remedy is to enforce the terms of the settlement agreement, e.g. by applying to court for an order for payment of money. Once bound by a settlement agreement, a party can only get out of it in very rare circumstances. As a result, the original dispute is generally a matter of history.[7] New legal proceedings will be unnecessary if the settlement agreement was

---

[6] Foskett (2019) [10-31] and *Zenith Logistics Services Ltd & Others v Coury* [2020] EWHC 774 (QB).
[7] Occasionally, the terms of the settlement restore the parties to their original rights if the terms are not performed.

made under a Tomlin Order or Agreed Award (see above). There are technical rules about the extent to which, if at all, rights against other parties who are also liable survive a compromise agreement with one party.[8]

6.11. Settlement and uncertainty

A settlement is intended to resolve the dispute. But it may carry uncertainty. The following are some of the possibilities. In cases concerning the payment of money only, the risk for the debtor is likely to be minimal, assuming the payment is affordable. For the creditor, there may be a risk of non-payment.[9] The creditor may have to consider any difficulties and extra cost in enforcing the settlement by legal action. Assuming no transnational issues of enforcement (see Appendix 1 page 182), the consequences of that outcome would include extra cost and delay, plus any attached to non-payment.

Where the settlement arrangements envisage longer-term performance by one party or both (e.g. a renegotiated distribution agreement), there would be risks from that non-performance, depending on the terms.

In some cases, the potential settlement terms may involve an alternative, or more than one alternative. For example, payment of £X or a new distribution agreement and payment of £X-Y. The uncertainty attached to each will differ and should be assessed before concluding the deal.

Ultimately, for a creditor the risks created by a default in payment under a settlement may be less than the risks created by the debtor's

---

[8] Foskett (2019) [6-26] – [6-61].
[9] In the case of payment by a company in financial difficulties, if it is a connected company there would be a risk of a liquidator being able to recover the payment in the event of an insolvent liquidation. See gen. on unlawful preferences: Gore-Browne (2020) 58 [19A-C].

default following an adverse money judgment and costs-shifting order.

6.12. Routes to settlement

6.12.1. Introduction

About 90% of litigation is settled out of court or dropped.[10] Court procedures require the parties to do their best to keep the dispute away from the courts and only litigate as a last resort (see Chapter 3 and Appendix 1 page 164).

6.12.2. Dispute resolution clauses

Many written contracts contain a disputes procedure that the parties have agreed to use. These are generally effective and subject only to limited exceptions, e.g. where something is wrong with the wording of the clause to make the clause unenforceable.

Those clauses may encourage the parties to settle their dispute. Typically, there is a prescribed period for negotiation between representatives of each business at one or more levels of seniority; followed by mediation if the negotiations are unsuccessful. Or there may be a clause for mediation on its own.

The contract may specify the method of dispute resolution if there is no settlement of the dispute after negotiation. The usual alternatives are court action, arbitration or expert determination (see Chapter 3).

6.12.3. Part 36 Offers and Calderbank Offers

Litigation may be brought to an end by a Part 36 Offer accepted by the recipient of the offer (see Chapter 5). Often, more than one Part 36 Offer is made in litigation, and claimants as well as defendants can do so. Part 36 Offers are also used in combination with other routes to settlement. For example, a last offer that is made but refused in a mediation (see below) may then be made as a Part 36 Offer.

---

[10] *Financial Times*, 14 August 2019, Kate Beioley.

In arbitration, an offer made 'without prejudice save as to costs' (known as a Calderbank offer) has a similar effect to a Part 36 Offer. The offer is not disclosed to the arbitral tribunal until after the award on the merits of the dispute. The tribunal may then see the offer and take it into account when deciding which party should bear the costs (see **5.5** above and Appendix 2).

6.12.4. Negotiation

A party may run a negotiation in parallel to litigation or an arbitration, whether actual or pending. The 'without prejudice' rule allows a party to continue to run its case, but to negotiate without the danger of the court or arbitral tribunal knowing about the content of the negotiations.

If an offer is made without prejudice, this means that the court or tribunal may not be informed of the offer even when assessing the costs of the case. The basic principle is that genuine attempts to settle a dispute should be hidden from the court and not admitted in evidence to the prejudice of one or other of the parties. The exceptions to the without prejudice rule are few.[11]

A without prejudice offer is therefore a means of conveying a 'commercial offer' to settle (i.e. not necessarily predictive of the outcome in court), while allowing the person making the offer to contest the litigation. If accepted, the offer will end the dispute, assuming that a binding settlement agreement is created (see above).

Correspondence in a negotiation is best marked 'without prejudice'. Face-to-face negotiations should also be conducted explicitly 'without prejudice.'

---

[11] See Appendix 1, section 6.

Negotiation is the most usual route to settlement, often carried out by with lawyers for each side.[12] How the negotiations are conducted will depend on the context and the preferences of the participants (see Chapter 7).

Round table meetings (RTMs) or joint settlement meetings (JSMs) have also developed informally as a result of the encouragement towards settlement in the civil justice system. Each party's legal team meets at the offices or chambers of one side's lawyers. The parties do not have a substantial input in the negotiations, other than to give the necessary authority to their lawyers.

6.12.5. Mediation

Mediation is a structured process by which the parties to the dispute consent to the appointment of a neutral known as a 'mediator' to facilitate settlement of the dispute. *'A skilled mediator can bring an independent perspective that can cut through the positions taken by the parties, identifying middle ground or new solutions.'* [13]

The basic model is based on a mediation day, when the parties and their lawyers go to an agreed venue. The mediation is conducted under a mediation agreement. The day generally consists of a sequence of 'joint meetings' and separate 'party only' meetings, with the mediator. If a deal is done, the parties sign a settlement agreement that day or soon afterwards.

The Covid-19 pandemic has led to many mediations being conducted by video-conferencing, with positive reports of mediations conducted in this way. Participants can meet in, and also be separated into, virtual rooms. The mediator can move between rooms, meeting each side privately or in joint session. This type of mediation may be best conducted over more than one day. The

---

[12] Litigation brought to an end under the procedures in CPR Part 36 does not require a settlement agreement. If used, CPR Part 36 constitutes a self-contained framework for the disposal of litigation.
[13] *Garritt-Critchley v Ronnan* [2014] EWHC 1774 (Ch).

conferencing facilities should be private and secure, and participants require a good internet or other communications link. The Centre for Effective Dispute Resolution (CEDR) has published a useful Guide to Online Mediation for Barristers, Solicitors and Clients.

In addition to video-conferencing, there are other so-called 'Online Dispute Resolution' ('ODR') tools. To date, these have been mostly confined to consumer disputes or those of low value. Developments in the technology of Artificial Intelligence are likely to influence mainstream mediation and online mediation generally is likely to grow.

Settlement rates through mediation are high. The most recent published figures show that about 74% of commercial disputes settle at the mediation and a further 15% settle within a few weeks after that.[14] Mediation is *'a user-friendly, adaptable and highly effective dispute resolution process, so long as its scale and extra cost is proportionate.'* [15]

The mediator is usually a person with appropriate training in mediation skills and is often a lawyer, but not always. Surprisingly, there is no statutory regulation or licensing of mediators. The Civil Mediation Council operates a system of voluntary registration for mediation providers and mediators. Mediation providers include CEDR, Independent Mediators, In Place of Strife and ADR Group. The ICC offers mediation under its Mediation Rules.

The mediation agreement will generally provide for the 'without prejudice' and confidential nature of the discussions and information provided for and during the mediation. The agreement may, and should, provide that any settlement agreement must be in writing to be valid and binding.

---

[14] *CEDR Mediation Audit 2018*, based on a survey of mediators in the UK. The overall percentage for the previous audit by CEDR (2016) was 86%.
[15] CJC ADR Working Group (2018), section 3.5.

The mediator will usually contact and speak to the parties before the mediation day by phone or video-conferencing. These are separate calls or meetings with each party (the contents of which are usually confidential), but sometimes the mediator meets with both parties. In more complex cases 'process design' may be necessary to get the best out of the mediation. Typical topics discussed in pre-mediation contact with the mediator are a brief overview of the dispute, initial thoughts on how it might be resolved, discussion about the representatives who should best attend, their authority to conclude a settlement, whether there will be an opening joint meeting and if so whether an oral opening statement will be made and who will make it.

How is a mediation set up? Lawyers can set up the mediation in contact with the other side. If parties have not engaged lawyers, the easiest approach is to contact a body (e.g. CEDR) which provides mediation services and they can guide participants through the process for setting up a mediation. CEDR also has on its website model settlement documents for use. Bear in mind that these are not a substitute for legal advice on the terms of settlement. A mediation provider can also provide a selection of mediators for the parties to choose from or appoint a mediator if they cannot agree which person to engage.

On the mediation day, the mediator directs the process in consultation with the parties. In a minority of cases ill feeling may point against an opening joint meeting with all present. Even then, profitable opening sessions can still be held between the lawyers and the mediator, for example. Caucus meetings are an opportunity for confidential discussions between the mediator and each party.

The mediation process is not just a negotiation moderated by the mediator. The mediator should facilitate exploration of commercial interests, of settlement options and engage in the 'reality-testing' of each side's position. Reality-testing is generally done privately and in confidence with the mediator. Essentially, it is an opportunity to reflect on the commercial implications of litigating (see Chapter 7).

Using the tools of the mediation process, a mediator can often reduce the adverse effects of emotion driving a dispute and help the parties to see their dispute more objectively. In many cases, parties settle because pursuit of the legal process is commercially too dangerous because of the risks.

If funds are limited, a party may take legal advice before the mediation day but not engage a lawyer to attend. Costs can be kept costs down if a party's lawyer does not attend, but is available to advise by telephone, if necessary. That said, it is best that the lawyer does attend. If a party is not legally represented on the day or does not have access to legal advice, the best course is often to agree terms in writing but expressly (and in writing) 'subject to contract' and 'subject to legal advice.'

6.12.6. Early neutral evaluation

Early Neutral Evaluation (ENE) is a process by which the parties engage a neutral, typically a judge or other senior lawyer, to give their opinion on the likely outcome of the case or one or more issues in it. Until recently, ENE had been of more theoretical than practical interest. ENE might become more used, however.

An ENE assessment can examine the key issues in the dispute through a focused time-limited process, avoiding much of the time and cost of a trial. ENE requires the evaluator to read the papers provided by the parties and to give an opinion (generally non-binding) on the likely outcome of the case, though the parties may agree that the opinion is binding or binding for a certain period, e.g. up to trial. ENE has been used in the USA, with significant success.[16] Evaluation based on percentage prospects of success is the form of evaluation of most use to litigants. The ENE process can be designed

---

[16] Brazil (2012) gives a detailed analysis of ENE.

to suit the parties, so for example, there may or may not be a hearing. If there is one, it would likely be short (e.g. half a day).

ENE is particularly productive at an early stage of a dispute, before significant legal costs have been incurred. It can work well where it is about some legal point, such as the meaning of a contract. It may be less useful where there are complex issues of fact, where an outcome in court might depend on an assessment of witness evidence.

However, an experienced neutral may give a useful forecast of how a court would decide a dispute involving issues of fact so typical of the general run of cases.

The opinion given by the neutral may help the parties settle the case by negotiation. A mediation may be unnecessary. However, the evaluation may result in one party becoming entrenched in its position as a result of the ENE, if the neutral's opinion favoured its case. That may make settlement more difficult, particularly if the other party considers that the neutral was wrong. Equally, the evaluation may inject a dose of reality where one side has unrealistic expectations.

The CPR authorises judges to direct ENE.[17] Although ENE has been used rarely to date, that has the potential to change. In *Lomax v Lomax*[18] (an inheritance dispute) the Court of Appeal directed that ENE be used even though one party objected.

ENE may be conducted outside court rules. It does not require an order from the court if both parties agree to it. The ENE would best be carried out under a written agreement made between the parties (and the evaluator).

---

[17] CPR 3.1(2)(m).
[18] [2019] EWCA Civ. 1467.

Some courts have specific schemes for ENE. These include the Chancery Division and the Commercial Court.[19] If a scheme is used, the evaluating judge would generally take no further part in the case. Rules provide for the 'without prejudice' nature of the process. In the case of ENE, particularly ENE outside a court scheme, the ENE agreement should specify such matters as the confidentiality and 'without prejudice' nature of the process. ENE under a court scheme may address these considerations by way of directions issued by the court or the evaluator.

6.12.7. Financial Dispute Resolution

The courts of the Chancery Division have a procedure for an ADR tool by which the judge facilitates negotiations and may provide the parties with an opinion about the claim or elements of it. Financial Dispute Resolution or 'FDR' is generally confidential and 'without prejudice'. [20]

6.12.8. Dispute Boards

A 'Dispute Board' ('DB') is a permanent body (of one or more members) set up by parties to a contract. DBs assist in avoiding or overcoming disagreements and disputes. They are particularly suited to long-term contracts, such as infrastructure projects, shareholder agreements and research and development contracts. Depending on the particular procedures chosen by the parties, a DB may assist them to reach an agreement to resolve the dispute, or make recommendations (or a decision that may be binding on the parties: see **3.4.4** above).[21]

6.12.9. Mediation-Arbitration (Med-Arb)

Mediation may be carried out alongside an arbitration. Med-Arb, however, is a process by which the parties agree to mediate and if

---

[19] *Chancery Guide*, [18.7] – [18.15], Commercial Court Guide, G2. See also *Telecom Centre (UK) Ltd v Thomas Sanderson Ltd* [2020] EWHC 368 (QB).
[20] Courts in the Chancery Division; see *Chancery Guide*, [18.16] - [18-18].
[21] See e.g. ICC Dispute Board Rules: www.iccwbo.org.

the mediation is unsuccessful, the mediator becomes an arbitrator of the dispute. It is not widely used in this jurisdiction, principally because of the difficulties of fairly combining the two roles.[22]

---

[22] See Herbert Smith Freehills (2012).

7. NEGOTIATIONS

7.1. Introduction

As we have seen with Brexit, being 'bloody difficult'[1] has its limitations as a negotiating strategy. If one side issues a series of demands, the other is likely to do the same and progress is unlikely. Trying to hammer an opponent into submission by telling them they are wrong is not very effective.

There is a large body of literature on negotiation.[2] This chapter examines some of the more important points, for resolving a business dispute. It also explains the advantages of mediation as valued-added negotiation.

7.2. The Negotiations

Business-people are used to deal making. A commercial contract usually has an upside, the prospect of a profit or other commercial advantage. Negotiations to end a business dispute are very different. The choice facing each party is not between a good outcome and a bad outcome. It is generally between a bad outcome and one that is potentially worse. Bad, because a substantial payment or discount may be necessary to settle the dispute. And potentially worse, because a party may lose in court, pay two sets of legal costs and waste time and effort in losing the case.

But, for both sides there is usually a commercial advantage in being freed from the dispute by a settlement on the right terms. Settlement allows the parties to regain control of the dispute, as opposed to ceding control to a judge or other decision-maker. And solutions not available by legal action are possible in a negotiation.

---

[1] Ex-PM Theresa May's description of herself with reference to those negotiations.

[2] Some of that literature is referred to in the footnotes in this chapter.

Business disputes often result in a commercial divorce of the parties. The breakdown of commercial trust is often irretrievable and no future relationship possible. In these cases, the negotiation is often based on a search for a magic number x, the sum of money that fixes the problem.

On other occasions, a commercial relationship may survive the dispute. Where parties share interests in a continuing relationship (e.g. a joint venture), deal-making opportunities are often available and make court action particularly unattractive. Financial and other aspects of a dispute can be traded through changes to the ongoing arrangements, such as revised joint venture terms or new software licence terms.

Whether or not a continued relationship is feasible, a kind of 'alienation' often takes over once commercial trust has broken down. Each side sees the other as having behaved in way that is unacceptable, reprehensible or worse. The engagement of lawyers by each side, though often necessary to run a legal case, often adds fuel to the fire. Correspondence is 'hotted up' as each side's lawyers advocate their client's position. As we will see, the best chance of an effective negotiation is to reset the communications between the parties.

7.2.1. Preparation

Manner of negotiations and identity of participants

Having decided when to negotiate,[3] decide how the negotiation will be run. The negotiation may be between those at operational level, senior management or at board level. Face-to-face discussion at a physical meeting is usually the best course. The alternatives in descending order of likely effectiveness are video calls and conferencing, telephone calls or audio conferencing, and email.

---

[3] See Chapter 8, pp 148-151.

The Covid-19 virus has made face-to-face negotiation more difficult while social distancing is in place. During periods of lockdown or remote working due to Covid-19, video-conferencing will often be the best available method.

If lawyers are conducting the negotiation, lawyer to lawyer phone calls may take place, followed by correspondence containing or responding to an offer (see Chapter 6).

In negotiations, more than one representative of the business may be needed. For example, a financial director to deal with figures and a colleague with direct knowledge of the dispute. The negotiations should be attended by a person or persons with the authority to do a deal, who is/are objective and can make decisions in the best interests of the business. Those involved in the dispute are likely to be too partisan to distinguish effectively between those interests and a desire to be proved right in some way. For the same reason, conduct of the negotiation may be best left to another member of the team.

An in-house lawyer might have the necessary authority and be objective, if not involved in the dispute. Even so, there is often good sense in a commercial representative attending, who has not been involved in the dispute and can make a judgment on settlement based on all the risks in the dispute, legal and commercial. For negotiations without access to a lawyer, consider taking advice beforehand on the legal merits and - costs implications of going to law.

In assembling the negotiating team, personal relationships with the other side are key. Particularly bad relationships at one level indicate attendance by other representatives, while a good relationship between executive counterparts might be an obvious starting-point for a negotiation. If a previous negotiation has gone badly, a new mix of attendees might be appropriate, or a new spokesperson or negotiator.

NEGOTIATION

Each side to a negotiation should give the other reasonable notice of who is attending, and their role or position. The venue of the negotiation is also important, e.g. neutral and accessible to all attending. If the negotiation is to be online, appropriate and secure technology should be used, with each participant having access to a secure and adequate internet connection or other signal. It is also sensible to agree ground-rules for a remote mediation, e.g. no recording, back-up communication arrangements if there are communication issues, the 'chat' function to be used only for administrative matters, etc.

If lawyers (particularly external) are to be involved in a negotiation with clients present, what role are they to play? Although sometimes convenient to let the lawyer run the negotiation, the lawyer may not be best suited to that role.[4] Lawyers as negotiators sometimes reduce the breadth of discussions, which can become stuck on the legal merits.

Parties conducting in-person (including video and audio) negotiations without lawyers may wish to agree in writing (an exchange of emails suffices) that:

- the discussions are 'without prejudice', i.e. not to be referred to in legal proceedings,[5] and confidential;[6]
- No record or recording of the discussions is to be made by one side without the other's agreement.
- any settlement to be in a written agreement signed by or on behalf of the parties and is not legally binding without one – avoids confusion about whether or when a deal has been done.

---

[4] In mediation, parties sometimes use a mediation advocate, trained in the skills of persuasion in negotiation.

[5] See Chapter 6 and Appendix 1, section 6.

[6] What confidentiality should be clear; typically to exclude persons and entities not parties to the dispute or involved in its management. Steps may be necessary within an organisation to ensure that the information does not leak.

Alternatives to a negotiated agreement

Preparation should include an analysis of a party's alternatives to a negotiated end to the dispute. The best of these alternatives is known as the Best Alternative to a Negotiated Settlement (BATNA). The reader is also referred to Chapters 8 and 9.

A party's BATNA is generally to pursue a legal process and win the case. In a dispute, if a legal case were pursued and won, the win would generally be the BATNA. If money is the remedy claimed, the BATNA would be a court judgment for the debt plus interest and a costs-shifting order, with payment by the defendant. The BATNA will often be qualified by the delay, irrecoverable costs and wasted opportunity costs (staff and management time) of winning. In other cases, the BATNA may not be a 'win' in court, because litigation would be out of the question; as unaffordable or commercially undesirable. There, a party's BATNA might be its opponent paying up in response to a threat of litigation. Put the other way round, if a business would not go to court, its BATNA might be the claiming party giving up, persuaded that its opponent is likely to defend the case if it sued. Other situations would present different BATNA's. The likely value of the BATNA would depend on the probability of it actually happening.

The Worst Alternative to a Negotiated Agreement or 'WATNA' in two-party litigation is typically the financial and other commercial effects of losing the legal case with an adverse costs order. That is, a liability to pay the majority of the other side's legal costs and one's own; and, if a claimant, non-recovery of the sums claimed or if the defendant, a liability to pay the sums claimed. The litigation is likely to have other knock-on effects for the business, such as opportunity costs. All these are part of the WATNA.

Preparation should therefore include an analysis by a party of its own WATNA. It allows a business to understand the financial risk if the dispute were to go to court, arbitration, etc. There may be associated financial risks for the business, such as cash-flow and solvency.

There may be other unacceptable adverse outcomes, short of a WATNA. For example, adverse publicity from the dispute may be potentially so serious that the risk should be contained by an early settlement, if at all possible.

A BATNA is often intrinsically uncertain. That is particularly true in a commercial dispute, because of difficulties associated with accurately forecasting litigation outcomes (see Chapter 4). In *Getting Past No*, William Ury stated:[7]

> Keep in mind how easy it is to overestimate how good your BATNA is. Many business executives, listening to the advice of overconfident lawyers, have eschewed negotiations and taken a dispute to court, only to find themselves on the path to financial ruin. In any lawsuit, strike, or war, one contender – ... – discovers that his BATNA wasn't as good as he imagined.

To negotiate effectively, a party should understand the value of its BATNA. An analysis of the BATNA locates the point at which a party would walk away from negotiations, the 'reservation value.'[8]

What is the value of the BATNA? Take a case where the lawyer has advised the claimant it has a 70% chance of success on a claim of £1 million, including interest. An advice on the merits is a forecast, no more (see Chapters 4 and 9). How is the business to calculate an acceptable settlement figure based on a 70% chance of a win in court?

First, it is essential to understand what the claim is – an asset. The asset is not £1 million but a right to pursue a claim for £1 million by legal action.[9] With a 70% chance of success, the asset value might

---

[7] See Ury (1991), p 21.
[8] Malhotra and Bazerman (2007), p 20.
[9] In legal terminology, this asset is known as a 'chose in action.'

appear to be £700,000 i.e. 70/100 x £1 million. Assume that the legal costs to trial on each side were £200,000, a reasonable assumption in a case of any complexity. If a costs order were made and paid, it would result in payment of around £140,000, i.e. a shortfall of £60,000.[10] There is a 70% chance of obtaining that order, i.e. £98,000. Hence, £102,000 should be deducted from the £700K, leaving a value of £598,000.

To value the claim as an asset, the WATNA has to be priced in. There is a 30% chance of (a) recovering no part of the debt and (b) the claimant having to pay its own costs and the other side's. This would devalue the asset further. So, leaving aside any wider commercial considerations (particularly the opportunity costs of tying up staff in the litigation), the £1 million claim may be worth less than half its face value, even in a case where the legal merits are advised to be as high as 70%.

In preparation for a negotiation, a defendant should measure its potential (contingent) liability. A similar process as that for valuing a claim is required in reverse to estimate the extent of that liability. Account should also be taken of the opportunity cost of tying up staff in the dispute. Reputational damage, if any, would be difficult to quantify but should be borne in mind, as well as the other downside risks of a continuation of the dispute.

In a commercial negotiation, it is often possible to assess the other side's BATNA as well as one's own and then calculate the area where an agreement appears possible, the Zone of Possible Agreement known as 'ZOPA'. In business disputes, it is more difficult to locate a meaningful ZOPA beyond the effects of irrecoverable costs on each side if the dispute went to trial. Parties often have differing views of their chances of success (see Chapter 4)

---

[10] A costs-shifting order on the usual 'standard basis' would be for around two-thirds of a party's costs (see Chapter 5). A figure of 70% has been taken for convenience in the example given.

and are likely to give different weight to other commercial risks in a dispute.

A calculation of the other side's WATNA is helpful, however. What would be the financial result if the claimant or defendant (as applicable) were to lose the legal case? This can be used to calculate settlement offers, and to explain them.

As we have seen, the best and worst alternatives to a negotiated settlement may be based on positive and negative outcomes of a court case. However, these should not divert the business from making an overall assessment of the risks of not resolving the dispute.

7.2.2. Conduct of negotiations

It is generally a bad idea to start a negotiation by bargaining immediately. In starting the discussions, two things are key. That what you say is *heard* and that the other party considers it has been *understood*. 'People rarely change unless they feel understood.'[11] Effective negotiation is not therapy. It does not mean backing down, but it does require some persuasion of the counterparty.

Ask the other side to let you explain how you see the dispute and that they hear you out. And say that you want to hear them too, to understand their perspective. Both content and tone are important. If your message is delivered in angry tones, its content will be lost. The listener will hear the anger and lose interest in the message. Emotional venting should not be conducted at the counterparty.

For the other party to feel understood, they must believe that they have been listened to. When in conversation, how often are we not really listening? Thinking of something else or appearing to listen but thinking of what you are going to say next.

Richbell (2015), p 133.

Active listening is important. Show you are listening, so the counterparty sees that they have been understood. There are various techniques, such as paraphrasing, re-phrasing and the appropriate use of questions ("So, what you are saying is x?").

Listening addresses a further problem. Parties often feel devalued by their counterparts and this makes progress more difficult. It has been stated:[12]

> ... if we disagree with what the other person is saying, we may criticise the merit in whatever they say or do. We assume that part of the job of a negotiator is to put down the other side. All too often, we listen for the weaknesses in what the other person is saying, not for the merit. Yet everyone sees the world through a unique lens, and we feel devalued when our version of the world is unrecognised or dismissed out of hand. If we spent weeks putting a proposal together and the other side merely criticises it, we are likely to feel discouraged and angry.

Effective negotiation includes *due* acknowledgement of merit in the other's position. Interests can also be acknowledged, e.g. "I can see that ....". Consider the following. In a dispute between two songwriters over whether the claimant owned a share of the copyright in album lyrics, the defendant acknowledged their work together and said he had enjoyed working with the claimant. The defendant thanked the claimant for his contribution and offered to make a public acknowledgement on his website. He went on to say that though his lawyers advised that the contribution would not entitle the claimant to any share in the copyright, he wanted to find a sum of money to bring their dispute to an end.

Sometimes, acknowledgement extends to an apology, to the advantage of both sides. If a party considers that its basic grievance has been accepted, the compensation is often easier to agree, even where the parties disagree about the compensation. In a dispute

---

[12] Fisher & Shapiro (2007), p 27.

about faulty goods, for example, it may be to a negotiator's advantage to acknowledge the fault (assuming there is one) before moving to a subsequent discussion about compensation.

Effective listening should be combined with effective assertion of a party's own position. Once a party considers that it has really listened to their counterpart, the discussion can be taken up and contrary viewpoints communicated. Instead of 'but', use 'and' to introduce that viewpoint. Or pause and give time for the acknowledgement to be digested before the opposing argument is put. If the other side considers it has been listened to, it is more likely to listen to you. It is generally unwise to interrupt.

It is important how a party explains its perspective of the dispute. A common fault is to mix up effect and intention. It is easy and often wrong to assume that because the other side's actions have had an effect on the business, that the counterparty intended this to happen. Generally, what is called 'attribution bias' attributes underhand or other negative explanations for the other side's conduct, while allowing a party to view its own actions as justified.[13]

A message is more likely to be taken in if explained along the lines of, "When x happened, the effect on our business was Y." Concentrating on the effects of the other side's actions creates a better opportunity of being understood. Again, 'I' or 'we' sentences are preferable to 'you' sentences, which carry accusation.

Building trust in a negotiation can be very important. Even if relations between two organisations in conflict are very bad, individual negotiators often have an opportunity of building a personal rapport. That relationship does not downplay the difficulties but creates opportunities of joint problem-solving. This is typical of many political negotiations. Examples include the relationships in the negotiations to end the Cold War between

---

[13] Kiser (2010), p 92.

Presidents Reagan and Gorbachev and Secretary of State George Shultz and foreign minister Eduard Shevardnadze.[14]

Whatever approach one party takes in negotiations, the other may do something else. What is the appropriate response? Courtesy and firmness throughout are a sensible combination. If a counterpart becomes angry, for example, do not rebuke them. Take time out if necessary, to calm down. Try to understand why they are angry. It has been stated:[15]

> If you do not give an angry negotiator the opportunity to voice his frustration, he will likely become even more angry. – or at the very least, resentful. A much better approach is to encourage people to voice their anger and to help you understand its source. .. The key is to give legitimacy to the other person's feelings. You can (and should) question the legitimacy of what he believes, but you should not waste time questioning the legitimacy of a person's anger *given* what he believes to be true.

A negotiator may face manipulative tactics, such as artificial deadlines, 'good cop, bad cop' behaviour, wholly unrealistic offers, 'salami-slicing' tactics[16] and stone-walling. Name the tactic and refuse to negotiate on that basis. A threat to walk out, for example, may be met with a response, "I am sorry you see the negotiations like that. Can we work together to close the gap between us?"

In online negotiation the cues available to interpreting behaviour are absent or susceptible to misinterpretation from remote audio or video communication. It is worth giving counterparts the benefit of the doubt when there might be ambiguity, e.g. be slow to interpret silences as having some adverse motive.[17]

---

[14] Service (2015).

[15] Malhotra and Bazerman (2007), p 271.

[16] 'Salami-slicing' includes dealing with one issue at a time, rather than that issue and others. Salami tactics may result in a better deal for the user.

[17] See Shonk (2020).

Exploration

Consider the other side's commercial interests as well as your own. They will not do a deal unless it meets their interests. So, empathy (not sympathy) is important. The Cuban missile crisis in 1962 was a paradigm of empathy in negotiation. The dangers of continued escalation were obvious. A series of confrontational demands would have given each side no room to back down. But President John F. Kennedy took considerable steps to understand why the Soviet Union was engaging in the extremely risky behaviour of establishing nuclear weaponry in Cuba. He discovered that the Soviet Union was deeply concerned at perceived threats posed by missiles in Turkey and Italy and by how it had fallen behind in the nuclear arms' race. The result: the USA promised not to invade Cuba and in a secret protocol it agreed to withdraw its missiles from Turkey.[18]

To uncover interests, questions of the other side are appropriate. Tell them why information might be helpful: to uncover deal possibilities, not to find weaknesses in their position or to pry into confidential interests. Offer like information in return. Where the dispute concerns several issues, identify the important ones and the reasons why they matter.

Questioning may include the negotiating process itself. One side often needs to find out if there are limits to a counterpart's negotiating authority. If there are, insist on negotiating with someone with due authority.

Sometimes, one side needs information from the other to make an informed decision about settlement. Aspects of a claim may not be clear, or more information about losses claimed may be necessary. Ask for that information.

---

[18] Malhotra (2016), pp 122-126.

Much negotiated dispute resolution concerns a search for a magic figure of £X or in other currency. The 'pie' is often limited. However, in dividing it up there is a crucial distinction between a party's rights on the one hand and on the other, its motivations, interests and needs.

Possibilities of how a deal might be structured can be brain-stormed and representatives of each side tasked to do this. Realistic options may then be discussed further.

In disputes involving several commercial issues, the best course is usually to make packaged offers, linking the various elements. The discussions may reveal that the elements do not have equal importance for the parties. For example, in a dispute over termination of a distribution agreement, continuation of the agreement or even its extension might be more important to one side than the value of the goods in dispute. The more commercial issues can be linked, the greater the possibility for creating value in a negotiation.

The following examples (taken from my work as a mediator with one exception) show how discussions between counterparts can generate opportunities for settlement that would not exist if the parties simply started negotiating by reference to their opening positions.

Example 1. Motorbike distribution
The claimant was a motorbike distributor that had worked profitably with a manufacturer for many years. The manufacturer had the right to terminate the distribution agreement without cause and after some years did so. The distributor threatened a competition claim for £20M, based on a refusal to supply. There was a mediation. The key document was a handwritten note showing that the distributors were very angry by the way the commercial relationship had been ended. At a joint meeting, the manufacturers showed they understood this. They explained that their business

model had changed, they thanked the distributors for their many years of good work and regretted how they had ended the relationship. They said that they would not pay the £20M but would offer a fair sum of money to end the dispute.

A deal was done. The distributors did not need £20M but much less. Taking into account all the commercial considerations of the dispute, the distributors were able to settle at £500,000. The distributors also considered that they had been listened to and understood. This example also illustrates the importance of reciprocity. If one side gives something, the other is often motivated to do the same.

Examples 2 and 3. Disputes over royalties
In intellectual property disputes, talks may centre on royalties for future use. Should the rate be 5%, 6%, 7%? In a negotiation concerned with a new licence, one side demanded that the rate went up and the other wanted a reduction. The parties struck a deal that went both up and down. The top rate decreased over time but increased beneath the headline rates if sales went up. Each side's needs were therefore met.

In a dispute over the legal meaning of various licence agreements, royalty rates under different agreements for various products were fitted into a negotiation over a single rate and a deal was done.

Example 4. Dispute over a lease
In a long-running battle between landlord and tenant, arrears of rent, insurance and legal costs were claimed by the landlord. Exploration of the parties' interests resulted in the tenant being prepared to surrender the lease if the landlord paid a sum that would let her buy a new leasehold property with a mortgage. A deal was done on that basis.

Example 5. Ownership of an academic journal
The parties each claimed a share of the ownership of the journal. Each side's real interests lay in the underlying aspects of ownership,

such as editorial control and consultation, in addition to money matters. Once the dispute was broken down into its constituent parts, the binary dispute over ownership went away.

In disputes involving property, there are often opportunities to create value. A buy-out of a counterparty's property rights may create a solution, even where the dispute is about something else, such as the running costs of jointly owned property. The example of the academic journal also illustrates how the simple question 'why' asked of the other side can unlock a negotiation. The answer to why ownership was important to each party exposed their respective commercial interests.[19] So, if a negotiation becomes stuck on a figure, ask why a party insists on a particular sum of money. Also, see if the problem can be broken down.

Where parties are in dispute over compensation and legal costs, it is generally easier to look for a single sum of money to settle the entire dispute. But sometimes, if the compensation can be agreed in principle, the costs become easier to deal with through further bargaining.

There are other ways of dealing with arguments about legal costs. Under court procedures the costs can be assessed if a deal is done after litigation has started. The very expense of assessment proceedings can be a strong incentive to settlement.

There are 'costs only' proceedings available if the dispute is settled before litigation has started, if the parties have reached agreement on all issues, including which is to pay the legal costs.[20]

Where a party has engaged external lawyers, their fees may be part of the negotiation. A deal with those lawyers to reduce the fees may help to facilitate a deal with the counterparty, e.g. to close a gap in a deadlock. In cases where the legal case is funded by conditional fee

---

[19] See Fisher, Ury and Patton (2012).
[20] CPR 46.14.

arrangements, a claimant may well be able to negotiate with its lawyers over the level of success fee (i.e. the uplift on top of the basic fee).

Bargaining

The initial questions are what level of offer to make and which side should make it? In making its first offer, a negotiator should balance a number of factors. Preparation (see above) will have enabled the calculation of a *provisional* 'reservation value' translating into a 'bottom line', before the negotiation starts. Provisional, because a party should not be unnecessarily fixed on an outcome if the negotiation should merit a different settlement. New information may become available, justifying a modified risk assessment.

A deal is rarely done unless the other party has a way out, a means of backing down. It is important that a negotiator has this in mind. How can the other party be helped to climb down?

A first offer should be credible. An unrealistic first offer is likely to be met with an unrealistic counter-offer. Put yourself in the other side's position. What would be your reaction if you were them and received the offer you have in mind? A credible offer is one that can be justified with reasons, that should be given. A claimant could demand all the money in dispute less a discount of the costs it would save by not going to trial. That would risk being seen as not credible, even if explained to the counterparty. The offer would have assumed a zero risk of losing the case in court.

Who should make the first offer? It depends. The context may indicate which party should start, e.g. a defendant to open where a claimant has adequately quantified its claim.

A first offer creates an opportunity to 'anchor' a negotiation. Anchoring is a type of cognitive bias. When making a valuation or assessment we tend to latch onto an available figure which then influences the assessment. *'It occurs when people consider a particular value for an unknown quantity before estimating that quantity. What happens is one of the most reliable and robust results of experimental psychology; the estimates stay close to the number people considered – hence the image of the anchor.'*[21] Negotiators may gain an advantage from using this anchoring effect, particularly by making a well-considered first offer. Research shows that an anchor has influence even when the recipient knows it to be irrelevant.

An offer to anchor a negotiation should generally be accompanied by a suitable message. Offer and message should communicate that the offeror is making a serious proposal that moves *significantly* beyond its pre-negotiation position. How significantly depends on the context. There is little point in making an offer that either passes a point where a deal might be done (i.e. is over-generous) or would hamper subsequent bargaining. The latter danger can be addressed by the right message: for example, "We want to you to know that we are serious about ending the dispute. We expect to negotiate further, but an unrealistic counter-offer from you would be a mistake." Another tactic is to make an offer that reduces over time if not accepted. This is more appropriate where an offer is made in correspondence.

Once bargaining has begun, there are various techniques for responding to offers, e.g. ignoring an attempted anchor by making an offer that has already been prepared. Or to make an offer that attempts a counter-anchor accompanied by a persuasive justification for the proposal.[22]

If there remains a large gap between offers, 'bracketing' can be used. For example, where £1 million is in dispute and opening offers are £75,000 versus £750,000, one party could say, 'I would be prepared to offer £175,000 if you come down to £500,000.' Responses to

---

[21] Kahneman (2012), p 119. See also Chapter 9.
[22] See e.g. Malhotra and Bazerman (2007), pp 31-38.

bracketing include a party counter-offering its own bracket, consistent with its objectives or ignoring the bracket in other ways.[23]

Haggling is part of most bargaining. The further into the bargaining process, the smaller the concessions tend to be (though not always) and the more limited the room for manoeuvre. Deadlock is to be expected. 'Bottom lines' may have been reached and the parties may appear to have run out of road. In some cases, the gap may be too large to bridge.

What about cases where the gap might be bridgeable? Parties should not fixate on the 'fairness' of the negotiation, e.g. who has moved furthest. Though relevant to bargaining strategy and its execution, a party risks overlooking its own self-interest if too much is made of how a party has arrived at the deadlock point. Also, negotiations rarely end half-way between the parties' respective positions.

It is too easy to decide that the negotiation has failed because of deadlock. Language such as, 'That is my final offer', is unnecessary and can fetter a negotiator. Unless a position really is final, it prevents further discussion or risks a loss of negotiating credibility if a further offer is made.

Where deadlock has been reached, a reminder of how far the parties have come can strike a positive note and may help to keep a negotiation moving. A question worth asking your counterpart may be, 'As we are prepared to pay/accept the deadlock figure to head off the various commercial and legal risks, what is it about the amount in the gap that would make those risks worth running?' Or more generally, 'How can we work together to close this gap?'

Earlier discussions may have yielded information to justify a further move. Further consideration of the available information may

---

[23] See Geoff Sharp, LinkedIn.

produce different insights on risk. Often, parties simply do not want to lose a deal if the difference between them is comparatively small.

Uncertainty in the strength of the BATNA may persuade one or both parties to move further to reach a deal. By pursuing a negotiated outcome, each side is acknowledging the advantage of commercial certainty. The price of settlement may include a premium for certainty, to accept a bit less if a claimant or to pay a bit more if a defendant.

There are many cases where a substantial gap reflects completely different assessments by each side of its BATNA. Both believe they have a high chance of winning the litigation. Even then, that should not be an end to the negotiation. Commercial factors often dictate further movement. I have seen negotiations where one party has made a game-changing move based on commercial interests. It resuscitated the discussions that had become stuck several hundred thousand pounds apart because of rival assessments of the merits of the legal case.

Often, the difficulty with the deadlock is no more than one side wishing to 'win' the negotiation. A coin toss can work! However, settlement does not always suit the interests of parties. Sometimes, the other party's best offer is not good enough. Commercial or even tactical considerations may dictate that negotiations should end at that point.

7.2.3. The end of negotiations?
If terms are agreed, these should be set out in a written settlement agreement signed by the parties. Should a party wish to take legal advice before signing, the deal should be written up, headed 'Subject to Contract', but not signed (see Chapter 6).

If a last offer has not been accepted, it is often worth making clear that the offer remains open for a short period of time, e.g. 48 hours. Even if not then accepted, it may yet prompt a move from the other side that can be built on. If a last offer does not lead to a deal, it may be worth making a Part 36 Offer based on it (see Chapter 5).

There may be opportunities for further negotiations later during the legal process. But remember that legal costs on both sides may have increased, making a deal more difficult to reach. In some cases, however, one or other or both parties may need to feel more of the 'pain' of the legal process (money spent on legal fees and corporate time spent on the legal case) to be ready to do a deal.

7.3. Mediation: advantages

We have seen that mediation is a process with an independent, neutral person who assists the parties to reach a settlement of their dispute (see Chapter 6). The advantages of mediation and a mediator have been well described by Tony Allen as follows.[24] Mediation adds the following to settlement discussions:

- A managed process – no risk of partisan power struggle;
- Lawyers can concentrate on advising;
- Gives attention to non-legal matters, such as:
  - enabling frank and direct communication to be set up or restored (often obstructed by the litigation process);
  - attending to underlying emotion;
  - enabling parties to have their 'day in court', e.g. by encouraging contributions.

A mediator adds the following:

- Creation of a safe environment in which parties and advisers feel able to explore risks both together and privately and in the way they bid;
- Acts as a buffer against grand-standing – a different non-partisan mind and voice;

---

[24] *Choosing between RSMs and Mediation;* Tony Allen, CEDR. The summaries in the text reproduce most of the advantages identified in that seminar paper.

- Takes some of the heat that can develop out of the lawyer-client relationship;
- Relieving pressure of the moment – private meetings and time for reflection can be built in so as to avoid rushed decisions;
- To be an objective tester-out in private for each party's interests and positions without reactive devaluation;
- Synthesising the objective probing characteristics of a judge at trial, but with its being done by someone experienced and knowledgeable, who is *not* the decision-maker.
- Helping in privately defining and valuing risks;
- Enhancing negotiation efficiency and effectiveness by:
  - offering options for the ways offers might be conveyed – e.g. face-to-face or using the mediator;
  - getting and sharing (where permitted) intelligence for each team as to what might be regarded as insulting or credible offers;
  - helping each party to refine the message intended by any offer through better understanding of its likely impact;
- being able to receive each party's true position confidentially, so as to assess what the true gap between the parties may be when they need more persuasion to move towards each other.

7.4. Conduct of the mediation

At the mediation, a mix of joint and caucus meetings is generally the most productive. Joint meetings may be attended by clients, their lawyers, experts and others (e.g. insurers) or any combination of these. The discussions in the various meetings give the mediator a unique overview of the dispute. They also make each side better informed, enabling them to make an improved risk assessment in many cases. The results from these meetings can be brewed together by the mediator to generate the best prospects for settlement.

Caucus meetings allow each party to discuss privately and confidentially with the mediator the opportunities for settlement (i.e. exploration), the realities of the dispute and the bargaining stage. Groupthink can be avoided by the senior negotiator welcoming ideas and, on a devil's advocate basis, disagreement. A different approach may be agreed within the team for the private discussions with the mediator.

A joint meeting may be helpful as a platform to the start discussions at the mediation, particularly if used appropriately to re-set dialogue that had broken down. When deadlock has been reached later in the mediation, a joint meeting attended by the main negotiators may be used to close the gap. Joint meetings also take place during the mediation day, to lay the groundwork for bargaining, e.g. by acknowledging the concerns of the other side.

Mediation provides an excellent framework for handling party emotion. For example, a party may feel heard and understood once they have the opportunity to explain their views of the dispute to the mediator in the presence of the counterparty, who is given the same opportunity.

Mediators do not give legal advice, but they do 'reality-test.' There is sometimes a fine line between the two. Effective reality-testing can be done by the mediator's skilful use of questions or the offering of perspectives as to how a court might look at some of the issues. A mediator's perspectives on these matters (shared privately and confidentially) will not be subject to the same degree of reactive devaluation because they come from a neutral rather than from the other party.

What is the role of the mediator? First, to obtain the best available offer from each party. Second, to help each party decide whether or not to accept the best offer received. This second part of the role is generally conducted in private, i.e. in a caucus meeting. In effect, the mediator acts like a non-executive director, placing a mirror before a company's board, so the best decision can be made for the company by its representatives.

7.5.   Conclusion

Negotiations are an essential part of managing a dispute effectively. Whether or not mediation is used, careful thought is required in the preparation and conduct of the negotiations. Ultimately, a judgement is called for: whether to settle the dispute on the best available terms or to pursue a legal case or other alternatives. The final chapter in this book addresses that question. The next chapter looks at how to build a dispute strategy before that final decision is made.

8. OBJECTIVES AND STRATEGY

8.1. Objectives

Once a dispute breaks out, decisions have to be made. The business should ask itself: what is our objective? The ultimate goal is to ensure that the dispute is managed in a way that meets the best interests of the business, while also protecting its reputation and being cost-effective.[1] A dispute strategy is required to deliver that objective.

This goal will separate into a set of objectives depending on the details of the dispute. For a claimant owed money, the objective will generally centre on obtaining an outcome that delivers a sufficient payment within an acceptable timeframe by one or more dispute resolution processes. If there are other aspects of the dispute, such as termination of the contract, further objectives may be to obtain acceptable compensation from the counterparty and establish (by agreement or binding decision) that the business is free to stop performing the contract and to deploy resources elsewhere, e.g. on deals with other parties. The objectives might include an alternative, a new set of contractual arrangements with the defendant on better terms.

In other cases, the main objective for a claimant may be a vindication of its rights (contractual or property-based) to stop the defendant from invading those rights and to deter others, such as other employees or trade competitors.

The objectives of a defendant to a disputed money claim will include an outcome that limits its financial exposure to a minimum. The defendant to a wider contract dispute may decide that its objectives are to negotiate a new set of contractual arrangements,

---

[1] See Hogan Lovells (2019), p 5 with reference to a general dispute strategy.

obtain acceptable compensation for wrongful termination of the contract or both.

Alternative objectives of a claimant or defendant may narrow over time as the dispute strategy is pursued. A new agreement may not be possible. Negotiations may prove unsuccessful because commercial trust has broken down irretrievably. Hence, an acceptable financial outcome may become the main objective.

8.2. Dispute strategy

What strategy is required to deliver the objectives? It has been said that business strategy is essentially an integrated set of choices.[2] A dispute resolution strategy involves different choices from those of a usual business strategy. However, a co-ordinated and linked set of choices are also the key to an effective strategy for dispute resolution. As we shall see, those choices can only be made if the necessary information is to hand.

Many disputes are resolved by prompt discussion or do not escalate for other reasons. If the dispute does not go away, the answer might look deceptively simple: investigate the matter internally, try to negotiate and if that does not work, instruct lawyers. If the advice is that you are likely to win, pursue a legal case if you can afford it, but also if you can afford to lose it as well.

The best decision-making is not simply to hand over the dispute to lawyers. A legal strategy is necessary. But a dispute also creates non-legal risk that has to be addressed by an overall commercial strategy. Decisions based on that strategy will be based ultimately on a business's commercial appetite for risk (see Chapter 9).

8.2.1. The commercial strategy

Some businesses have well-developed systems for managing disputes. Particularly where litigation is routine or not unusual.

---

[2] Lafley and Martin (2014), p 3. A business strategy is aimed at delivering competitive advantage in the marketplace.

Others, particularly smaller enterprises, may have more informal approaches to dispute management, or no decision-making structure at all.

It is essential to know who the decision-makers will be, how they will obtain all the necessary information to manage the risk of a dispute, and how the strategy will be created and executed.

Most businesses want to end a dispute quickly, with an acceptable outcome. There are exceptions. Non-payment of a debt may be deliberate, the dispute generated to put off payment. Or litigation may be used to put pressure on a competitor, or to deter a take-over.

The following initial steps are likely to assist in the creation and execution of a strategy:[3]

- a prompt internal investigation into the facts;
- a legal analysis internal and/or external;
- identify the commercial interests at play;
- the available dispute resolution alternatives;
- the external costs of pursuing each of those alternatives;
- create a strategy for decision-making based on the above factors; and
- conduct regular reviews of commercial and legal strategies.

Risk analysis

An analysis should be made to identify all the potential risk factors, assess how likely each one is on its own and in combination with others, and what the cost and/or consequences to the business would be if one or more of them happened (see also Chapter 9).

Legal advice (see below) will address the risks from the legal process. What about the other commercial risks? Most disputes have direct financial implications. If money is owed but disputed, what is

---

[3] Herbert Smith Freehills (July 2017). These steps assume the presence of an in-house legal department, but apply (except for internal legal analysis) too where that advice is not available.

138   RESOLVING BUSINESS DISPUTES

the potential cost to the business in pursuing payment? If money is claimed but the claiming party has not done what it promised to do under the contract, what is the financial impact on the business?

If legal action is to be pursued or defended, the cost implications have to be measured against the likely benefit and potential risks of the legal action. Negotiations, whether direct or by mediation, may prove unsuccessful. If the legal action had to go to trial, the loser would have to pay two sets of legal costs. Other considerations include the risk of non-recovery of all or part of a disputed debt or of a delay in recovery, the risk of the dispute interfering with a larger project (e.g. a joint venture or long-term contract) or adversely affecting the commercial relationship with the defendant where the claimant intends to maintain it after the dispute has been resolved.

For both claimant and defendant, there may be solvency concerns about the other, i.e. enforcing a court judgment if the legal action or defence to it succeeds and the potential extra costs of doing so.

For a defendant, the risks include having to pay the disputed debt with interest, bear its own legal costs and having to pay most of the claimant's costs under a costs-shifting order. Win or lose, there would be the opportunity cost of staff being tied up in the legal case and possible damage to the broader commercial interests of the business.

Legal action requires management and staff time, particularly employees who are potential witnesses. They will be required at various stages before and at a final hearing, to provide information for the lawyers, in the preparation of witness statements and giving evidence at the trial. How much time may be judged from an estimate from lawyers. Wasted salary is one measure of the cost. Another is the lost opportunity of bringing in new business or doing other productive work, i.e. opportunity cost.

An effective dispute strategy may anticipate legal action and a settlement (though not assume one) before any trial. A time/cost analysis would show how much time is likely to be spent, by whom and at what cost, as the case progresses. A settlement before preparation of witness statements, for example, may avoid much wasted time.

Research has shown that disputes have serious adverse effects on productivity. A typical £1 million dispute takes up three years of management time (those directly involved and others who become involved); and four times that of in-house legal teams. Other consequences for senior management recorded in a separate study included increase of individuals' stress levels, loss of sleep and decreased motivation in varying percentages up to 46%.[4] Other potential effects include staff becoming distracted from their 'day-job' and wanting to move job.

A dispute may present a wider set of risks to the business than can be managed by litigation, other legal action and settlement discussions. There may be regulatory or reputational risk. An assessment may be required of how to eliminate these threats or reduce them.[5]

If there is a reputational risk, how severe is it likely to be? Examples are defective product allegations, claims of poor service, regulatory concerns or issues of commercial integrity. Would the public filing of documents in the case cause problems, if picked up by the press, a competitor or a regulator? If media interest is likely, the media reports what is interesting to readers and viewers. It may be damaging enough if one day's press report is no more than the other side's case. But then again, this may not matter.

There may be a risk of endangering commercial relationships by pursuing legal action at all. Are there risks from evidence that might be given in court and would it matter if the judge or the opposing

---

[4] Massie (2014), pp 200-204.
[5] Reuvid ed. (2014).

advocate made adverse comments? Hostile cross-examination of the other side's witnesses may endanger relationships. But that may not matter either, because the relationship has broken down irretrievably; or has it?

What is the strategy?

In most cases, some form of legal advice is necessary for a full picture of the available strategy options, their cost, likely benefits and disadvantages. Having identified all the various risks and their potential significance on the business, the best course in most cases is to pursue a strategy for achieving a settlement of the dispute. There may be exceptional cases, where a court judgment is necessary, e.g. to establish a contractual precedent or to make competitors aware that a business's intellectual property rights have been recognised by a court.

To execute a strategy aimed at settlement, a claiming party often has to threaten and then begin litigation if a negotiated outcome is not available beforehand. In other words, it has to spend more money. To be taken seriously by a claimant, a defendant often has to engage lawyers and pursue a robust defence if a settlement cannot be achieved before legal proceedings begin.

To mix the metaphors from previous chapters, legal proceedings are like a game of poker played on a train that passes through the stations towards the terminus, the trial of the legal case. As each stage in the journey is passed, more money is spent on lawyers to progress the case. The winner of the game will be revealed when the trial judge gives judgment. Some or all of the burden of funding the case may be transferred to a third-party funder or to the lawyers (see Chapter 5). But if the game of poker (i.e. the case) is lost, the business will generally have to pay most of the other side's legal costs. If a claim is made to recover money, losing the case would mean recovering none of the debt. Even if it is won, is there a risk that the other side becomes insolvent, and if so, what does that mean for the successful litigant?[6] All the financial risks must be thought through.

As most legal cases settle, it seems rational to assume that there is a good prospect of a compromise to end the dispute on reasonable terms. There are *caveats* to this. Although most cases do settle, that does not tell you whether your dispute is likely to. It might be one of those that do not. A deal on acceptable terms may not be possible. The other side may be unrealistic in its approach. What then? A party may have to make a Part 36 Offer and go to trial unless it gives up the litigation and pays most of the other side's legal costs.

Not every dispute presents a choice between litigating or not, though possible litigation may be a factor. Decisions about termination of a contract are a typical case. First, it is necessary to decide whether the contract may be validly terminated in law. If termination would be lawful, is that sensible? What are the business implications of bringing the contract to an end? Could the termination intensify the dispute and what is the percentage risk that the termination would be unlawful? On the other hand, what are the risks of not terminating the contract?

But there may be immediate opportunities for containing and ending the dispute. The contract may contain a dispute resolution clause requiring negotiation and if that fails, mediation (see Chapter 2). The clauses may then go on to state how the dispute is to be resolved if neither work, by litigation, arbitration or expert determination. Inclusion of these clauses in a contract is itself a pre-emptive strategy for dispute resolution. In long-term projects, the parties may have specified that a Dispute Board be appointed under the contract (see Chapter 6). If the contract does not provide for a dispute resolution mechanism, a proposal of prompt negotiation once the dispute has blown up may be well-advised anyway.

---

[6] See Chapter 5 in particular.

Decision-making processes

In substantial disputes the decision-makers may best include senior management, or an appointed body such as a risk committee, with the involvement of the board of directors if the business is corporate.

A person of appropriate seniority and independent of the dispute should be appointed to instruct outside lawyers, particularly if there is no in-house legal team.

As indicated (see Chapter 7), those directly involved in the dispute are generally not well placed to make decisions that are in the best interests of the business. They tend to be too partisan or motivated to justify their conduct that led up to the dispute. If they are managing the dispute, steps should be taken to guard against a lack of objectivity, e.g. by internal reporting and reviews.

Reporting structures to a company's board or to senior executives may be required, to prevent disputes that are being managed at the operational level from causing damage to the wider commercial interests of the business, such as its reputation or commercial relationships.

Where an enterprise is divided into business units, the unit may bear the cost of the dispute and any resulting losses. The policy may be that the unit resolves its own disputes, with the help of an in-house legal team if necessary. Senior management from outside the unit may need to check and be kept aware of the financial and other risks raised by the dispute.

The legal strategy (see **8.2.2** below) should be integrated into the overall strategy. When legal advice is sought, internal, external or both, a decision-making process is necessary, to consider that advice in combination with the other commercial factors. Legal advice as the dispute progresses should be fed back to the business and then fresh instructions given to the lawyers and other decisions taken to manage the dispute and contain or manage any wider commercial risks.

An effective strategy requires regular reviews as the dispute progresses. In particular, the reviews should consider whether any additional risks have been presented and their impact on the strategy.

8.2.2. The legal strategy

When external lawyers are engaged, the client will need advice and legal representation. The instructions will be recorded in a client care letter.

The first conversation with the external lawyer should identify the client's objectives (see above). For most disputes, the strategy is likely to include some form of twin-track approach, involving the legal process or the threat of it, plus negotiations or mediation at the appropriate time.

The client will need advice on a range of matters, including the available choices for the progress and disposal of the dispute. Having received that advice, the client is able to instruct the solicitor on the steps to be taken.

Legal advice

Where litigation or other legal action is taking place or is in prospect, a client should *insist on* the following core (written) advice:

- clear advice on the prospects of success;
- the legal costs the client will have to incur to pursue the claim or defend it, as the case may be;
- a detailed explanation of the client's risk and exposure on legal costs;
- the process options and choices open to the client in the pursuit or defence of a claim.

A solicitor has an obligation to consider and take account of the client's attributes, needs and circumstances.[7] For example, dispute

---

[7] *Code of Conduct for Solicitors* [3.4]. Bear in mind that lawyers also have duties not to impede the administration of justice.

resolution advice should take into account the client's financial capabilities.

Legal advice is given in many different forms. Many are of little practical use. Expressions such as 'good prospects', 'reasonable chance', 'very good' or even 'likely to win' are imprecise and mean different things to people. The most helpful advice gives a percentage chance of success or a bracket of two percentages. The advice must also identify the percentage chances of each potential outcome. The information and assumptions on which the advice is based should also be made clear (see Chapter 4).

Competent legal advice should include a discussion and explanation of the various legal options, the cost implications of each, with a cost/benefit analysis. The options may relate to different types of dispute resolution, or procedural steps within the litigation. Clients need to be able to make informed decisions: to decide whether it is in their best interests to continue with litigation and if so, how to proceed. This should be done at the outset and the analysis updated as the case progresses.[8]

Use of a particular arbitration scheme, such as CIArb's Cost Controlled Arbitration Rules, might be an option to consider, to keep the legal costs down (see Chapter 3). If confidentiality is important, arbitration may also be appropriate. The other side would generally have to agree to this if there is no arbitration clause in the contract.

In some disputes, more than two outcomes may be possible, beyond a win or a loss. The result may be some form of draw or other

---

[8] *Code of Conduct for Solicitors* [8.6] requires that clients are given 'information in a way they can understand. You ensure they are in a position to make informed decisions about the services they need, how their matter will be handled and the options available to them.' See too *An ombudsman's view of good costs service*, section 4; Legal Ombudsman; legalombudsman.org.uk.

outcome no-one wants. If there are several defendants, the claimant may obtain a judgment against one but lose against others. How likely is each of these outcomes?

The following are examples of specific matters where legal advice should or may be given. A check (if possible) on the solvency or assets of the other party is often appropriate. Registered companies and limited liability partnerships are required to file annual accounts at Companies House. There may be no point in taking legal action if the other side is near insolvent.

Contrast the position of a defendant faced with a claimant in financial difficulty. To give up the litigation against a near insolvent claimant would risk an adverse court judgment. But security for costs might be available to gain some protection from the risk of the insolvency (see Chapter 5). If the litigation is funded by a third party, e.g. a director of the company, would a costs order be made against the director (see Chapter 5) and is there information about their available assets? Any potential difficulties of enforcing a judgment abroad should be mentioned, with an indication of further costs to take that step.

Other questions if acting for a claimant might be whether claims could and should be made against additional defendants if there are solvency concerns about the main defendant. What are the prospects of success against these parties? Multi-party litigation can be very risky. A typical situation would be a claim against a company with solvency issues, with possible claims against one or more of its directors. Although the directors might be 'good for the money', the claims against directors are often much less likely to succeed.

Decision-analysis tools may assist in more complex litigation (see Chapter 4). These can also provide insight into where best to allocate resources. If there is a high probability of success on issue X, but a lower probability of success on issue Y (e.g. important issues of fact), it may make sense to expend resources on evidence-gathering to increase the probability of success on issue Y.

In many disputes, the key question is likely to be: when to negotiate or mediate? See page 148 below.

Some of the more important considerations about legal costs are set out in Chapter 5. Unless there is a third-party funder, the funding of the client's costs will depend on the arrangements made between the client and solicitor. It is essential that the client is given clear advice about the funding choices and their implications. Is costs insurance available, and if so, on what terms and what do they mean? The client should be advised that even success at trial can have its risks about the recovery of costs (see Chapter 5).

The advice should identify the appropriate procedural steps in any legal process. As we have seen (Chapter 3), in litigation cases going to trial must pass through basic procedural stages. Some cases may merit additional steps, for example:

- additional disclosure of documents;
- security for costs;
- interim injunction; and
- summary judgment /strike out of all or part of an opponent's case.

Sometimes it suits a financially stronger party to make the other side spend money in the litigation to persuade it to settle. Whether that will work is quite another matter. On the other hand, to keep costs down, the client should instruct their lawyer not to engage in unnecessary lengthy correspondence. Too often there is pointless lawyers' correspondence that argues the case or over-indulges in satellite disputes, generating large legal bills. Even if the other side writes such letters, there is generally no need to do the same.

Procedural steps may be necessary to protect the client's position in the dispute resolution process. Others may be suggested to deliver a tactical advantage. The client should consider the likelihood and significance of that advantage. Would the money be well spent? For some procedural steps that may aid negotiations, see page 150 below.

Reviews

The legal advice and resulting strategy should be set out in writing and reviewed regularly (every three months or so as a guide), with adjustments to the cost/benefit analysis. The written legal advice should be a dynamic document, taking account of developments in the case such as new evidence.

Who will handle the case?

The client should understand who is going to handle their case. This affects its cost and effective conduct. Is it the solicitor to whom they are giving the instructions? If that person is a partner in the firm, they may delegate the day-to-day running of the case to a more junior solicitor, perhaps assisted by a trainee. Although the partner should be overseeing their work, how does the oversight actually work? Does this division of labour reduce costs for the client and is it really for the client's benefit? Where such arrangements are in place, a varied approach may be suggested. Who will be taking statements from the witnesses? Such is the importance of witness 'proofing' that the client may wish the partner to do that work. Work on disclosure of documents may be suitably delegated to a less senior lawyer.

Use of ADR and when to negotiate/mediate?

A key issue in the strategy is whether there is good reason *not* to negotiate or engage in ADR at a very early stage and if not then, when. As we have seen, court procedures specify that litigation should be a last resort, the parties being required to consider whether negotiation or some other form of ADR might allow them to settle the dispute without starting court proceedings.[9]

Lawyers cannot be expected to predict everything that the other side will do. A strategy will have to respond to action or inaction by the other party. For example, if a mediation fails, the next step may be to make a Part 36 Offer after the mediation, perhaps reflecting your last offer at the mediation.

A party might be advised to make a Part 36 Offer early in the process, to gain a measure of protection in costs (see Chapter 5). If the offer is not accepted, mediation may take place later (see Chapter 6).

In deciding when to engage in mediation or negotiation, the main consideration is whether sufficient information is available to permit an informed risk assessment. A number of points are worth bearing in mind.

First, the different attitudes to risk of business-people and lawyers. Clients may be used to making decisions based on an amount of information, while lawyers often require more. As long as legal advice has been given competently, with the advice being appropriately qualified, *the client* can decide whether more information is necessary before a negotiation or mediation, after discussion with their lawyer.

A lawyer may say that mediation should take place once the issues in the case have become clear; after the litigation has begun and after case statements have been exchanged. There are cases where details of a claim are important in order to know at what amount to settle a claim; typically, where a defendant needs details of the loss claimed against it.

---

[9] See Chapter 3 and Appendix 1, Practice Direction – Pre-Action Conduct and Protocols [8].

Many disputes do not raise those issues. The writer has conducted mediations in reasonably complex disputes where only the basic information was available. An early deal suited both sides, where the legal claims were arguable. Leaving aside cases such as where a defendant needs to know more about a claim, there are many disputes where a commercial view may be taken early in the dispute. Each side has an arguable legal position and realism dictates a prompt settlement.

Sometimes successful procedural steps create a negotiating advantage. For example, a successful application for an interim injunction can be a platform for settling the dispute. If the other side has unrealistic settlement expectations, it may be best to go to court to strike out part of its case first and if that step succeeds, to mediate afterwards.

In one case, the trial judge stated:[10]

> Experience suggests that many disputes … are resolved before all material necessary for a trial is available. Either parties know or are prepared to assume that certain facts will be established, or, during the course of a mediation, such information is made available on a without prejudice basis … the parties being prepared to compromise without necessarily having as complete a picture of the other parties' case as would be available at trial.

In another case the trial judge stated:[11]

> The trick in many cases is to identify the happy medium: the point when the detail of the claim and the response are known to both sides, but before the costs that have been incurred in reaching that stage are so great that a settlement is no longer possible.

So, if important information is not yet to hand, request it from the other side. If mediation takes place too late, there are two disputes,

---

[10] *PGF II SA v OMFS Company* [2012] EWHC 83 (TCC) at [45.1].
[11] *Nigel Witham Ltd v Smith* [2008] EWHC 12 (TCC) at [32].

the original one and one about who should bear the legal costs. A late settlement may be a detrimental to both sides. Each is exhausted by the substantial legal costs it has paid, with the prospect of even more should the case go to court and an uncertain outcome if it did. Equally, legal costs can make it impossible to settle the dispute.

ADR is a means of managing risk. ADR may keep costs to a minimum, deliver a speedy outcome, allow parties to control the process (e.g. confidentiality), facilitate non-money objectives in the resolution, and sustain commercial relationships. But ADR (mediation or other negotiation) at the wrong time can increase costs and may not be successful.

8.3.   The role of lawyers

Bear in mind the commercial incentives of external lawyers. True, they are obliged to act in the best interests of their client. But in most cases, their commercial interests are not aligned with the client's, particularly when billing at hourly rates. A settlement means that lawyers forego profitable work (going to trial). That said, dispute resolution lawyers also know that clients may be more likely to return as clients if the service meets their needs, i.e. delivering a settlement on acceptable terms as opposed to court action.

It is not that lawyers deliberately give advice that is in their own interests and not in a client's (of course a few may do). But be aware of this potential misalignment between a lawyer's duty and interest when pursuing a dispute strategy. The client should be particularly vigilant about advice in a case that has begun where further expensive work is recommended before a mediation can take place, such as disclosure and witness statements.

Ultimately it is the client, informed by legal advice, who should decide when to mediate or engage in negotiations at a particular stage. The lawyer is there to act on their client's instructions.

8.4.   Covid-19 – Considerations

The pandemic has created commercial emergencies that have had to be sorted out very quickly. This is likely to continue in the near-term at least. In other cases, its effects on the performance of contracts and other commercial arrangements have been no less profound. Many parties will have been simply unable to afford to perform their contractual obligations because of the effects of the pandemic.

The commercial risks presented by pandemic-caused interruption of transactions will be specific to each case. In developing a strategy for disputes that have arisen, each risk must be identified and addressed.

The following are examples. What are the commercial and legal risks of (a) terminating and (b) not terminating a contract for an innocent party because of a counterparty's non-performance due to Covid-19? In some situations, the advantages of a contract renegotiation will be clear, to keep a contract alive. Where there is little prospect of a contract continuing, recovery of financial compensation is likely to be the objective. In other cases, an innocent party's best interests may lie in continuing with a contract but recovering compensation for its losses by a negotiated settlement or subsequent litigation.

The objective for a party unable to perform its contractual obligations will generally be to minimise its financial exposure, by striking a deal with the counterparty on acceptable terms at the right time. If litigation ensues, a key factor may be whether the defaulting party can establish a defence of sufficient strength to overcome a claimant's application for summary judgment or for a sizeable interim payment (see Appendix 1 pages 168 and 171). Where a defendant succeeds in defeating such an application, the tactics of each side up to trial may be influenced by a combination of the defaulting party's ability to continue to afford to defend the litigation, the ability of the claimant to pursue it and whether either side can afford to lose it. These factors are likely to affect the timing and outcome of attempts to settle the litigation before any court judgment.

If a defaulting party has solvency issues, strategy is likely to be affected by other factors, such as attempts to raise money for the business. The implications for dispute strategy may also be complex where third parties are involved. If the supplier is in a supply chain, the default of third parties may come into play.

A negotiated outcome may not suit the parties in every case. In disputes concerned with business interruption insurance for example, the commercial interests of both sides may drive them to a resolution through the courts. In connection with SMEs, the Financial Conduct Authority has announced that it proposes to take court proceedings for declarations to resolve contractual uncertainty over selected policy wordings for such insurance.[12]

There are other considerations. A business facing difficulties in performing an agreement due to Covid-19 may be in breach of contract. Both parties may be suffering losses. But in some cases, it may not ultimately matter much which side 'is in the right' legally. Going to court may not be a practical option, or if it appears to be, the risks too great. For example, if the innocent party were to force the other side to litigate as well as to find money to compensate it, might this risk driving the other party to insolvency or making it unable to perform future obligations under the contract; and if so, what further risks would be created?

In considering the value of their BATNA (see Chapter 7), claimants should bear in mind any additional outcome risk from the strain on the court system due to a rush of Covid-19 claims , and the potential

---

[12] *FCA Statement – insuring SMEs: business interruption*, 1 May 2020. See too **3.4.5** above with reference to the Financial Ombudsman.

uncertainties as the law develops in the field of pandemic-caused interruption (see **4.3.10** above).

In many disputes, a tolerable negotiated outcome is likely to be better for the business, rather than waiting for the law to take its course. Nonetheless, claimants are likely to see value in litigation, either to obtain the best settlement terms or because resolution by the courts is the only realistic option.

9. MAKING THE DECISION

A decision whether to settle or litigate a dispute is essentially a choice between two things. Generally, these are:

- the commercial terms and implications of a settlement ('settlement');
- the consequences of pursuing the litigation or other legal process ('litigating').

How is the choice to be made? We have seen (Chapter 7) that preparations for a negotiation should include an assessment of the Best Alternative to a Negotiated Agreement or BATNA. This chapter provides more information for that assessment and to guide decision-making between the BATNA on the one hand and on the other, the settlement terms that may be offered to a party or those that may be in a party's interests to propose.

9.1. Uncertainties

The choice between settlement and litigating involves a number of uncertainties. How should these be addressed? In *Smart Choices, A Practical Guide to Making Decisions,* the authors stated:[1]

> Some people make their decisions based on the most likely scenario, attempting to eliminate complexity by ignoring uncertainty altogether. Without bothering to make a risk profile, they just assume that the most likely chain of events will occur, determine their best choice under those circumstances, and pursue it .... Effective decision-making takes all viable possibilities into account.

A risk analysis is necessary to address all the risks of the dispute (see Chapter 8 and **9.2** below).

A prime consideration is how to approach the uncertainties addressed by a litigation forecast. The following considerations arise from the more detailed discussion in Chapter 4. A forecast is not a

---

[1] Hammond, Keeney and Raiffa (1998), p 156.

prophecy. To believe that it does is to create a false sense of security. An advice on the merits is an assessment of the probabilities of both winning and losing a legal case. A 70% chance of winning implies a 30% chance of losing. The use of numbers should not distract from the essential nature of a forecast. It is a judgment call based on a reasoned analysis of available information that may not be as objective as it appears, particularly due to various biases at play in the information-gathering for the forecast, in the forecast itself, or both.

The more information there is to hand, the more informed the forecast will be. However, it is often unnecessary to pursue all the avenues in the legal process (e.g. to witness statements) to have sufficient information on which to base a worthwhile forecast.

We have also seen that the advice should provide a percentage forecast of each potential outcome in the legal case. Any further uncertainties associated with the legal process (particularly foreseeable difficulties of enforcement) should be factored into the advice. The financial risks, including any risk of the counterparty's insolvency, and all other risks should be taken into account in the overall commercial risk analysis to be made by the business (see Chapter 8). Although an incentive to settlement is to end the dispute, the settlement may itself carry uncertainty (see Chapter 6).

Litigation is often settled after a first attempt at negotiation. In deciding between settlement and litigating at that stage, a party might consider that there is a prospect of being able to settle the dispute later on improved terms. That prospect would itself be an uncertainty, that should be taken into account in a risk analysis. Sometimes, parties are not ready to settle. They need to 'feel the pain' of the cost and inconvenience of running a case to trial. Against that, the legal costs will have increased by the time another attempt at settlement is made.

9.2. Identifying and balancing the considerations

There are numerous models, theories and books on decision-making tools in business matters. The suggestions in Benjamin Franklin's famous letter to Joseph Priestley written in September 1772[2] are now modelled in what is called a 'T-Chart'. This is a listing of matters 'for' and 'against' alternative courses of action, a brief description of the purposes or reasoning behind each of those matters and the weighting of each. Other models include Decision Matrix Analysis, Paired Comparison Analysis, Decision Trees and forms of Cost-Benefit Analysis or models for assessing returns on investment, sometimes displayed in tabular form. The following are key factors in any analysis:[3]

- identification of each potential outcome;
- the percentage chances of each outcome occurring;
- the consequences of each outcome; and
- whether the consequence would be advantageous or disadvantageous for the objectives of the dispute strategy (see Chapter 8).

The outcomes are not limited to the direct outcomes of the litigation, win or lose. They include all the other commercial factors, such as opportunity cost, damage to commercial relationships and reputational damage, as well as other possible outcomes such as non-recovery of money under a judgment.

The consequences of the outcomes should be measured financially, if at all possible, and given a percentage likelihood. A 'win' for a claimant might equal the sums claimed less one third of the legal costs, based on a costs-shifting order in its favour. If the legal advice predicts a 70% chance of success, that percentage would be identified in a separate column.

---

[2] See at https://www.founders.archive.gov/documents.
[3] Hammond, Keeney and Raiffa (1998), Chapters. 3-8.

An estimate may be made of the likely cost of lost management and staff time if the case went to trial. The percentage likelihood of that consequence would generally be near certain, i.e. 90-100%.

Outcomes difficult to quantify in money terms may be susceptible to financial estimation. Potential damage to reputation or customer relationships might be compared to the sum the business would pay to be free of that risk. If financial evaluation would not measure the consequence of an outcome, the consequence may be measured (albeit subjectively) by a non-monetary grading, e.g. Standard & Poors risk ratings or other ratings.[4]

Some decision analysis tools envisage a separate desirability score for each consequence, informed (i.e. multiplied) by the percentage chance of occurrence for each. The desirability score may be graded from 0-10 or 0-100 and when multiplied by the relevant percentage, a weighted score is generated.[5]

The analysis from decision tools may generate useful information for making the choice between litigating or settlement. Sometimes, it is clear that the only sensible option is to settle the dispute on those terms, or to litigate as the case may be. But often, the choice is not obvious.

9.3. Decision frames, biases and other behaviours

The degree of acceptable risk for a decision-maker may be affected by the way in which the decision is framed. Framing is generally seen as unhelpful. Thus:

> Unless there is an obvious reason to do otherwise, most of us passively accept decision problems as they are framed and therefore rarely have an opportunity to discover the extent to which our preferences are *frame-bound* rather than *reality bound.*[6]

---

[4] Hammond, Keeney and Raiffa (1998), pp 73 and 130.
[5] Hammond, Keeney and Raiffa (1998), Chapters 7 and 8.
[6] Kahneman (2012), p 367.

Conclusions from studies in behavioural economics (also examined in the field of litigation)[7] indicate that humans facing economic choices are risk-averse faced with losing a prospective gain but risk-seeking to avoid a loss. This inclination was illustrated in the studies by Randall Kiser and others, referred to in Chapter 4. There the financial consequences of defendants' decision-making errors were many times greater than those of error-making of claimants. Thus, claimants may be more inclined to settlement and defendants less so. In *Thinking Fast and Slow*,[8] Kahneman refers to the following choices:

Problem 1: Which do you choose?
Get $900 for sure OR 90% chance to get $1,000.

Problem 2: Which do you choose?
Lose $900 for sure OR 90% chance to lose $1,000.

The authors point out that most people would take the $900 from the first problem but gamble on the chance if faced with the second. They make this wider point:[9]

In bad choices, where a sure loss is compared to a larger loss that is merely probable, diminishing sensitivity causes risk seeking.

A defendant is generally presented with a choice between losses. On the one hand, payment of a settlement sum to the claimant plus incurring its own legal costs. On the other, a loss which is either (a) bearing some of its own costs despite winning the case (plus opportunity costs of litigating) or (b) payment of the sum awarded by the court plus all its own legal costs and two-thirds of the other side's, in addition to opportunity costs. The prospects of (a) or (b) occurring are assessable by litigation forecasting (see Chapters 4 and 8).

---

[7] Kiser (2010), pp 111-115.
[8] Kiser (2010), p 279.
[9] Kiser (2010), pp 280 and 285.

Framing also happens due to the *anchoring effect*. Studies have shown that when making a valuation or assessment we tend to latch onto an available figure which then influences the assessment – see Chapter 7. There are many examples in the literature. One was an experiment with estate agents split into two groups and given different asking prices in the sales information for the same house. When asked to advise on a reasonable buying price and the lowest selling price, their responses were significantly affected by the anchors.[10] In dispute resolution, anchors are particularly important in negotiations as we have seen and may also play a role in a court's assessment of the claims before it, e.g. for damages.

The making of a final choice to settle or pursue a dispute is unlikely to be a purely rational exercise, however much we attempt to debias our judgment.[11]

The biases referred to below are explained in Chapter 4. In deciding whether to settle or litigate these and certain behaviours may include the following:

- self-serving bias – tendency for the recipient of a settlement offer to believe it is not 'fair';[12]
- devaluation bias – tendency to downgrade the value of an offer made by an opposing party;
- sunk-cost bias – disposition to carry on with litigation when significant legal costs have already been invested;
- groupthink – in context, the potential for decisions by groupthink made within the business and/or with (legal) advisers;
- the collection of biases and their effects in estimating the overall chances of success in the litigation;

---

[10] Kiser (2010), p 124.
[11] Lotto (2017), pp 164 and 222. There are various ways to counter these biases. See e.g. for groupthink, **7.4** above and Kiser (2010) p 375.
[12] Kiser (2010), p 103.

- competitive bidding – studies in behavioural economics show that people tend to engage in 'nonrational escalation of commitment' the higher the stakes, even where the sum at stake is low in comparison to the stakes placed; in context, the effect of increasing legal costs as the case progresses.[13]

9.4. Making the decision

The ultimate decision will depend on the decision-maker's appetite for risk. The judgement call is based on a comparison between the relative advantages and disadvantages of each of the two choices, settlement or litigating. Commercial people well understand risk and are used to making risk-based decisions. Organisations may have their own risk tolerances.

Using decision analysis with weighted scores (see above), the judgement may be assisted by a comparison between the weighted scores of the comparative advantages and disadvantages of settlement and litigating.[14]

If decision-making tools are not used, the comparison between the relative advantages and disadvantages will require a reasoned judgment to enable the decision-maker to strike the balance between them so that the decision would fit with the objectives of the dispute strategy (see Chapter 8).

Even if decision tools are used, before a decision is finally made a reasoned cross-check should be carried out of the balance that has been struck between the comparative advantages and disadvantages of settlement and litigating.

The cross-check should include what has been described as a 'projection', 'run ... the experiment in your mind and see what

---

[13] Malhotra and Bazerman (2007), p 115.
[14] Hammond, Keeney and Raiffa (1998) Chapter 8. Weighted scores may be translated into money to produce a rate of return; see pp 146-154.

happens.'[15] If the provisional decision is to settle the dispute on particular terms, imagine how settlement of the dispute would fit into the future operations of the business, and whether that imagined world would meet the declared objectives of the dispute strategy and so be in the best interests of the business. Against that, consider the imagined world of pursuing the litigation or other legal process. Cross-checking may also include discussion with colleagues who are tasked to argue against the proposed decision. The cross-check also allows the decision-maker(s) to look for bias and other matters that may taint the decision, with a view to excluding these as far as possible.

9.5. Conclusion

A decision whether to settle or continue a dispute by legal process may be difficult. But it is hoped that the reader will now be in a better position to understand and respond to the challenges of dispute resolution, get the best from their lawyers' during a dispute and make better decisions for the benefit of their business.

---

[15] de Bono (2009), p 32.

Appendix 1 – LITIGATION

1. Introduction and pre-litigation procedures

The UK does not have a single judicial system. The court system for civil claims in England and Wales does not include Scotland or Northern Ireland, which have different civil justice systems.

Business disputes will generally be allocated to one of the Business and Property Courts ('BPC').[1] These include the Chancery Division of the High Court, the Commercial Court, the Technology and Construction Court and the Circuit Commercial Court. The courts are in London, Birmingham, Cardiff, Leeds, Liverpool, Manchester, Newcastle and Bristol. The work of the BPC is divided into various courts and specialist 'lists.'

As a general rule the High Court (which includes the BPC) considers the highest value and most complex cases. Money claims valued at £100,000 or less must be started in the County Court. County Court claims are managed and heard by District Judges and Circuit Judges. High Court claims are managed and heard by Masters and High Court Judges.

There are CPR parts that specifically apply, e.g. Part 63 for Intellectual Property. Court Guides also apply (e.g. the Chancery or Commercial Court Guides), detailing further procedures. This Appendix mainly deals with the general provisions of the CPR. Where reference is made to further procedures, these are by way of example only. Thus, the Appendix does not include every litigation pathway. It concentrates on the framework for disputes with claim values above £25,000. Excluded are Small Claims (including the Online Civil Money Claims for disputes up with claims up to £10,000), and Fast Track cases.

---

[1] CPR Pt. 57A, PD 57AA.

APPENDIX 1 – LITIGATION

The CPR requires the parties to take steps designed to encourage early settlement and avoid the need for litigation. Those are set out in a *Practice Direction – Pre-Action Conduct & Protocols* and may involve significant legal costs. Parties are required to investigate cases before proceedings are started.

The claiming party must set out its claim in writing with concise details, including the basis of the claim, a summary of the facts, what the claimant wants from the defendant and, if money, how it is calculated. This is often referred to as a 'letter before action' and will be seen by the trial judge, if the dispute is not settled. It is a critical step in the litigation process and its accuracy is important.

A response is required from the proposed defendant within 14 days for a simple case and no more than three months for a very complex case. That party should state whether the claim is accepted, and if not the reasons why, with an explanation as to which facts and parts of the claim are disputed, with details of any counterclaim. Copies of the essential documents must be supplied by each side to the other.

The Practice Direction states that 'litigation should be a last resort.' Each party must actively consider whether negotiation or some other form of ADR might enable them to settle their dispute without litigating. Parties are required to consider the possibility of reaching a settlement at all times, including after proceedings have started. Part 36 Offers may be made before proceedings have been started. A Part 36 Offer is part of a regime to encourage settlement (see Chapter 5).

There are exceptions to the principle of 'last resort'. For example, where urgent court intervention is needed by interim injunction. Another is where a claimant has to bring proceedings to avoid a time bar, a defence of 'limitation'.[2] Any potential litigant should consider if their claim is subject to a limitation period (usually six years for claims in contract though sometimes less) generally as set out by the Limitation Act 1980, to avoid commencing proceedings that are 'time-barred.'[3]

2. The start of litigation and up to trial

Most business disputes involve an argument about the essential facts involved. For these cases the litigation starts with a Claim Form. The Claim Form is 'issued' by the appropriate court and has to be properly 'served' on the defendant within a specified period.[4]

Some disputes involve non-domestic elements of one sort or another. This may be the place of domicile, residence or principal place of business of one or more parties to the dispute. A contract, if there is one, may stipulate the courts of which country are to have jurisdiction over disputes.[5] In the absence of a contract specifying the jurisdiction that will apply to a dispute, there are a number of rules that apply to determine whether the English courts are the appropriate jurisdiction for the claim.

There is considerable uncertainty in litigation between parties domiciled in the UK and those in the EU post-Brexit implementation period. As at 31 December 2020, if trade talks have not borne fruit

---

[2] Even then, the proceedings should be put on hold ('stayed') to allow the parties to explore ways of disposing of the dispute without troubling the court further. This can be achieved by a formal stay of proceedings if issued or if pre-issue by a standstill agreement: *Cowan v Foreman* [2019] EWCA Civ 1336.

[3] See Limitation Act 1980, section 2. For example, there may be a limitation period in the contract of less than six years.

[4] Special rules and regulations apply to service on defendants outside the jurisdiction. These apply to defendants in Scotland and Northern Ireland: CPR 6.30-52, PD 6B.

[5] The wording of those clauses is important; e.g. if those courts are to have 'exclusive jurisdiction.'

there will be a lapse of key treaties that allow UK businesses to litigate at home and within the EU, EFTA States and Switzerland

with relative ease. The implementation period is fixed by the EU (Withdrawal Agreement) Act 2020 s39 and the UK's political rhetoric is that it is not subject to extension. If no agreement is reached (including the UK becoming an independent signatory to the Lugano Convention 2007),[6] the parties will only be able to rely on the domestic laws in each country. This creates significant uncertainty.

How to sue a defendant based outside the jurisdiction
The claimant will have to show prescribed matters concerning the claim and/or the location of the defendant. In some cases, the permission of the court is required to start the proceedings. It is likely permission will be required for any state (other than Scotland) post the Brexit implementation period. Jurisdiction is different from the 'proper law of the contract', i.e. the system of law that governs the interpretation and other principles of law affecting a contract.

Statements of case
Once the litigation has begun, the first stage is to complete the sequential exchange of written 'Statements of Case.' These set out the essential facts and matters alleged by a party in support of its case or in response to the other's.[7] A timetable is laid down for this. Usually, following the Particulars of Claim (which may be served with the Claim Form), a Defence is served by the defendant and after that the claimant may serve a Reply. Where a defendant has a cross - claim, this often arises out of the same transaction as the claim; e.g. a claim for compensation for defective work in answer to a claim for payment of the contract price. This 'Counterclaim' is

---

[6] *Convention on jurisdiction and the recognition of judgments in civil and commercial matters* dated 21 December 2007.
[7] CPR 16 and Practice Direction.

usually served with the Defence and there follow mutually responsive Statements of Case to the Counterclaim.

A defendant may make another type of claim against a third party, by claiming an indemnity or contribution or making some other claim to offset any liability which the defendant may have.[8] Statements of Case are exchanged between the defendant and the third party. This often arises where sub-contractors are to blame for the alleged breach but only the principal contractor has been sued by the end client. These proceedings often track the main case and are tried with, or immediately after, trial of the main claim. A counterclaim or additional claim has a life of its own and may continue even if the main claim is settled or discontinued.

A two-year Disclosure Pilot operates in the BPC from 1 January 2019. The Disclosure Pilot can be conveniently broken down into two parts: Initial Disclosure and Extended Disclosure. Each party serving a Statement of Case must give 'Initial Disclosure' of the key documents on which it relies, subject to certain exceptions. This will apply to most cases started in the BPC.[9] Heavier claims with documents exceeding 2000 pages are excluded from these initial requirements but may be the subject of a request under part two of the Disclosure Pilot for Extended Disclosure. This is far more specific and cannot be avoided unlike Initial Disclosure. Parties need to be alive to this as disclosure is an intrusive and labour-intensive process. As it is a pilot, the requirements and rules may change as the court considers it in practice.

An early end to the case?

There are reasons why a case may not proceed to the next stage, or at least not immediately. The defendant may apply to challenge the

---

[8] Any additional claim, whether a counterclaim against the existing claimant or an additional claim against a third party, is governed by Part 20 of the CPR.

[9] The Disclosure Pilot does not apply to proceedings set out at PD51U [1.4].

jurisdiction of the court or for an order that the court should not exercise its jurisdiction, e.g. because the case would be more conveniently tried in a different jurisdiction (country). Or a defendant may say that the claim should proceed no further, because there is a prior agreement that the dispute be referred to arbitration. There are important technical rules about when such applications may be made, the procedural steps to be taken and their timing.[10]

A defendant may fail to serve a Defence in time and the claimant obtain judgment in default of defence.[11] A default judgment may be set aside if the defendant can show there would be a real prospect of successfully defending the claim or some other good reason why the judgment should be set aside (or varied) or the defendant be allowed to defend the claim.[12]

Summary judgment and strike-out

There are two separate and alternative procedures known as 'summary judgment' and 'strike out' that allow a party (claimant or defendant) to stop a claim or obtain judgment at an early stage on the claim, a claim or an issue. For summary judgment, the applicant will succeed if the other side's case has no real prospect of success and there is no other compelling reason why there should be a trial. Each side may rely on written evidence (there is no 'live' evidence) and there is a hearing at which each side may appear or be represented to argue their case.

If the claimant or defendant is successful, there is no trial at all or only a trial of part of the case.[13] The successful party will generally obtain a costs-shifting order in their favour.

---

[10] CPR 9.2(c), 10 and 11. Special rules may apply to some claims, e.g. in the Commercial List.
[11] CPR 12.
[12] CPR 13.3(1).
[13] CPR 24.

A party may apply to strike out all or part of a Statement of Case or seek an interim payment, as opposed to summary judgment.[14] Defending parties often apply for both summary judgment and strike out in the alternative at the same time. It is an effective tool to put pressure on a claimant and bring hopeless proceedings to an end promptly. Likewise, an application for summary judgment can be combined with one for interim payment (see below).

Interim remedies

The CPR provides a range of interim remedies.[15] A party applies to the court if it wants an interim remedy. Generally, each side may file written evidence and participate in a hearing before a judge.

Interim remedies are mainly designed to 'hold the ring' until trial or to allow the claim to be tried fairly. An order for an interim remedy may even be made before proceedings have started but also after judgment has been given.[16] The following are examples.

Interim injunction

An interim injunction may be granted by the court at an early stage, sometimes before proceedings have started and may be sought 'ex parte,' i.e. without the respondent party being on notice. This may be required to avoid the respondent taking action that will undermine the injunction, or in cases of extreme urgency. However, there are important restrictions and conditions attaching to such applications.

As it is generally unclear which side will win at trial, the court usually makes or refuses an interim order depending on which side has the most to lose if an order is made or refused. If one side has no less to lose than the other, the court may maintain the 'status quo'. The merits of the case may be relevant too. A 'mandatory' injunction

---

[14] CPR 3.4 and see later in the text for interim payments.
[15] See the list at CPR 25.1.
[16] CPR 25.2(1).

is usually more difficult to obtain before trial than a 'negative' or prohibitory injunction.

A party applying must usually give a 'cross-undertaking in damages' before the court will make an interim order. This requires that party to compensate the other party if it is later shown that the order should not have been granted and that other party suffers loss as a result of the order. The cross-undertaking must be of financial substance. The court may direct a speedy trial of the case, whether or not an interim injunction is granted.

Applications to court for an interim injunction can generate very large legal bills. There are a number of costs-shifting orders available to the court, depending on who wins the injunction application. If an injunction is obtained, this can present a very good opportunity for settling the case.

Freezing orders

A claiming party may be concerned that the opposing party has taken, or is about to take, steps to move or dissipate its assets to frustrate any court judgment. A freezing order prohibits the party to whom it is addressed from dealing with their assets up to the value of the claim and anticipated legal costs. The claiming party must give a cross-undertaking in damages. Notice of the injunction is given by the claiming party to any bank holding assets of the injuncted respondent and a bank is likely to comply with the order of the court.

A freezing injunction usually allows the party against whom the order has been made to deal with their assets in the ordinary and proper course of business and individual defendants are permitted to spend so much a week on ordinary living expenses and a reasonable sum on legal advice and representation. The orders are usually made without giving notice of the application to the opposing party. To do so might prompt the other party to take the very steps which the injunction is designed to prevent. The applicant owes a duty of full and frank disclosure to the court and has to show what is called 'a good arguable case'. The standard-form injunction envisages that the order will be made for a short period, until a 'return date' when the court can consider whether it should be continued.

Security for costs

In some circumstances, the court will order that financial measures be put in place to protect a party against a risk that, if successful at trial, it will not recover costs from the opposing party. This is called a 'security for costs order'. If the order is not complied with, the proceedings may not progress further. Security for costs is only available for a defendant to a claim or a counterclaim. See Chapter 5.

Interim payment

The court may order an interim payment if satisfied that, if the claim went to trial, the claimant would obtain judgment for a substantial amount of money (other than costs).[17] This is different from a summary judgment application. Following the end of a trial, the winning party is entitled to seek an interim payment on account of costs pending agreement or determination of those costs by detailed assessment unless there is good reason not to have such a payment so ordered.[18]

Case allocation

All defended cases are allocated to a particular 'track' after they have started, which has its own procedures. The following commentary is directed at Multi-Track cases (claims for over £25,000). Multi-Track cases are heard in the County Court and High Court, including the BPC.

---

[17] CPR 25.7(1).
[18] CPR 44.2(8).

Disclosure of documents

Once Statements of Case have been exchanged, each side has to 'disclose' all documents in its 'possession, power or control' that tend either to assist or undermine its case. A party to litigation, whether claimant, defendant or other party, must generally submit to an intrusion into its affairs which requires it to produce such documents.

The other party or parties to the litigation are subject to what is known as a 'collateral undertaking' to use disclosed documents only for the purpose of the proceedings in which they have been disclosed.[19]

Given that cases in the BPC are now (with exceptions) subject to the two-year Disclosure Pilot from 1 January 2019, disclosure at this stage may be more limited. So, preparation and related costs are usually incurred earlier in the litigation (see above). In cases within the Disclosure Pilot, Initial Disclosure may be followed at this stage by Extended Disclosure,[20] e.g. where one side considers the Initial Disclosure given to be inadequate or the parties did not have to comply with Initial Disclosure due to specific exclusions from that stage. The procedure in the Commercial Court is different, where a case-specific approach applies to what arrangements for disclosure best fit the case.[21]

'Documents' include those electronically stored. Disclosure requires a reasonable and proportionate search to be made. In cases outside the Pilot, if one side considers that the disclosure given is inadequate, it may apply for what is called 'specific disclosure.'[22] As

---

[19] CPR 31.22(1), (2): the exceptions to the rule include where the document has been read to or by the court, or has been referred to, at a hearing held in public. That exception may itself be disapplied by the court.
[20] CPR PD 51U para. 6.
[21] *Commercial Court Guide*, E2.1.
[22] CPR 31.12.

most documents are now in electronic form, diligent searches must be made of email accounts, archives and other sources where electronic documents are stored.

A litigant is not required to produce copies of privileged documents to the other party (see section 5 below). If a document is confidential, e.g. contains trade secrets, arrangements may be made to limit the disclosure to the other side's legal advisers only.

Case management directions

For cases allocated to the Multi-Track, 'directions for trial' are given by the court. These are the steps to be taken by the parties before the trial. The directions fix a date for the trial or a period ('window') within which it will take place.

Instead of simply issuing directions, the court may fix what is called a 'Case Management Conference.'[23] This will deal with outstanding procedural issues and the court gives directions (e.g. permitting the parties to call expert evidence) and rules on any outstanding issues, e.g. applications for specific disclosure or Extended Disclosure. Once the trial date or window has been fixed, it is difficult to move either. The directions for trial may include directions for use of ADR, particularly mediation.[24]

A 'costs management order' or 'CMO' may be made by the court to limit the amount of recoverable costs. Such an order is made by reference to costs budgets prepared by each party. See **5.2** above.

Court support for ADR

The court's duty to manage cases actively includes encouraging parties to use an ADR procedure if appropriate, and to facilitate its

---

[23] This is mandatory in the Commercial Court.
[24] CPR PD 29 [4.10(9)] and standard directions.

use as well helping the parties to settle the whole or part of their case.[25]

This may include a disclosure order, trial of a preliminary issue or a 'split trial' with liability to be decided first, and a subsequent hearing to assess financial compensation if liability is established.

There are court-based ADR schemes. For example, in appropriate cases and if the litigating parties agree a judge in Chancery Division proceedings may conduct an Early Neutral Evaluation ('ENE'). The parties are given an opinion about the legal merits of the dispute or an issue or issues in it. A related service is Financial Dispute Resolution or FDR. A judge plays the role of a facilitator and evaluator at a short hearing, to assist the parties to settle the dispute. Both processes are generally 'without prejudice'.[26]

Case management orders often require a party refusing to engage in ADR to explain why its refusal. An unreasonable refusal may later be penalised in costs. ADR in this context is generally mediation but it does not have to be.

The law in this area is in a state of development. The court has directed ENE on the application of a party, where the other side opposed it and argued for mediation.[27] The decision re-opens the question of whether the court will order a party to engage in ADR, particularly mediation.

Witness statements

Exchange of witness statements is generally the next main step in the process. The basic rule is that the evidence of a witness must be set out in a Witness Statement. It must contain a 'Statement of Truth' (i.e. a statement by the maker that he/she believes the facts stated are true) and be signed by the witness. If the evidence of a witness

---

[25] CPR 1.4(2), (e), (f).
[26] See *Chancery Guide*, [18.7] – [18.19]. See Chapter 6 above.
[27] *Lomax v Lomax* [2019] EWCA Civ 1467.

cannot be established at this stage (e.g. a *subpoena* is to be served on the witness), a party may serve a 'Witness Summary'.

In most cases, the preparation of witness statements requires a lot of time and care by the witnesses. Draft statements may have been taken before the case started. Witness statements generally follow disclosure. This allows the witnesses for each party to consider the documents from each party.

The witness statement is the key document by which the weight of a witness's evidence will be measured by the trial judge. In turn, the weight given to that evidence will be tested against what lawyers refer to as 'the contemporaneous documents'. These are the documents brought into existence at the time of the transaction in dispute. Therefore, in putting forward his or her account of relevant events, a witness must read or re-read (as the case may be) the contemporaneous documents with particular care. A witness statement must be the witness's own account of events. This is often a party's first opportunity to set out at length the particular events relevant to their case. It is undertaken away from the pressure of the court environment and can be considered with care. However, for that same reason, mistakes in witness statements may be picked up at trial by the opposing side and so accuracy is paramount.

Witness evidence generally carries more weight if the maker of the statement goes on to give evidence orally at the trial. But written evidence may be relied on without calling the maker of the statement. Uncontentious matters are often proved by not calling the maker of the statement. Where there is a conflict on an important issue of fact, greater weight is usually given to the oral evidence. Judges often place much less weight on hearsay evidence on contentious issues, as the opposing party will be prevented from testing the evidence by cross-examination.

Expert evidence

Expert evidence is evidence in the nature of opinion and is generally contrasted with evidence of fact, i.e. witness evidence. Examples of expert evidence include the condition of contract goods or the adequacy or amount of work done under a contract; or forensic accountancy evidence to calculate loss in more complex cases. Expert evidence significantly increases the costs of litigating a dispute.

Permission of the court is needed to rely on expert evidence. Expert evidence is generally presented in report form. Reports generally follow witness statements, several weeks later.

It is the duty of an expert to help the court on matters within their expertise. This duty overrides any obligation owed to the person from whom the expert has received instructions or by whom they are paid.[28]

An expert witness should provide independent assistance to the court by way of objective unbiased opinion on matters within his expertise and should never assume the role of an advocate.[29]

Although the CPR makes provision for the court to be assisted by a 'single joint expert',[30] cases often proceed on contentious issues with each party using its own expert. Following reports in advance of trial, the experts may be required to meet with a view to narrowing disputed issues of expert opinion. Supplemental reports may be allowed by the trial directions.

---

[28] CPR 35.3.
[29] *National Justice Compania Naviera SA v Prudential Assurance Co Ltd ('The Ikarian Reefer')* [1993] 2 Lloyds Rep 68, 81.
[30] CPR 35.7 and 35.8.

The lead-up to trial

By the time that trial is about a month away, trial preparations on both sides are likely to be underway and if not, soon will be.[31] This is a time of intense activity for litigation lawyers and trial advocates. Often there is a meeting between the clients and the lawyers at this stage to discuss the running of the case, issues that need addressing for the trial, and likely prospects of success.

Bundles of documents for the trial are being prepared, last minute conferences held with expert witnesses and the advocates are preparing their written arguments for the court, so–called 'Skeleton Arguments'. A running order for witnesses is finalised and a day or so before the hearing starts the parties are generally informed who the judge will be.

The witnesses for trial have more work to do at this stage. They will have been asked to read and comment on the other side's witness statements. That allows the lawyers to know what their own witnesses will say in answer to points made by the other side. No side wants to be in the position of finding out in court for the first time what its witnesses will say. This underlines the essential importance of witnesses being full and frank in their preparation of witness statements.

3. Trial

Many readers will have some idea of a court trial from television. The basic rule is that the hearing is in public.[32] In a civil trial there is rarely a jury. A trial is before a single judge, who will generally have read the Skeleton Arguments prepared by the trial advocates and

---

[31] Depending on the complexity of a case and its length, the court may direct a pre-trial review shortly before the start of the trial to resolve any procedural matters before trial and avoid delays at trial.

[32] The courts have been given power to conduct trials by remote hearings (including video-conferencing) due to the Covid-19 virus. See Chapter 3, fn 3 and accompanying text.

core documents identified by the parties. In heavier trials, the trial bundle may contain thousands of pages. Therefore, it is critical that the court is taken to key documents. Legal representation at trial is the norm. An individual may represent him/herself without legal representation and may be assisted by a lay person, known as a 'McKenzie Friend', who may give them reasonable assistance, e.g. note-taking.[33] A company may be represented by an employee if authorised to do so by the company and if the permission of the court is given.[34] That should be cleared in advance of the trial. Company employees cannot conduct litigation otherwise they may fall foul of conducting a reserved activity,[35] which is a criminal offence.[36] The company must conduct the litigation. The Board authorises its employees to carry out the steps and functions which enable the company to conduct the litigation.[37]

The claimant generally 'goes first'. Their advocate opens the case, then calls evidence. The defendant will then present its case in the same way. The evidence relied on by both sides is likely to be oral, documentary, and where relevant, expert evidence.

After that, each side is given the opportunity to make final closing submissions in which each seeks to persuade the judge why their case should succeed in the light of all the evidence.

There are three stages in the oral evidence of a witness: evidence in chief, cross-examination and re-examination. As the witnesses will generally have made witness statements, the questions asked 'in chief' are likely to be few. They may extend to events after the date when the statement was made. Generally, advocates like to ask a few introductory questions to 'warm up' the witness to make them

---

[33] See *Civil Procedure*, Vol. 2 pp 13-18.
[34] CPR 39.6.
[35] Defined by Legal Services Act 2007 s 12.
[36] Legal Services Act 2007 s 14.
[37] *Ndole Assets v Designer M&E Services* [2018] EWCA Civ 2865.

feel more at ease before cross-examination. However, the advocate will require the court's permission to ask further questions.

In cross-examination, the witness may be asked any question relevant to the issues. They may also be cross-examined on wider matters that go to 'credit', i.e. their credibility as a witness. Once cross-examination has ended, the party who called the witness may 're-examine' the witness, to ask questions limited to those arising out of the cross-examination. The judge sometimes asks questions of the witness and follow-up questions may be asked. Witnesses should be prepared to be asked uncomfortable questions by the other side. For instance, they may be challenged as to their truthfulness.

It is generally a good idea to exclude witnesses from the court until they have given evidence; to avoid a suggestion that their evidence may have been 'tailored' by the witness in the light of evidence given by previous witnesses. Equally, once a witness has given evidence, they may remain in court to listen. However, they must not discuss their evidence or any other evidence heard in court with witnesses who are yet to give evidence.

If there is expert evidence, the witnesses of fact for both sides may be called to give evidence before that happens, so the court has before it the oral evidence of fact before the experts give evidence. Experts often give evidence back-to-back; for the claimant at the end of its case with the defendant's expert giving evidence at the start of the defence's case.

The expert evidence is generally given in a similar way to the evidence of fact, based on reports written by each expert. Experts are allowed to remain in court and listen to the evidence of fact to enable them to give instructions to the advocate on issues arising relating to their expertise. This often leads to helpful questions on technical points being put to witnesses.

As the case progresses through its various stages (opening, evidence and closing submissions), the judge may intervene, asking questions of the witnesses or experts, making observations and asking questions of the parties' advocates. These may show where the judge's thinking is at that particular point. The judge will generally be astute not to appear to have made up their mind.

Each side will be trying to read the judge. The trial can be a very volatile environment, the case appearing to swing one way and then another as the evidence 'comes out', especially when the judge makes interventions. Experience shows that judges often try to play 'devil's advocate' to test both parties' evidence and cases.

Following closing submissions, the judge will usually end the sitting with a view to giving judgment later that day or in most BPC cases, at a later date. If the hearing is adjourned, a draft judgment is often made available to the parties' lawyers a few weeks later. The draft is generally 'embargoed' (being confidential to the parties and their lawyers) until formally handed down in open court at a later hearing.[38] Arguments on costs are sometimes made after the parties have considered the judgment, though in simple cases the judge may have received submissions on costs before giving judgment.

The judge will rule on costs at the later hearing when the judgment is formally given in open court.

The result of the trial is a therefore generally a written judgment and orders of the court made by the trial judge. The judgment contains the judge's reasons. These include their findings of fact, crucial to the outcome.

If the claim and/or counterclaim is successful, the judgment will grant one or more of the remedies sought by the claimant, and/or counterclaimed by the defendant. The judgment is followed by a

---

[38] PD 40E. A party breaching the embargo will be in contempt of court and could be subject to punishment by the court.

written order of the court that details the steps giving effect to the judgment; e.g. the defendant to pay the claimant £x and the claimant's costs, to be assessed on the 'standard basis' if not agreed (see Chapter 5).

The judge also deals with any application for permission to appeal and other matters arising, e.g. whether the judgment should be stayed.

In some cases, the court will decide liability only and leave the assessment of any financial compensation or 'quantum' to a further stage of the proceedings. It will grant an injunction or other relief, if appropriate. The successful party may, however, apply to the trial judge for an interim payment, if the court has ordered compensation in the form of damages to be assessed.[39] However, in many cases it is not possible to fix the minimum level of likely financial compensation at this stage so no interim order would be made.

The splitting of trials in this way provides a particular incentive to parties to settle disputes. Faced with the prospect of effectively two trials, both parties may want to avoid the cost and prolonged uncertainty of that process.

The court should make an interim order on account of costs, where it has made a costs-shifting order, unless there is good reason not to do so.[40]

4. Appeals, enforcement and assessment of costs

Obtaining a judgment from the court is not an end of the process. The winner must still get their money. The winner may have to use the court procedures of enforcement if the loser does not pay up.

---

[39] CPR 25.7(1)(b).
[40] CPR 44.2(8).

Enforcement

A judgment may be enforced against the assets of the loser. There are different procedures for different types of asset. If assets are located abroad, the winner must invoke cross-border procedures of enforcement. Although judgments are often enforceable outside England and Wales, in some jurisdictions the judgment has to be registered and there may be defences available too within that jurisdiction.

Enforcement of court judgments outside England and Wales is by a patchwork of arrangements. Enforceability of EU judgments in civil and commercial matters in other Member States is enabled by a number of EU Regulations. These will cease to apply to the UK after the implementation period of Brexit ending on 31 December 2020. Arrangements are not yet in place after this date.

There are reciprocal agreements with other states, but no reciprocal agreement with the USA, where enforcement of an English judgment is possible but not always straightforward.

Costs assessment

There is a process for the assessment of costs. However, it is expensive and is used in a minority of cases. Claims for costs over £75,000 are assessed by a costs judge. Usually, the parties attempt to agree the costs, particularly once an interim costs order has been made by the trial judge.

Claims for costs under £75,000 can be assessed initially by a costs judge without a hearing using a process called provisional assessment. If a party disagrees with the result, it may ask for an oral hearing but if they fail to achieve a shift of 20% or more than the result at that hearing, they will pay the other party's costs (subject to any Part 36 offers).

Appeals

A losing party does not have an automatic right of appeal, except in very limited cases. Permission to appeal must be obtained from the court. For decisions of a trial judge to an appeal court, permission to appeal may only be given where the appeal would have a real prospect of success or there is some other compelling reason for the appeal to be heard.[41] Time limits apply to bringing an appeal and to applications for permission to appeal. There is a voluntary Court of Appeal Mediation Scheme that applies to all contractual claims up to a value of £500,000. Mediation may be done outside the scheme and the parties are at liberty to settle the appeal and their wider dispute.

Although an appeal court has broad powers and will allow an appeal where the decision of the lower court was wrong,[42] the grounds on which an appeal may succeed are narrow. Generally, the appeal court will not hear oral evidence or receive any evidence that was not before the lower court.[43]

An appellant will generally be unable to challenge successfully the findings of fact made at trial. The trial judge is considered to have been in the best position to assess the quality of the evidence, particularly the oral evidence on which so many cases turn.

An appeal may succeed if the judge has made an error of law (i.e. of legal principle) of sufficient relevance to the trial outcome. If the appeal is directed at the exercise of a judicial discretion, the decision will be difficult to challenge where the judgement shows that the trial judge has taken into account all the relevant factors and not taken into account irrelevant considerations.

An appeal, even if permission is given, does not allow the loser to prevent the winner from enforcing their judgment (for money and costs). In legalese, there is no 'stay' of the orders made by the lower

---

[41] CPR 52.6(1).

[42] CPR 52.20 and 52.21(3)(a). A second ground is where the decision was unjust because of a serious procedural or other irregularity in the proceedings: CPR 52.21(3)(b).

[43] CPR 52.21(1), (2).

court, unless the court orders otherwise.[44] Security for the costs of an appeal may be obtained against the appellant in some cases.

The hearing of the appeal is usually much shorter than the trial. The court and the advocates will refer to the trial transcript where necessary, as well as the other documents in the case, particularly the judgment of the trial judge. There are various tiers of appeal, depending on which court dealt with the trial. However, it is rare for a case to get beyond one tier of appeal. The final appeal (for which permission is required) is to the Supreme Court, generally from the Court of Appeal. Until 31 December 2020, questions of European law may be referred to the European Court of Justice for a preliminary ruling. There is no right of appeal from a national court to that court.

5. Other courts and trial schemes

The Shorter and Flexible Trials Schemes

If parties require a court decision faster than in ordinary litigation, there are other possibilities. The Shorter Trials Scheme ('STS') is apt for a number of cases which would not last longer than four days at trial, including judge's pre-reading time. Disposal by STS is not normally appropriate if extensive disclosure, witness evidence or expert evidence is necessary. A CMO may be made if the parties agree, or the trial judge will 'summarily' assess the costs after judgment has been given.[45] Cases under the STS may be dealt with in less than a year. Pre-action exchange of information is limited and the Pre-Action Protocol does not apply, assuming that the defending party agrees to trial by the STS.

The Flexible Trials Scheme ('FTS') allows the parties to adopt trial procedures suited to the case. The scheme is designed to limit disclosure and oral evidence to what is necessary for the fair

---

[44] CPR 52.16.
[45] CPR PR 57AB, 1.1 – 2.60.

disposal of the case.[46] Dedicated procedural rules apply to both schemes. The CPR is disapplied to the extent inconsistent with those rules.

Intellectual Property Enterprise Court

The Intellectual Property Enterprise Court (IPEC) deals with intellectual property disputes where the money claims do not exceed £500,000, excluding interest and costs. The parties may agree to the court having jurisdiction if the claim is higher.[47] Its interest for present purposes is the costs regime. Costs-shifting recovery is generally limited to 'scale costs', a maximum of £50,000 for the trial on liability and no more than £25,000 for the second stage, when financial compensation is decided. The scale costs also have limits for each stage of the litigation.[48]

6. The without prejudice rule and other forms of privilege.

The law recognises the public interest in parties to a dispute being able to negotiate without their settlement communications being placed before the court, to the prejudice of the case advanced before the court. This 'without prejudice rule' allows each party to pursue its case without fear that statements or concessions made by it in settlement communications will damage their case. As a result, written or verbal communications made in a genuine attempt to compromise a dispute between the parties are generally inadmissible in evidence.[49]

---

[46] CPR PR 57AB, 3.1-3.9.

[47] CPR 63.17A.

[48] CPR, 45.31.

[49] There are limited exceptions to the without prejudice rule, e.g. where the issue is whether a binding agreement has resulted from the negotiations or to explain a party's delay in which case the fact of the negotiations may be referred to, and sometimes their content. There are also exceptions where the privilege is abused, e.g. blackmail: see generally, Phipson (2017) [24-13] – [24-36].

APPENDIX 1 – LITIGATION

The without prejudice rule is an aspect of what is called 'privilege'. There are different kinds of privilege. For present purposes, there is a general public interest in preserving the secrecy or confidentiality of communications made between lawyer and client whether or not legal proceedings are in existence or contemplation ('legal advice privilege') and communications made in contemplation of litigation ('litigation privilege')). In rare cases, use of express words in a statute may operate to remove privilege in a particular field. Otherwise, the secrecy of these communications can only be opened up in limited circumstances, e.g. if the privilege has been waived.

Litigation privilege allows preparation of a case without the communications in question coming to the attention of the court or the other party to the dispute. Once litigation is in prospect or pending, communications between a client and his solicitor or agent or between one of them and a third party, will be privileged if they come into existence for the sole or dominant purpose of either giving or getting legal advice with regard to the litigation or collecting evidence for use in it.[50]

---

[50] Hollander (2018) [18-01].

APPENDIX 2 – COMPARISONS: LITIGATION, ARBITRATION AND EXPERT DETERMINATION

This Appendix sets out differences between litigation and arbitration and between those forms of dispute resolution and expert determination. It supplements **3.5** above.

1. Litigation and arbitration compared

The essence of an arbitration is the same as court proceedings: a set of procedures resulting in a binding decision given by an independent and impartial decision-maker.

As we have seen, trials in litigation are generally in open court, whereas the basic rule is that arbitrations are private and confidential.[1] Occasionally, that confidentiality will be lost on an appeal. In practical as well as legal terms, privacy and confidentiality are not absolute. Some arbitration awards do 'leak' into the public domain.

Arbitration procedures can often be tailored to reduce legal costs and the time for a decision. The tailoring may be in institutional rules chosen by the parties or in an arbitration scheme that applies to their dispute. Or the procedures can be tailored by the arbitrator, after consultation with the parties.

The parties may agree to a 'documents only' arbitration, i.e. an award made without an oral hearing, where the award is based on written representations, information and evidence provided by them. The Business Arbitration Scheme of the Chartered Institute of Arbitrators (CIArb) *'offers a final and legally binding award in less than 90 days from the appointment of an arbitrator and is simple enough to*

---

[1] Under other (i.e. non-English) systems of law, an arbitration may not be confidential and private. However, the rules of the arbitration agreed by the parties may contain those or similar requirements.

allow most businesses to present their case without legal representation[2]. Arbitrations under CIArb's Cost Controlled Expedited Arbitration Rules are to be decided within 180 days. Both schemes allow for oral hearings, though encourage disposal of the dispute on a documents-only basis.

In international disputes, arbitration is often agreed on in advance within the terms of the contract, rather than leaving disputes to be litigated. Arbitration will cost more than litigation in some cases and the parties may expect this.

The fee to start an arbitration where there is one (institutional arbitrations) is often lower than the fee to start a court case. The fees payable to an institution will depend on whether it is simply appointing the arbitrator(s) or whether it is also administering the arbitration. The parties pay for the arbitrator(s) and the arbitration venue.[3]

A sole arbitrator is sufficient for many cases. In high value cases there may be more than one arbitrator, usually three. In litigation, there is no single judge who takes the case from the start to trial. The tribunal in an arbitration generally remains the same.

In litigation, the parties do not choose the judge. In arbitration, the parties may have that freedom of choice. If there is a disagreement, there may be an arbitral institution chosen by them to make the appointment. If not, the court may make the appointment.[4]

As in litigation, the time when an arbitration commences may be important for the purposes of time-barring; i.e. because a claim must be brought within a certain period of time. As in litigation, if an arbitration is started outside the period, the opposing party may

---

[2] CIArb website: https://www.ciarb.org.
[3] In complex cases, a tribunal secretary may be appointed.
[4] AA 1996 s 18.

have a complete defence to the claim.[5] A contract may provide for how and when an arbitration is to be started. The 1996 Act contains default provisions stating when the arbitration commences.[6]

Where a party starts court proceedings despite an agreement to arbitrate, the court will generally enforce the agreement and 'stay' the case.[7] A contract containing an arbitration clause may require the parties to engage in negotiation and/or mediation before starting any arbitration. If there is no arbitration clause, the contract may specify negotiation and/or mediation before the start of any litigation.[8]

The CPR contains a comprehensive list of procedures leading to trial. The flexibility of the 1996 Act is based on the tribunal's duty to act fairly. For example, disclosure of documents is not required in every case, though fairness may require disclosure. It may be necessary to go to court for certain types of procedural measure, e.g. an interim injunction, because of the limitations in this area in the 1996 Act. But some arbitral laws and rules provide for a wide range of interim measures, akin to an interim injunction. Some arbitration institutions have in place arrangements for Emergency Arbitrators, who may make interim orders even before the main tribunal has been constituted.

The steps in an oral hearing with witness evidence are often very similar to a court trial, though the formality of the court room is absent. Arbitrations are generally conducted in offices that are part of an arbitration centre. Venues in London include the International Dispute Resolution Centre, and CIArb.

---

[5] AA 1996 ss 12 and 13.
[6] AA 1996 s 14.
[7] AA 1996 s 9(1), (4), CPR Part 11.
[8] Unless a 'standstill agreement' can be reached with the other party, consideration may have to be given to starting proceedings if the claim would become time - barred.

The arbitral tribunal considers each side's written cases, evidence and submissions and makes its decision or award. Reasons for the award must be given, unless the parties have agreed to dispense with them.

The powers of an arbitrator are similar to court powers. Unless otherwise agreed, the tribunal may order the payment of money in any currency (with pre- and post-award interest), an injunction or specific performance (an order to take specified action) and a declaration (i.e. an order declaring rights, such as the existence of a binding contract).[9]

As in litigation, the loser will generally be ordered to pay the winner's costs. The basic position under the 1996 Act is that this is a reasonable amount of the other party's legal or other costs reasonably incurred.[10] The recoverable costs also include the arbitrator's reasonable fees and expenses, unless these have been agreed by contract in which case the contract rate will apply.[11] There are also costs-limiting rules in litigation (see Chapter 5).

A costs award allows the winner to shift its liability for the fees and expenses of the tribunal (and any of an arbitral institution) onto the loser. If, or to the extent that, the loser does not pay, the winner is still liable for the arbitrator's fees and expenses.[12]

'Without prejudice' offers to settle can be made. Such communications would not be seen by the tribunal. Parties can make offers 'without prejudice save as to costs', however. These can be seen by the tribunal once it has delivered its award on the issues other than costs. The effect is similar to the regime under CPR Part 36 (see Chapter 5). A claimant who does not 'beat the offer' could be

---

[9] AA 1996 ss 48, 49.
[10] AA 1996 s 63(5)(a).
[11] AA 1996 s 64.
[12] AA 1996 s 28.

RESOLVING BUSINESS DISPUTES

liable for the respondent's costs from the last date when the offer could have been accepted.

The right of appeal from an arbitral award applies to errors of law. In court proceedings an appeal may also relate to the facts, though such appeals are generally difficult to win. The arbitral right to appeal may be excluded by the arbitration agreement.[13] Any available arbitral process of appeal must be exhausted before an appeal and permission of the court is then required, unless all other parties to the proceedings agree that the appeal may be brought. Time limits also apply.[14]

If a litigant obtains a judgment or award, the loser will generally comply, e.g. by paying money to the claimant. In litigation, a judgment can be enforced by the different methods in the CPR; e.g. a charging order on land. However, to enforce an award permission of the court must first be obtained. After that, the award may be enforced in the same manner as a judgment or order of the court.[15]

To enforce an award abroad, the laws of that jurisdiction may be relevant and there may be mutual recognition of judgments. The UK is party to the United Nations Convention on the Recognition and Enforcement of Foreign Arbitral Awards 1958 ('the New York Convention'). It has over 159 contracting states (including the USA) and provides a generally efficient means of enforcing arbitral awards outside the UK.

Enforcement of court judgments outside England and Wales is by a patchwork of arrangements. Enforceability of EU judgments in civil and commercial matters in other Member States, European

---

[13] AA 1996 s 69(1). The arbitration agreement may provide for further grounds of appeal. There are additional rights of challenge to an award based on jurisdiction and serious irregularity under AA 1996 ss 67 and 68.

[14] AA 1996 s 69(2) and s 70(2), (3).

[15] AA 1996 s 66(1), (2).

Economic Area EFTA[16] member states ("EFTA States") and Switzerland are enabled by a number of EU regulations and treaties. Following the UK's departure from the EU, these will cease to apply to the UK at the end of the implementation period (i.e. at 11pm GMT on 31 December 2020) unless the implementation period is either extended or a new arrangement is agreed in trade talks. The agreement between the EU and UK maintains the *status quo* in the implementation period.[17]

There are reciprocal agreements with other states, but no reciprocal agreement with the USA, where enforcement of an English judgment may not be straightforward.

2. Litigation and arbitration compared to expert determination

Litigation or litigation-like procedures generally do not apply to expert determinations. However, the contract terms may provide some procedures to enable each party to have an opportunity of placing its case before the expert. There is no equivalent to the 1996 Act, with a reservoir of procedural powers. The expert's powers largely derive from the contract appointing the expert or from the terms of the appointment contained in a separate document.

If the parties cannot agree on the expert, the contract will only work if it nominates an appointing institution or gives the parties the right to go to court to obtain the appointment. This is unlike arbitration, where the court can generally plug the gap and make the appointment.[18]

A reference to expert determination does not 'stop the clock' for limitation purposes unless the contract says so; and a 'standstill

---

[16] European Free Trade Association.
[17] EU (Withdrawal) Act 2018 ss 1A to 7C and EU (Withdrawal Agreement) Act 2020 s 39.
[18] AA 1996 s 18.

agreement' or other measures may be necessary for a claiming party to stop time running. Otherwise, the limitation period might expire during the process.[19] That would result in the claim being defeated.

The expert usually gives directions to the parties as to what information and documents are required, with a timetable. It is not clear if litigation privilege applies to expert determination.[20] However, there is no obligation to disclose documents adverse to one's case unless the contract requires disclosure. Even if the privilege does not exist, it would not follow that a disclosure order would be made for a document that would otherwise be covered by it.

Sometimes, there is a hearing where the parties can argue their position. If not, the expert may request written submissions. The giving of oral evidence is rare.

The expert procedure should lead to a speedy decision. Reasons for the decision are not required unless the contract states that they are. Whether an expert determination is confidential and private is not clear,[21] unless the contract states that it is confidential and/or private.

There is no costs-shifting in favour of the winner unless the contract says so. The expert has a (contractual) right to be paid their fees and expenses. The losing party will generally comply with the expert's determination. But if it has to be enforced, that must be done by litigation.

There is no appeal against an expert's determination. Defences to enforcement are generally limited and depend on the contract. For example, the contract may state that the decision is binding 'save for

---

[19] Kendall (2014) [12.2] – [12.3].

[20] Kendall (2014) [12.7-5].

[21] Russell (2015) para. 2-032 says not it is not confidential unless the contract says so. Kendall (2014) suggests that the expert determination is private and confidential; [1.2-6] and [6.11-7].

manifest error'[22]. There is an implied duty of procedural fairness, but its extent is unclear. At any rate, the unfairness must be material to the outcome. Defences based on fairness are often related to the expert's departure from the contractual procedure, if there is one.[23]

The only further remedy for a party disappointed by an expert's decision is a court claim against the expert for negligence. This is generally even more difficult to show than establishing a right of appeal in litigation or arbitration. It also requires litigation. An arbitrator has immunity from claims, except in very limited circumstances.[24] For the position on appeals, see above.

Expert determinations are well suited to issues of valuation where the decision-maker is expert in the field. Expert determination, as used for decisions by lawyers of litigation-type issues, may have advantages over litigation and arbitration; e.g. speedier decisions at reduced cost. However, the better course is likely to be arbitration. As we have seen, arbitration can be tailored to deliver fast and cost-effective decisions, while retaining clear safeguards necessary for a fair resolution of the dispute.

---

[22] An error that is 'obvious or easily demonstrable without extensive investigation': *IIG Capital LLC v Van der Merwe* [2007] EWHC 2631 (Ch) at [52].
[23] *Ackerman v Ackerman* [2011] EWHC 3428 (Ch), see gen. Kendall (2014) [14.14].
[24] AA 1996 s 29.

Reading list

Albright, Thos. D (2017) 'Why eyewitnesses fail', *Proceedings of the National Academy of Science*, USA 2017 Jul 25, 114(30).

Bailey, HHJ Edward et al (2013), *A Handbook for Litigants in Person*, www.judiciary.uk/publications/handbook-litigants-person-civil-221013/.

Bar Council (July 2018), *CFAs and DBAs in Public Access Cases*, barcouncil.org.

British Institute of International and Comparative Law (BIICL), *(April 2020), Breathing Space – a Concept Note on the effect of the pandemic on commercial contracts*, 27 accessed at www.biicl.org.

Bingham, Sir Thomas (1985), 'The Judge as Juror: the Judicial Determination of Factual Issues', *Current Legal Problems*, Volume 38, Issue 1, 1985.

Bingham (2000), *The Business of Judging*, Oxford University Press, Oxford.

Bingham (2010), *The Rule of Law*, Penguin, Harmondsworth.

Brazil, Wayne (2012), *Early Neutral Evaluation*, American Bar Association.

Campbell, Keith, Sedikides & Constantine (1999) 'Self-threat magnifies the self-serving bias: A Meta-analytic integration', *Review of General Psychology* (1999).

Charlesworth & Percy on Negligence 14th ed. (2018), Sweet & Maxwell, London.

Chitty on Contracts 33rd ed. (November 2019), Sweet & Maxwell, London.

CJC ADR Working Group (November 2018) *ADR and Civil Justice* www.judiciary.uk/wp-content/uploads/2018/12/CJC-ADRWG-Report-FINAL-Dec-2018.pdf.

Cordery on Legal Services (1996), looseleaf, Lexis Nexis, London.

Cuthbert, Leslie (2016) *Cognitive biases: 15 more to think about*, judiciary.gov.uk.

de Bono, Edward (2009), *Teach yourself to think*, Penguin Books, Harmondsworth.

Fisher & Shapiro (2007), *Building Agreement,* Random House Business Books, Harmondsworth.

Fisher, Ury and Patton *(2012) Getting to Yes*, Penguin, Random House, Harmondsworth.

Foskett on Compromise 9th ed., (December 2019), Sweet & Maxwell, London.

Furlong, Gary T. (2006), *The Conflict Resolution Toolbox, Models and Maps for Analyzing, Diagnosing and Resolving Conflict*, Wiley.

Goodman, Andrew (2018), *How Judges Decide Cases;* 2nd ed., Wildy, Simmonds & Hill.

Goodman-Delahunty, Loftus, Hartwig and Granhag (2010), 'Insightful or Wishful: Lawyers' Ability to Predict Case Outcomes', *Psychology, Public Policy and Law*, 2010, Vol 16 No.2.

Gore-Browne on Companies, 45th ed (2020), Lexis Nexis, London.

Guthrie, Rachlinski, Wistrich (2001) 'Inside the Judicial Mind', 86 *Cornell L. Rev.* 777.

Halsbury's Laws of England, 5th ed, (2017), Lexis Nexis, London.

Hammond, Keeney and Raiffa (1998), *Smart Choices; A Practical Guide to Making Better Decisions*, Harvard Business Press, Cambridge Mass.

Hastie, Reid and Dawes (2001), *Rational Choice in an Uncertain World*, SAGE Publications, London.

Herbert Smith Freehills (July 2017), *Improving Conflict Management*.

Herbert Smith Freehills, 28 February 2012, *Med-Arb – An Alternative Dispute Resolution Practice*.

Hogan Lovells (March 2019), *Implementing an effective dispute resolution strategy which promotes the use of ADR.* www.hoganlovells.com.

Hollander (2018), *Documentary Evidence* 13th ed., Sweet & Maxwell, London.

Howe and Knott (2015), 'The fallibility of memory in judicial processes: Lessons from the past and their modern consequences'; *Memory*, 23, 633.

Jones Elizabeth, QC and Clark, John 'Analysing Risk' Part 2, Ch.8, pp 317-324 of *Richbell (2015)*, Bloomsbury, London.

Jowitt's Dictionary of English Law (2019), Sweet & Maxwell, 5th ed., London.

Kahneman (2012), *Thinking Fast and Slow,* Penguin, Harmondsworth.

Keating on Construction Contracts 10th ed. (August 2019), Sweet & Maxwell, London.

Kendall on Expert Determination 5th ed. (2014), Sweet & Maxwell, London.

Kiser (2010), *Beyond Right and Wrong: The Power of Effective Decision Making for Attorneys and Clients,* Springer.

Kiser, Asher and McShane (2008), *Journal of Empirical Legal Studies,* September 2008.

Korobkin and Ulen (2000), *Law and Behavioural Science,* 88 Cal. L.R. 1051.

Lafley, A.G. and Martin, Roger (2014), *Playing to Win, How Strategy Really Works;* Harvard Business Review Press, Cambridge, Mass.

Levitin Daniel J. (2014), *The Organized Mind*, Viking, Harmondsworth.

Lotto, Beau (2017), *Deviate*, Weidenfeld & Nicholson, London.

Malhotra, Deepak (2016) *Negotiating the Impossible,* Berrett-Koehler Publishers Inc.

Malhotra and Bazerman (2007), *Negotiation Genius,* Bantam Books.

Massie, Graham (2014), *Risks for Financial and Corporate Managers,* pp 200-204 of Reuvid (2014).

Merkin & Flannery on the Arbitration Act 1996, 6th ed. (December 2019), Informa Law from Routledge.

Mnookin, Robert H (2004) *Beyond Winning,* The Belknapp Press, Cambridge, Mass.

Myers, David (2014) *Exploring Social Psychology*, 7th ed., McGraw Hill Education.

Newman & Garry (2014), 'False Memory'; *Sage Handbook of Applied Memory*, Ch. 7, ed. Perfect & Lindsay, SAGE, London.

Phipson on Evidence, (2017) 19th ed., Sweet & Maxwell, London.

Plous, Scott (1993), *The Psychology of Judgment and Decision Making*, McGraw – Hill.

Pronin (2007), Perception and misperception of bias in human judgment, *Trends in Cognitive Sciences 2007*.

Rachlinski, J (1996), 'Gains, Losses and the Psychology of Litigation', 70 *S. Cal. L. Rev.* 115 1996-1997 (Cornell Law Faculty).

Randolph, Paul (2015), *'The Psychological Resistance to Mediate'*, UK *Mediation Journal* Issue 2, London.

Reuvid, Jonathan ed. (2014) *Managing Business Risk: A Practical Guide to Protecting Your Business*.

Richbell, David (2015) *How to Master Commercial Mediation*; Bloomsbury, London.

Roediger & McDermott (1995), 'Creating False Memories: Remembering Words Not Presented in Lists', *Journal of Experimental Psychology*, Vol. 21 No.4, 803.

Russell on Arbitration 24th ed. (2015), Sweet & Maxwell, London.

Service, Robert (November 2015) *The End of the Cold War*, Pan Macmillan.

Shonk, Katy *Online Negotiation in a Time of Social Distance*, Harvard Law School, Daily Blog, 26 March 2020.

Stafford, Tom (2017), *Biases in Decision Making* www.judiciary.uk/wp-content/uploads/2018/02/stafford-biases-in-decision-making-winter-2017.pdf.

Tetlock and Gardner (2016), *Superforecasting; the Art & Science of Prediction*, Penguin, Random House, Harmondsworth.

Teversky and Marsh (2000), 'Biased Retellings of Events Yield Biased Memories', *Cognitive Psychology* 40-1-38.

Ury, William (1991*), Getting Past No*, Penguin, Random House, Harmondsworth.

Vos, Sir Geoffrey and others, (November 2019), *Legal statement on cryptoassets and smart contracts*, UK Jurisdiction Taskforce, www.judiciary.uk/wp-content/uploads/2019/11/LegalStatementLaunch.GV_.2.pdf.

Zander, Michael (2015), *The Law-Making Process*, 7th ed., Bloomsbury, London.

Index

Adjudication 37

ADR Group..................................107

Agreed Award..............................103

Alternative Dispute Resolution ....
....26, 33

Arbitration 34
    Chartered   Institute   of
       Arbitrators 35
    costs 95
    Calderbank Offer *96*
    Dubai   International
       Arbitration Centre 36
    International   Chamber   of
       Commerce..........................36
    London Court of International
       Arbitration.........................36
    Singapore   International
       Arbitration Centre 36

Best Alternative to a Negotiated
Settlement (BATNA)................117

Bias......................................50, 62, 158
    attribution 122
    blind spot 62
    confirmation 63, 68
    devaluation 160
    optimism 64
    representative.........................56
    selection..................................65
    self-serving...................63, 160
    sunk-cost 64, 160
    witness.....................................62

Business Arbitration Scheme.35, 187

Business disputes
    challenges for decision-makers
   5

financial interests....................7

forms of......................................5

legal advice.............................7

negotiated settlement..............9

Centre   for   Effective   Dispute
    Resolution 97, 107

Chartered Institute of Arbitrators
    (CIArb) 187

Civil Mediation Council 107

Civil Procedure Rules 24

Civil rights................................11

Comparisons
    Litigation, Arbitration, Expert
       Determination.................187

Competitive bidding....................161

Contract disputes...........................16
    pandemic 20

Court of Appeal Mediation Scheme
....183

Covid-19...v, 20
    arbitration...............................35
    breach of contract 153
    commercial   risks   created   by
   152
    court hearings 24
    FCA 38
    mediated settlement............106
    negotiations 115

Decision frames 158

Decision whether to settle or litigate
....155
    Cost-Benefit Analysis..........157
    Decision Matrix Analysis ... 157
    litigation forecast 155

Paired Comparison Analysis 157
T-Chart 157
uncertainties 155

Dispute strategy
commercial 137
legal 144

EU (Withdrawal Agreement) Act 166, 192

Expert determination 36
costs 95

Financial ombudsman 37

Finding the facts 40

Forecasting
advice on the merits 51
assumptions 56
best use of 67
bias 62
decision trees 59
limitations on outcome predictions 64
outcome prediction software 61
probability 54

Groupthink 160

In Place of Strife 107

Independent Mediators 107

International Dispute Resolution Centre 189

Lawyers
role of 151

Legal costs
barrister's charges 79
conditional fee agreement 81
costs management order 88
costs-shifting orders
Pre-Action Protocol 87
costs-shifting orders 86

damages-based agreements .. 84
exposure management
security for costs 94
exposure management: 91
funding your own costs 77
insurance
after-the-event 85
before-the-event 85
Legal Aid 77
non-parties 90
pre-trial 90
pro bono legal representation 77
recovery of fixed costs only .. 90
solicitor's bill of costs 78
third party funding 83
unreasonable refusal to mediate 89

Legal Ombudsman, The 77

Legally binding decision 24

Litigation
ADR procedure 173
appeals 182
Case Management Conference 173
Claim Form 165
costs assessment 182
Counterclaim 166
court proceedings 24
disclosure 172
disclosure pilot 167, 172
enforcement 182
expert evidence 176
Flexible Trials Scheme 184
Intellectual Property Enterprise Court 185
interim remedies
freezing order 170
interim injunction 169
interim payment 171
security for costs 171

INDEX

Multi-Track cases 171
outside the jurisdiction 166
Part 36 Offer 30
Particulars of Claim 166
Practice Direction – Pre-Action Conduct & Protocols 164
pre-litigation procedures 163
Shorter Trials Scheme 184
Skeleton Arguments 177
Statement of Case 169
Statements of Case 166
strike out 168
summary judgment 168
trial 177
without prejudice rule 185
witness statements 174

Lugano Convention 2007 166

McKenzie Friend 178

Mediation 30
advantages 132
conduct of 133

Negotiations
alternatives to a negotiated end 117
bargaining 128
conclusion of 131
conduct of 120
exploration 124
preparation 114

Non-payment
insolvency 31
refusal to pay 33

Objectives in a business dispute . 136

Online Dispute Resolution 107

Pandemic .... *See* Covid-19

Privilege
legal advice 28, 186
litigation 28, 186

Remedies
declaration 23
further questions 23
injunction 22
payment orders 21
Rights 11
causes of action 11
English civil law 11
EU laws 11
sources
contracts 12
property rights 13
statutory rights 15
torts 15
trusts 14

Settlement
Calderbank offers 104
commecial terms 99
confidentiality 100
definition 97
Dispute Boards 111
dispute resolution clauses .. 104
dispute resolution procedures 101
during legal action 102
Early Neutral Evaluation ... 109
Financial Dispute Resolution 111
international elements 101
legal requirements 98
mediation 106
Mediation-Arbitration (Med-Arb) 111
negotiation 105
Part 36 offers 104
payment terms 100
rights under the settlement agreement 102
terms of 97
uncertainty created by 103

Singapore Convention 101

Solicitors Regulatory Authority ... 78

Standard & Poors risk ratings..... 158

Tomlin Order 102, 103

Trial

    findings of fact 70

        documents 71

    judicial decision-making 70

    legal principles

        common law 72

        equity 72

    oral evidence........................... 71

Video-conferencing.........35, 107, 115

Witnesses

    bias 50

    credibility 71

    false memories........................ 45

    perception 43

Worst Alternative to a Negotiated Agreement (WATNA) 117

Praise for *Un*

C000128300

"When people know you are a Witch, 1
tion and to break curses and attacks, 1
tunate to see Katrina Rasbold work her .... and uncrossing magic
firsthand, and I am grateful to have her teachings, tips, and methods—
hard won from years of experience—in one place where we can benefit
from her wisdom. Let her guide you in helping yourself and helping others if you are called to do the work of uncrossing."

—Christopher Penczak, co-founder of the Temple of
Witchcraft and author of *The Witch's Shield*

"If you've been crossed, jinxed, or hexed, you need to clean up that mess!
Katrina lovingly guides you through all the means and methods from
various magical paths on removing negativity from yourself, your loved
ones, and your environment. I consider this book to be a 'must have' on
any magical bookshelf and am confident that it is one that you will turn
to again and again to change your bad luck to good."

—Madame Pamita, author of *The Book of Candle Magic*
and Madame *Pamita's Magical Tarot*

"Just as you wouldn't head out on a multi-day hike without a first-aid kit,
so, too, you wouldn't practice magic without having the tools to treat
a psychic attack. Life happens, and whether because you have enemies
or you're your own worst enemy, recovery from malicious magic is of
paramount importance. With Katrina Rasbold's experienced step-by-step
advice on how to heal from everything from curses and hexes to psychosomatic self-sabotage, *Uncrossing* is your indispensable magical first-aid
handbook for not if you fall victim to psychic attacks, but *when* you fall
victim to them."

—Tomás Prower, author of *Queer Magic*,
Morbid Magic, and *La Santisima Muerte*

"*Uncrossing* is an important work in today's uncertain times. Katrina Rasbold's clear, concise style is refreshingly to the point and ultimately practical. *Uncrossing* approaches energetic involvements from the receiving end

UNCROSSING

© Myk Aero

About the Author

Katrina Rasbold is the author of twenty-seven books on various aspects of the magical arts. She also pens the popular fictional series *The Seven Sisters of Avalon* as well as other fiction and nonfiction works.

Born in the hills of Kentucky and raised in folk magic, Katrina studied the magical arts all over the world before settling in her current home in the remote mountains of California. She lectured at Pantheacon in San Jose, Sacramento Pagan Pride, and PanGaia Festival in Fair Oaks, California, and currently offers online and in-person classes.

She and her husband, Eric, are co-creators of the CUSP spiritual path and are co-authors of the Bio-Universal Energy Series. Their first book, *Energy Magic*, spent several weeks on the Amazon best seller list in the category of Neopaganism upon its release in 2013.

Eric and Katrina own Crossroads Metaphysical Store in Shingle Springs, California, where they offer their handmade magical products and services such as spellcasting, healing, and cleansing. You can contact Katrina via www.crossroadsoccult.com.

Katrina and Eric have six adult children who are grown up and loose out there in the world.

KATRINA RASBOLD

UNCROSSING

**Identify, Cleanse, and Heal from
Hexes, Curses, and Psychic Attacks**

Llewellyn Publications
Woodbury, Minnesota

Uncrossing: Identify, Cleanse, and Heal from Hexes, Curses, and Psychic Attack © 2021 by Katrina Rasbold. All rights reserved. No part of this book may be used or reproduced in any manner whatsoever, including internet usage, without written permission from Llewellyn Publications, except in the case of brief quotations embodied in critical articles and reviews.

FIRST EDITION
First Printing, 2021

Book design by Samantha Peterson
Cover design by Shira Atakpu

Llewellyn Publications is a registered trademark of Llewellyn Worldwide Ltd.

Library of Congress Cataloging-in-Publication Data (Pending)
ISBN: 978-0-7387-6672-0

Llewellyn Worldwide Ltd. does not participate in, endorse, or have any authority or responsibility concerning private business transactions between our authors and the public.
  All mail addressed to the author is forwarded but the publisher cannot, unless specifically instructed by the author, give out an address or phone number.
  Any internet references contained in this work are current at publication time, but the publisher cannot guarantee that a specific location will continue to be maintained. Please refer to the publisher's website for links to authors' websites and other sources.

Llewellyn Publications
A Division of Llewellyn Worldwide Ltd.
2143 Wooddale Drive
Woodbury, MN 55125-2989
www.llewellyn.com

Printed in the United States of America

Other Books by Katrina Rasbold

Aster of Avalon

Crossing the Third Threshold

Crossroads of Conjure

CUSP: A New Way to Walk an Old Path

Days and Times of Power

Energy Magic

Get Your Book Published

Goddess in the Kitchen: The Magic and Making of Food

How to Be a Queen

How to Create a Magical Working Group

Iris of Avalon

Leaving Kentucky in the Broad Daylight

Lily of Avalon

Magical Ethics and Protection

Properties of Magical Energy

Reuniting the Two Selves

Rose of Avalon

Spiritual Childbirth

Tarot for Real People

The Art of Ritual Crafting

The Dance Card

The Daughters of Avalon

The Magic and Making of Candles and Soaps

The Sacred Art of Brujeria

Weather or Not

Weather Witchery

Where the Daffodils Grow

Forthcoming Books by Katrina Rasbold

Jasmine of Avalon

DEDICATION

I gratefully dedicate this book to everyone who ever cursed, hexed, or crossed me because without your malice, I would never have learned how to help others or to relate to what my clients feel when someone goes after them.

I also dedicate this book to my mentors who taught me—most times patiently and other times not—how to heal and track energy and, most of all, how to trust myself. Thank you for seeing something in me that I could not yet see myself and for calling me into a service that I had no idea I would ever pursue. You blessed me beyond what any of us could ever know with your faith in me and by sharing your wisdom and talents.

Many thanks to Eric Rasbold for all his hand-holding and tear-wiping as I struggled through writing this book during the COVID-19 global pandemic. Honey, I could not have done it without you.

CONTENTS

Disclaimer ✦ xi

Introduction ✦ 1

PART ONE: ABOUT PSYCHIC ATTACKS
Chapter One: Psychic Attack within Modern Culture ✦ 11

Chapter Two: When Life Feels Like an Attack ✦ 25

PART TWO: TYPES OF ATTACKS
Chapter Three: Incidental Attacks ✦ 39

Chapter Four: Deliberate Attacks ✦ 55

Chapter Five: Controlling Others through Magic ✦ 69

Chapter Six: Self-Crossing ✦ 83

PART THREE: IDENTIFYING AN ATTACK
Chapter Seven: Is This an Attack? ✦ 99

PART FOUR: MANAGING THE ATTACK
Chapter Eight: What Can I Do? ✦ 117

Chapter Nine: Preparing the Healing Area ✦ 133

Chapter Ten: The Initial Exam ✦ 145

Chapter Eleven: The Egg Cleansing ✦ 157

Chapter Twelve: Flying Solo ✦ 171

PART FIVE: HEALING AFTER PSYCHIC ATTACK

Chapter Thirteen: After the Healing ✦ 187

Chapter Fourteen: Protection and Retribution ✦ 197

Chapter Fifteen: Staying Clean ✦ 213

DISCLAIMER

The purpose of the information in this book is to supplement—not replace—professional medical and psychological care. If you have physical or mental health issues compromising your quality of life, please contact a health care professional immediately.

INTRODUCTION

There is a game that people play on the internet where you describe what you do for a living in the most literal yet absurd terms possible. In my case, I rub eggs on people to pull demons and curses out of them and I set things on fire to help others manifest their deepest desires. In short, I am a professional Witch for Hire.

My day job is casting spells on behalf of others, usually through candle magic, and cleaning out their energetic systems after they are exposed to psychic attack or other contamination. This is also my night job and my side hustle, because true Witchcraft lived as a profession takes nearly all of a person's time and energy. There are plenty of charlatans out there who will happily relieve a person of their money, light a candle, and walk away calling it good service, but real magic takes time. You sit with the client's energy, pray over their candles, brainstorm with them, counsel, reframe, and guide them to the best approach for a positive outcome. In addition to time and energy, it is an investment of emotion, education, experience, sweat, tears, and, above all, patience.

One of the most satisfying parts of my job is when I perform a spiritual cleansing on someone and free them from a negative influence that has troubled them for years. Seeing the visible results as the color returns to their cheeks and the light comes back into their eyes is truly rewarding. I am excited to share with you the techniques I have used over many years to assist others in releasing the negative energies that influence their vitality, their prosperity, their relationships, and their potential.

The best part of all of this is that anyone can do it. Sure, it is helpful if the person doing the cleansing has experience working with energy and a natural proclivity to any kind of psychic awareness. That is a bonus. I have, however, handed an egg to a novice wife and said, "Rub the egg on your husband like this." With no prior knowledge of energetic cleansing, she did a fine job and, to this day, she emails me photographs of the excellent work she does on her husband and children. Spiritual cleansing does not require expert or even experienced hands to produce the desired effect.

Considering that things like hexes, curses, and hitchhiking entities are a huge part of my everyday life, it is strange to consider that a few decades ago, I never imagined such things even existed. I spent a third of my magical life calling in quarters, honoring the Wheel of the Year, and casting an occasional spell to get my electric bill paid or to free up a parking place at the grocery store. I was a Witch and I loved magic, but I was completely oblivious to the fact that I was only skating the surface of the metaphysical world.

At the time of this writing, I have worked in the Pagan community for almost forty years, engaging various magical people on many levels. Back in the first decade or so of my practice when I was a baby Witch, I believed that people rarely cursed or hexed one another.[1] If anything, I thought they might inadvertently throw negativity in someone's direction by wishing them ill with the energy of normal human thoughts and emotions. I even taught my magical students that as responsible practitioners, they must be mindful of their thoughts and intentions because they could work magic with the blink of an eye. And yet, I had no clue.

Most of my mindset at that time came from my mistaken idea that all Witches embraced the Wiccan concepts of "As it harms none, do what you will," threefold law, and karmic return. My magical practice began in the United Kingdom and when I returned to the United States, I followed the Wiccan path, which originated in England. Therefore, my perspective on the issue of cursing or crossing at that time derived from the European approach, which represents a geographically and culturally isolated view of Witchcraft. As my study of Witchcraft deepened beyond the Neopagan and Wiccan presentation of the Craft, the depths of my naivety became clear, as did the cultural singularity of my experience with magic.

The active persecution of any activities related to Witchcraft, including astrology and divination, drove the practice underground throughout Europe until it was revived in the 1940s in the sanitized form of Wicca. Aggressive marketing of Wiccan books and classes

---

1. I take the approach in this writing that when someone suffers a deliberate attack, the primary aggressors will likely be Witches and other magical practitioners. I use the terms *Pagan* and *Witch* loosely to identify magical practitioners. This is for convenience's sake, and no inappropriate labeling is intended to those who identify otherwise. I also use the words *hex* and *curse* interchangeably throughout the book although, as you will see in chapter 3, there are subtle differences between the two. Again, this is for the sake of word flow, and any distinguishing differences are inconsequential to the individual word usage.

throughout the 1970s and 1980s solidified the public impression of Witchcraft as a benevolent, even passive, nature-based practice where Witches lived in harmony with all, governed by the dictate that we may do whatever we wish so long as we harm none.

At its heart, the Wiccan concept of harming none extends beyond physical harm and includes harm on all levels of existence, including mental, emotional, spiritual, sexual, and social. It is an ambitious undertaking to live one's life in such a way that we never cause harm to anyone on any of those levels, and some feel it sets unrealistic and unreachable goals for those who follow the Wiccan path. To always hold in your mind the idea that you must never harm anyone is admirable and if everyone followed those premises, our world would be a more peaceful place. The dark side of this idealism is that when others in our world do not embrace those same philosophies, it is easy to fall victim to the slings and arrows of their responses to normal human conflict.

As Wiccan premises began to overtake the historical impression of Witchcraft in the minds and hearts of the public, the fear of and belief in psychic attack—although prevalent throughout many centuries of prior history—began to diminish. If Witches truly had no intention or willingness to harm, why should anyone imagine they would be attacked? Many, like myself, lived in complacency and relative unawareness, presuming Wiccan theologies and practices onto all Witches without considering that there are Witches out there who do not embrace Wiccan beliefs. I certainly never considered concepts such as incidental psychic attacks or disincarnate entities that can compromise the energetic system.

The average Pagan person talks about curses and hexes in hushed tones, wondering if this person is "casting" against them or if that person "sent something" to them. They will often brush off the notion of a deliberate attack and leave it as the last possible thought for why their life has gone sideways. Ideas of cursing or hexing have the same levity in most conversations as stories told around a campfire with a flashlight shoved under the narrator's chin. When a client comes to me with the idea that someone may have attacked them, they suggest it almost shamefully and offer qualifiers before they even suggest the idea, saying things like "I know this sounds silly, but ..." and "It isn't likely, but what if ...?"

The reality that I now work in every day is that people attack one another on a spiritual and energetic level *all the time*. People pick up entities walking through a store the same way one picks up a cold or flu virus *all the time*. Generational curses exist and incidental crossings happen *all the time*. If the victim does not seek professional help or take measures to remove these contaminations from their energetic field, their life can be affected in minor to profound ways. Attacks such as these can destroy your prosperity and good fortune, sap away your vitality and energy, and create tension and turmoil in your interpersonal relationships.

Often, these maladies intensify so gradually that the victim does not realize anything is wrong with them energetically. For most people, the effects of a curse, hex, or crossing—whether deliberate or incidental—do not slam into them like a freight train. That occasionally happens, but more often, it is a gradual deterioration of their quality of life that accumulates over time. The victim becomes like the frog in a pot of cold water on the stove: as the burner heats, the water warms in such tiny increments that the frog is boiled before he knows it. A curse or entity lives inside the victim like an energetic parasite, draining away life's joy with the host never suspecting or acknowledging that it is there.

In addition to intentional psychic attacks and incidental entity infiltrations, people also suffer from past and current traumas, hooks to unhealthy relationships, and destructive habits that contaminate their spirits and create obstacles to their success. In these cases, it is even possible to curse yourself!

As society shifts, a rapidly growing number of people seek to control the thoughts, emotions, and behaviors of others. I know because my email inbox is full of requests for services like "Make him think about me all the time," "Get her to let me explain why we should get back together," "Make my boss give me a raise," and "Force my partner to stop cheating on me."

When a person's desired outcome hinges on the behavior and choices of someone else, the human impulse is to pressure that person to do what you want them to do. When you fail to elicit the responses you want from those people through mundane means, you might turn to energy work to force your will onto the one that you feel controls your destiny. Most who attempt this do not consider what they are doing to be a deliberate psychic attack, and yet it is.

I consider deliberate psychic attack to be a willful energetic assault upon another person, or an attempt to forcefully influence the thoughts, emotions, or actions of someone through the manipulation of energetic forces.

To expound on that definition, if someone …

+ Works magic with the intention of harming or inconveniencing another person

+ Works magic to attempt to force another person to do what they do not want to do

+ Works magic to attempt to force another person to *not* do what they want to do

✦ Works magic to attempt to force someone to feel something they do not organically feel

✦ Works magic to attempt to prevent someone from feeling what they organically feel

… then it constitutes a deliberate psychic attack, no matter how passionately the person believes in the justification of their actions.

It is quite telling that when my husband and I offered a class called "A Witch Scorned: Hexing, Cursing, and Crossing," the room was filled. A month later, we offered a class on "Uncrossing: Removing Psychic Attack" and the room was again filled—with entirely different people! People are fascinated by the idea of magically controlling or influencing others, and their ears perk up if you mention that someone else might be the cause of their misfortunes and maladies. A potential dodge of accountability for the problems in one's life can be quite seductive.

While it may seem daunting to know how vulnerable we are to potential psychic attack, the good news is that there are curative and preventative steps that can be taken to resolve the effects of both deliberate and incidental attacks and to help get the victim back on track to leading their best life.

The even better news is that those situations are managed using the same techniques. Each experience with psychic attack is unique, but there are some trends that can be anticipated and tracked, which helps with the management of these types of cases. Following the techniques described in this book will resolve almost any energetic crisis.

Better than that, if you use the information and techniques contained in this book with the intention of healing someone from a psychic attack and, by chance, they were not attacked, only good can come of it. You cannot harm a person with a spiritual cleansing or protective work, even if the work is done by a novice or amateur. This allows you the freedom to err on the side of caution and incur no penalty.

If you, in fact, move forward with an open mind, a willing spirit, and a positive outlook, you can assist your friends and loved ones with their challenges and make the world a better place, one cleansing at a time.

PART ONE

❖

ABOUT PSYCHIC ATTACKS

CHAPTER ONE

PSYCHIC ATTACK WITHIN MODERN CULTURE

Most of written human history contains ongoing mention of Witches, and I would hazard a guess that there have been Witches for as long as there have been people. I feel comfortable in furthering that guess by saying that for as long as there have been Witches, there have been Witches who have no compunction about cursing and will do so without hesitation. To pretend or believe that they are not there in no way reduces the efficacy of their work.

Throughout history, various cultures treated their Witches in different ways, ranging from respect to fear. Most places where Catholic churches hold dominion have a strange dissonance in their opinion of Witches. On one hand, their power is minimized and ridiculed, yet they are feared and denigrated as minions of Satan who can enact great harm. Even now, when people come to see me to address their problems, they do so as if on a covert mission, making certain that I practice the utmost of confidentiality (I do) and that no one will ever know they were there (they won't).

Sometimes I feel like I am my clients' best-kept secret. I own and work out of a busy metaphysical store and find it interesting that the people who come in to purchase the products we make are usually a whole different crew than the people who come to me for healing or spell work. This might be because Witches do their own work for the most part; they purchase products to support their magical intentions. Typically, those who come to me for spell work and spiritual cleansings are not people who would ever identify as a Witch. In fact, they usually identify as Christians or lightworkers.

The anonymity that people want when they seek my assistance is as much about who I am as it is about what they intend to do. They do not want anyone to know they sought out the services of a Witch, but they also do not want anyone to know about the sorts of things they would like done. In my experience, they either want to use magic to harm or influence other people or to have a suspected attack managed. In either of those cases, they likely do not wish to alert the presses, so confidentiality is key.

The inherent desire of people to harm and control one another for their own gain is an unfortunate but easily observable human trait. Since people avail themselves of every resource accessible to them, especially those in which no tangible evidence of their personal culpability can be shown, psychic attack is a handy way to harm someone with no provable weapon in sight. This makes it a popular tactic, whether a person launches the attack themselves or has someone do it on their behalf.

The Impact of Wicca on Witchcraft

What we know about Witches throughout history comes as much through literature as it does through historical documentation. If you believe historical accounts and the tracking of human behavior expressed through literature, it is safe to say that for most of history, Witches were feared for their ability to interact with energetic forces (divine or profane, depending on who you were talking to) to achieve a desired outcome. This is a reasonable fear if you consider the notion that if a Witch could harm, a Witch could heal. If they had the power to kill, they had the power to also cure. These abilities and the societal interpretation of them formed the overall perspective about Witches.

Within the past century, the image of Witchcraft in the public eye shifted dramatically due to the aggressive, widespread arrival of Wicca. Wicca single-handedly transformed a feared and eccentric practice into a socially accepted, sanitized, and viable spiritual path. Suddenly, housewives, lawyers, doctors, and revered professionals identified as Pagans or Witches under the far-reaching umbrella of the Wiccan Rede: "An' it harm none, do what ye will."

My impression after years of working with Wicca is that it is a vibrant spiritual path that celebrates the forces of nature and honors the God and Goddess as divine male and female balancing forces. Its practice is rewarding and lovely. There is no denying, however, that Wicca effectively co-opted Witchcraft through its marketing practices and, in the public eye, tied an ancient and heavily nuanced practice to the relatively new tenets of Wicca. The reality was and is that while most Wiccans correctly identify as Witches, far more Witches *do not* identify as Wiccans or follow Wiccan theologies and philosophies. This means that we have a growing number of people out there who are dedicated to the study of energy movement and manipulation who do not acknowledge or adhere to the "harm none" dictate.

Throughout most of the 1970s and 1980s, books that were specifically Wiccan in nature bore titles identifying them not as Wicca, but as Witchcraft. *The Complete Book of Witchcraft* by Raymond

Buckland, *The Truth About Witchcraft Today* by Scott Cunningham, *Witchcraft Today* by Gerald Gardner, and *What Witches Do* and *Eight Sabbats for Witches* by Stewart Farrar are all famous books about Wicca, but through their titles they implied that they spoke for all of Witchcraft. The content inside these books also supports the idea that Wicca and Witchcraft are synonymous, backing up the misleading titles and furthering the confusion between the two practices.

The aggressive campaign to legitimize Wicca and Witchcraft as nonthreatening with a unified modus operandi of harming none swayed many non-Pagans to believe that all Witches subscribed to the same code of ethics. Interestingly, it also convinced most Pagans of the same myth, including myself. The truth is that there are and always have been plenty of Witches out there who will hex you to the Summerlands and back and not think twice about it.

If you push your thumb and forefinger tightly together, you would not create a small enough margin to represent the presence of Wicca in the total spectrum of Witchcraft throughout human existence. Relative to most Witchcraft practice, Wicca just got here! Plenty of hexes and curses have gone on before—and since—Wicca arrived on the metaphysical scene.

Other Popular Theological Concepts

If the preponderance of Witches throughout history do not follow the rules of "harm none" or embrace concepts such as the Laws of Attraction, the threefold law, or even the power of karma, do any of those theories even belong in a conversation about psychic attack? I believe they do, to some degree.

Even though historical Witches likely did not have knowledge of ideas such as these, when we incorporate new concepts into our collective conversation about energy work, their pertinence to the existing infrastructure automatically comes into question.

The Law of Attraction, the belief that the energy we put out into the world affects us and our environment, does seem to hold true. From my own observable and anecdotal perspective, when you surround yourself with positive, uplifting, motivated, high-vibing people, your fortunes and outcomes tend to change for the better. When you spend time with people who drain you, depress you, and encourage your negative behaviors, your fortunes and outcomes diminish. I see this at work every day through the people who come into my shop. Based on what I have witnessed throughout decades of work, the energy you put out attracts your tribe to you. Likewise, your willingness to take responsibility for your environment and the influences you allow into it positively affects the opportunities that come to you and the future you can create for yourself.

Despite the mention of threefold law throughout many cultures, I have not seen adequate evidence to convince me that the arbitrary number of three applies to the tripling of return on what you put out into the world. If you hit someone on the head, I do not believe that, as a result, you will get hit on the head three times or hit three times as hard. By power of suggestion, it is possible that someone's belief that this is the case could manifest that experience, but I have seen nothing that convinces me that the natural world creates that outcome. I do, however, embrace a different theory involving the idea of a threefold law: What you do affects the mind, the body, and the spirit as a threefold impact. I do not accept that the threefold premise was ever intended as a quantifier, but instead identifies the ways that you absorb and process the energy and impact of what you say and do. Your words and deeds define you and, in this case, I am confident that they shape who you are. To push this idea even further, every act and action on your part changes you in some way. The goal, of course, is that you change for the better. In my practice, threefold law is neither punitive nor is it quantitative. It is simply cause, effect, and creation.

There are so many layered ideas and theories about karma that those are best left for you to consider on a personal level. Think of all the factors that come into play in a conversation about karma: Do you process your karma all in one lifetime? Do you experience abundance or misfortune in one life because you earned it in a previous life? Can you take on the karmic debt of someone else? Is there a universal concept of good or bad, justified or unjustified, that karma follows? How does karma change between two people who have different ideas of right and wrong? Is a mentally impaired person subject to the same karmic standards as a mentally sound person? The overall karmic idea is "What goes around, comes around," and this is subject to the personal concepts of good and evil, the interpretations of which vary profoundly. Even within the same spiritual path, what one person considers good or evil is different than the impressions of another. The concept of karmic return requires deeper consideration of afterlife concepts and butterfly wing effects, and with all those moving parts, it is well outside of the scope of this book.

The culture in which someone is raised and the one that they ultimately embrace as an adult greatly influence how a person engages with the concept of psychic attack. Some cultures are more accepting of the practice; others actively renounce it. My own approach to the management of a potential psychic attack is influenced, to a degree, by the client's predominant culture.

Witchcraft and Psychic Attack

In most of today's society, there is little stigma to practicing Witch-craft in any of its many forms. Someone who self-identifies as a Witch may suffer an askance glance, a handful of derisive quips, or rolled eyes, but for the most part, in the civilized world, people do not experience persecutions for their practice to the degree that was once common.

This relative freedom allowed for the prolific propagation of various forms of magical practice and resulted in more people learning how to use their personal energy to manifest desired life changes. The outcome is that we have more people using magic throughout the world than we have had in many generations because there is less fear of reprisal. My impression is that this also raised the number of psychic attacks flying from person to person, both deliberate and incidental.

Witch Wars

Another form of psychic attack are Witch wars, which, I assure you, are a real thing. Although they were especially prevalent in the 1980s and 1990s before Paganism, Wicca, and Witchcraft were as public and accepted as they are now, there are still occasional rounds of Witch wars. Witch wars are when two Witches or two covens have a skirmish and begin attacking one another magically.

During those years, covens were more territorial than they are now, with a handful holding to the Wiccan covenstead principles of specific covens having a controlling area of three miles in all directions from the primary coven location in a sort of Wiccan-gang-land-turf arrangement. The competition for new seekers could be fierce, and poaching newcomers from another coven was grounds for retribution. Often, that retribution happened on a magical level.

Lately, there are enough seekers for everyone, so rather than squabbling over Craft newcomers, Witch wars usually flare up over personal slights, real or imagined. Someone could say something untoward about another group or a public Pagan. A friendship or coupling may end badly, requiring friends and associates to take sides. More often, a business arrangement goes sideways and someone feels taken advantage of or misused, so angry spells start flying. Pagans tend to forego written agreements and, as a result, misunderstandings often arise. As soon as the armies divide, trouble usually follows.

This behavior is no different than non-Pagan grudges and arguments except that it involves people who are trained in the practice of using energy to create an effect. This type of magical attack comes with social meddling as well, such as rumormongering and attempts to coerce those not involved with the conflict to take sides.

The next thing that tends to happen is a primary altercation that divides the parties involved firmly into one camp or the other. Amid dramatic allegations and righteous indignation, someone within one of the camps will eventually take a magical shot at a person in the other camp. There may even be a group working where an entire coven sends negative energy to the other side or to specific people involved in the conflict.

Once the first shot is fired, it is game on. The other side arches its eyebrows and says, "Oh really? It's like *that*, is it?" and hurls back their own magical fireball. This is followed by a flourish of "Oh no they *didn't*," and a retaliatory attack ensues. Does this remind you a bit of the 1881 Gunfight at O.K. Corral? Or a tennis match at Wimbledon? Witch wars can literally go on for *years*, ending only when someone accidentally brokers peace or when one side tires of the game and finds a new focus for their attention.

Because Witch wars are rarely limited to two people, there are ample opportunities for whipping an opposing side into a magical frenzy, especially if the participants are naturally predisposed to drama and paranoia. In the Pagan community, I regret to say that there exists a high level of jealousy, pettiness, and competitiveness. This is likely because humans are jealous, petty, and competitive in their less-evolved forms, and Paganism embraces people of all kinds and all levels of evolution. Paganism does not demand the improvement or actualization of anyone who identifies as Pagan and accepts everyone as they are, where they are. In my opinion, this is both a strength and a weakness of the path.

When offense occurs, even if it is valid and difficult to overlook, it is always the better part of valor to reject the energy and turn your attention to managing your own life. Allow the other party to look petty and vindictive while you take the high road. Ground the energy outside of your wall of protection or simply return it without adding to the discord. This eventually defuses the potential war.

It is not easy, especially when others attempt to fan the flames of your insecurities and frustrations. It is, however, the best way to maintain your own dignity, both publicly and privately, and to avoid missteps. If you ever have the misfortune of being the target of a Witch war or are caught in the crossfire, be prepared for everyone with information about the "other side" to feel compelled to share with you what they know. This makes it easy to get sucked into the drama. When you know someone is actively working to disparage you, word of their downfalls or missteps may be welcome; when you refuse to participate, you always create a better outcome.

There is only ever a Witch war or battle of any kind if both sides engage. When one side refuses to participate, it becomes a tantrum—often a very public one—on the part of the aggressor who is attempting to coerce a fight, which only serves to make them look infantile. The truth always comes out if you just trust the process.

Everyday Psychic Attack

If we only had to think about Witches and other energy workers as the sole sources of potential psychic attack, this book would be a different conversation than what it is. The reality is that one does not have to have any experience in magical work to energetically attack someone. The effect of their attack can be just as devastating as that of a trained practitioner. The desire to attack another person is unnecessary to causing an inadvertent or incidental attack.

Even for those who do not self-identify as magically inclined, words and emotions still influence the environment. I am sure all of you know people who are not energy workers who can suck all the air out of a room when they are unhappy. Have you ever walked into a room where two non-practitioners are arguing and felt the uncomfortable energy generated by the disagreement, even if not a word was said? Sure, this means that you are empathically sensitive to the energy and can feel it, but you did not create that energy—they did. As such, when someone deliberately hurls angry words at another person, the energy goes straight to its target and *energizes*. It creates outcomes big and small, whether the sender intended for it to do so or not.

You might think that normal expressions of frustration are meaningless, but when a huge ball of anger comes flying in your direction, you feel its impact. This type of energetic influence born from the intense emotions of another person and directed at a victim is a psychic attack, and it is quite prevalent in our modern life. The victim does not even have to be aware that the energy hit them to suffer its effects, and yet the outcome can be the same as if a person deliberately hexed them.

Road Rage

The most common place where a person experiences this kind of energetic impact is on the freeway. Road rage sends a giant burst of negative energy toward a total stranger for driving in a way that someone else does not like. The on-ramp of a freeway is a hotbed of crossings that are usually incidental. If someone tries to merge onto the freeway in heavy traffic, they get frustrated with other drivers who cannot (or will not) let them enter the flow of vehicles: "Let me in!"

Drivers who are already on the freeway get frustrated with those trying to merge: "Wait your turn!" Despite legal dictates for who has the right of way, it creates a no-win situation for all involved and results in strong negative energy hurled in both directions.

Road rage itself is a situation where normally rational and calm people feel justified to express their outrage to others. It is little wonder people come out of a traffic jam feeling anxious and tense. They were likely just crossed by multiple people, especially if they weren't a perfect driver!

Politics and Social Media

The United States is an evolving hotbed of divisive and destructive political conflict. Social media creates a mask of relative anonymity, giving people the freedom to express their most hateful and aggressive rampages, some of which they might be hesitant to reveal if a person sat in front of them face-to-face instead of behind a monitor and keyboard. These two factors combined create a hotbed of negative energy assailing people on a daily basis.

Watching the news for even five minutes results is an overload of horrible, distressing information with little that is positive to offset it. Evolutionarily, humans are people of the village mentality; for many generations, we were limited to the news of what happened in and around our own village. Before the world grew smaller with cars, phones, the internet, and air travel, people rarely heard news from more than a hundred miles around them. News of faraway tsunamis, wars, and earthquakes did not reach or affect daily life. Now, people process traumatic reports of natural disasters and atrocities committed upon other humans on a regular basis. The human sense of fear cannot help but be stimulated by this onslaught of information about danger to fellow humans.

Social media and televised news are forms of trauma that the mind, body, and spirit instinctively respond to. The level of toxicity encountered daily is unprecedented; it is little surprise that there is a preponderance of depressed, anxious, and emotionally volatile people in society. Add to that the economic struggles that besiege people every day and the pall of hopelessness and anxiety that permeates everyone until it becomes palpable. People react on the spirit level to such a degree of ongoing anxiety and fear in our collective species, and this itself is a form of psychic attack that grows from a situation rather than from an individual.

When people feel helpless, they begin to turn on one another. Dismay and fear cause people to begin looking for reasons outside of themselves for why they are failing and why they feel no hope for recovery. In times of struggle, especially on a global level, it is difficult to find recourse for life improvement, and the mind may naturally drift toward the idea of being cursed—or, in fact, of cursing someone else.

At least once a week, I receive a request from someone asking me to bind or curse the president of the United States. Recently, a client asked me to bind the governor of New York. A few months ago, a man asked me to destroy everyone in the United States who was of a specific ethnicity he did not appreciate.

Part of my practice involves separating out my own political and sociological views and meeting my client where they are. It is imperative that I suspend judgment and act as the client's advocate, even if they are only a prospective client. I do not feel it is my place to label the client as "right" or "wrong," but to advise them on the best use of energy in regard to their goals and whether or not I am the best person to help them achieve their desired outcome.

The energetic component in the client-healer interaction requires that a neutral position remains present in my words, my body language, and even my thoughts. I cannot for one moment cause the client to suspect that I am dismissive of them or that I feel they are inappropriate in requesting such a thing of me. What I do instead is discuss the effective use of energy with the client and suggest that we work toward a peaceful resolution that brings about the best outcome for those concerned, then leave the particulars up to the Universe. I encourage them to trust the process and to let me help them find the most effective use of the energy we invest.

In the case of the governor of New York, for instance, I could guide the client toward a peaceful, healthy resolution of the conflict rather than attacking the person. This perspective also lets me remind the client that political issues have multiple moving parts and that targeting just one component limits influence. By working toward a positive outcome, we send our energy to any who might present obstacles to our goals rather than to just one person.

People are frustrated, scared, and angry, encouraged into a conflagration of emotions by various media outlets. This anxious energy force has a power that is impressive and destructive. When someone comes to me for help, they are not looking for a teaching moment or for criticism. They want results. When I choose to take on a client, it is my job to guide them into actions that potentially create positive outcomes with as few casualties as possible. Most people—even those with the most hateful, bigoted, uninformed perspectives—believe that their perspective is the correct one, so opening the work up to "the greatest and highest good" allows them to believe, by default, that the greatest and highest good will uphold their own desires.

CHAPTER TWO

WHEN LIFE FEELS LIKE AN ATTACK

When so many ever-shifting ethical and moral boundaries influence and inform society's concepts of right and wrong, how do we determine energetic high ground in a conversation about psychic attack? Where is the boundary between defensive and offensive spell work, and when is each one a reasonable response? The answer is that you should not interact with anyone magically in a way that you would not interact with them mundanely, and that is subject to your own integrity and personality.

My acceptance of a client's case hinges on one pivotal point: Is their desire justified, or is it unjustified? This is, of course, a case-by-case decision and is based on *my* assessment, not theirs. There is a waiting list for my services, and I am selective about where my energy goes. I conduct an extensive intake interview to give a prospective client the opportunity to convince me that whatever they want done *needs* to happen.

This process is a lot like an attorney interviewing a potential client. I ask myself: Does the client have a case? If they do, am I the right person to help them "win" it? What are the risks and what are the benefits? Is there a different way to mitigate the situation? Is the client accurately and truthfully representing the situation, to the best of their knowledge? Do they have the stamina and resources to see this through? Are they genuinely invested in moving forward? All these considerations come into play.

If I cannot find the justification for a client's work, I refer them to someone else or I simply let them know that I am not the person to help them. If the work they want done is not something I can justify in my heart and spirit, the hesitancy I feel will contaminate and hinder the work. If I cannot give a client a body of work done to the best of my ability without compromising my own integrity, then I will not take the job. My goal is always to give the client realistic expectations and let them know our best strategy for managing their case and whether or not I can be an asset to them.

This is never more so than in the case of responding to a psychic attack. The question is not about my ability to clean their energetic field and heal the traumas they sustained, but more about what they want to do next. Chapter 13 discusses retribution after a psychic attack. Sometimes it is warranted; other times, it is best to let the energy ground and get on with one's life. Clients do not always agree with this advice, unfortunately.

Equally, it is challenging when I inform a client that I find no sign of psychic attack and they jump to the conclusion that this is a failing on my part rather than considering that perhaps they were not attacked at all and possibly caused their own symptoms. I have learned never to argue with a client, but that does not mean I will pretend something is there when it clearly is not.

Sensitivity to a client, especially one who is under the duress of a perceived attack, is vital, so I do try to choose my words carefully. Words can be one of the most valuable tools at our disposal, but when emotions take over, ousting out rational thought, they can also be a formidable weapon.

Words Have Power

I believe most people accept the idea that words are powerful tools or weapons. A person trained in magical practice can generate and channel even greater power with their words than the average person. When such a person allows their emotions to overtake their behavior and influence the words they speak or think, the power of those emotions directs a strong energy force.

For this reason, it is essential that people who undertake a serious study of magic engage in determined mindfulness about the language they use and the energy they throw around. A person's words, thoughts, and emotions can create unintended outcomes that could harm someone else if they use them haphazardly. This opens the avenue not only for the increase in deliberate psychic attack previously mentioned, but also for incidental attacks.

In magic, your words and thoughts are imbued with power. Frankly, you cannot have it both ways: your words are powerful or they are not. You do not get to pick and choose when your words count. I see so many strong practitioners who speak carelessly when they are not involved in active, intentional magical work, believing that if they are not practicing magic or focusing their attention at the time, it does not matter.

To represent oneself as a Witch, a Wise One, a practitioner of the Craft, a Mage, or any other sort of energy worker implies that you use your thoughts, words, and actions to weave the fabric of magic into the world around you. You use energy to create form and experience. You manifest change, regardless of whether your words and actions unfold inside a sacred, cast circle or in the bustle of the mundane world. You have the strong capacity to shift outcomes whether you intend to do so or not. You have trained your energies to follow the flow of your words and actions and you have asked your gods and divine sources to listen to you.

Misfortune Is Not Always an Attack

With so many kinds of challenging and destructive energies flying around, it can be difficult to distinguish simple misfortune and course-correcting life events from psychic attack. As previously stated, treating general misfortune or malaise as a psychic attack harms no one, least of all the victim. In fact, a person who suffers a true psychic attack receives the same energetic treatment as someone who has symptoms that resemble a psychic attack when none occurred. For this reason, you do not have to know if an attack occurred, what kind of attack it was, or even who sent it. The techniques will help regardless.

If a person is under psychic attack and someone close to them follows the instructions in this book to heal them, you have an excellent outcome. If a person is *not* under psychic attack and someone close to them follows the instructions in this book to help them, they will relieve tension, clear their inner vision, and create balance in their energetic system, which is also an excellent outcome. There is no treatment outlined in this book that is harmful to anyone. These are curative techniques that can only heal, not hurt.

In the magical community (and life in general) there are always people who thrive on being the perennial victim. They are the ones who always seem to have a persecutor of the week who is doing them wrong while they revel in stories of ongoing drama and intrigue. Within that same klatch of people, you can usually find the eternally fearful, those who believe that no matter where they turn or what they do, misfortune will befall them. These group arche-types draw a never-ending stream of abusive, dramatic, unfortunate experiences to them and attract others who, like themselves, enjoy participating in the excitement of the game play of victims, martyrs, and abusers.

Not everyone who struggles is in that cycle. There are also those people whose lives are going fine and then suddenly fly off the rails. A health crisis might lead to an employment crisis which might lead to losing a home or other form of stability. Partners grow apart, which leads to emotional distancing, which leads to disenchantment, which leads to separation, which leads to loneliness, and so on. There are any number of placating clichés that assure us that "into each life, some rain must fall," or "the wheel of fortune turns up, then down, then up again." The question I must consider is whether the negative run of luck a person is having is simply the turn of the wheel and a normal life experience … or the result of an attack.

On the other hand, some clients know precisely when an attack occurs. I clearly remember the following phone conversation with a client:

"This is Katrina, may I help you?"

"Yeah … Do you, like, take demons out of people?"

"Sure, how many do you have?"

"Um … Something like three and a half?"

"You have half a demon?"

"Um … Yeah, I opened a portal and three demons came out, and then when I closed the portal real quick, a fourth one got trapped coming through and is sort of dangling."

"..."

"...So I was wondering if you could get them out for me?"

"When you opened the portal, what had you planned on doing with the demons?"

"Um...I was going to send them after this girl? We had a fight, but then I felt really bad and decided to take them into myself instead of sending them to her. Then I closed the portal and the one got stuck."

"...Sure, come on in."

Sure enough, he had three and a half demons in him and half a demon that I tracked back to his house, hanging out of a half-open portal in his bedroom.

You know, just a day in the life...

Life Happens

Wise people tell us that it is not what happens to you, but how you respond that defines your character. The challenges you face may be aggressive redirections from the Universe to force you to move to a different place, to connect with different people who are essential to your life path, or to have specifically prescribed experiences that bring you closer to your manifest destiny.

The Universe is efficient, but it is not always kind or what people would perceive as fair. When the Powers That Be want you to be with another partner, to move to a different town, or to focus your attention elsewhere, the series of events that leads you there can be sudden and devastating. Often, this kind of Universal repositioning happens after you receive (and promptly ignore) ample coaching signals indicating that you should make the changes yourself.

When Universal repositioning occurs, you are not usually under psychic attack, but it can certainly feel as though you are. It might seem like the gods have turned against you and your security is crumbling around you. People who are eternal victims will find someone else to blame for their misfortune. The fearful ones will interpret their misfortune as validation that the world is a dangerous place. The smart ones look for opportunity in the rubble of their lives and are amply rewarded.

Life happens. No matter how wealthy or lucky you are, you are given no guarantee that you will go through life without hardship. People get injured or sick. Loved ones die. Pets do not live as long as their owners wish they did. Houses burn down. Jobs that were completely stable and assured go away. It happens.

I used to tell my students, "Everything happens for a reason, but those reasons are not always especially interesting." As you will learn in chapter 7, a series of misfortunes within a short time might identify a psychic attack, but sometimes it is just your turn to manage the usual struggles of life. Sometimes you ignored the gentle nudgings of the Universe and forced the Universe to take more drastic action.

Who, Me?

Occasionally, your own spell work and your innocent attempts to manifest a specific outcome result in the destruction of one lifestyle to create another. In 1996, I did an intense ritual to manifest joy for myself because in a moment of clarity, I realized that true joy was something I had never felt in my entire life. Within a month of doing the work, my husband of eighteen years unexpectedly announced he was leaving me and our children to be with another woman. Out of the blue, I was a single mother with minimal means. This did not feel like joy to me, and the anger I felt toward my Goddess was unparalleled. Why would she do such a thing to me? To mock me? To punish me for asking for joy? Was this punishment for my own arrogance? *Was I ... under psychic attack?*

It was not until more than a year later that I realized I could never have found true joy while married to the person I was with, regardless of how much I loved him or how disenfranchised I would be by the divorce. My life fell apart, but I was not cursed, crossed, or hexed. I was instead experiencing the outcome of the spell work I did to improve my life! It was Universal repositioning based on my own magic. Had I never done that spell work, there is no telling how long I would have gone on married to someone I loved who had no appreciation for who or what I was and who actively worked to keep me submissive to him.

Later that year, I met Eric Rasbold, the man who would become my friend, my next (and, I presume, last) husband, my magical working partner, my business partner, and the love of my life. Because my life fell apart, I was free to follow my fated path and become the person I was meant to be. The destruction of that life made way for the creation of a happier, more empowered one. Had I stayed with my first husband, I would have forever been a subjugated, fearful, stifled, closet Witch who fought constantly against the uprising of her own power.

The energies that you engage—whether you consider them to be divine forces, Universal flow, or simply your own manifest destiny—seem to have no understanding of or interest in the man-made concepts of money and time. Many people approach spell work as an ATM for life change, expecting a constant outflow of blessings without expense or inconvenience on their part. Rarely does it work out that way.

Growth is not normally convenient or painless. When you seek to create a new life for yourself and to better your situation, you often are blind to the ways that you have willingly entrenched yourself in the very circumstances you wish to be extricated from. "I want a better job" might mean you lose your current job and go through months of retraining to get the job you want. In my case, "I want to feel joy" resulted in the removal of a person I loved who stood in the way of my own actualization and ability to manifest joy.

Before I performed that ritual, were there clues that my first marriage was unhealthy and stifled my growth as a person? Every day. Would I have admitted that, even to myself? Never. To me, those moments were part of the overarching idea that "no marriage is perfect" and "into each life, some rain must fall." I was afraid to make the changes I needed to make. I convinced myself that it did not matter. I did not want to sacrifice or be inconvenienced to have my joy. Eventually, the Universe managed the situation in a way I would never have chosen for myself.

The Universe is efficient, but not always kind.

The destruction of my life did not come from an outside psychic attack, although I could have sworn at the time it was so. It came from me.

Misfortune as a Motivator

In crisis, you must step back to see the bigger picture. Where is this crisis taking you? How open can you be to where this experience could lead you? When you crumble into victimization, you lose all pretense of power and everything feels like a personal attack. Sometimes, however, life just happens. Often, it happens to motivate you to create something better.

When my husband Eric left the military in 2000, he finagled his way into a fantastic job with a well-known telecom company. As a military-trained telecom engineer in California, we knew he was well-positioned to get a good job, but *wow*—this was more money than we ever imagined he would make. We moved out of base housing and into a house that was commensurate with his pay. He loved his job and was good at it. For the first time in our marriage, we had more than enough money to meet our needs.

That lasted for around six months. Then the bottom dropped out of the dot-com industry in the Silicon Valley of California, which eliminated numerous clients from the telecom industry. Eric's company declared bankruptcy and, without notice, our family's primary wage earner was out of a job. We went from Easy Street to food stamps and eviction notices in nothing flat. We still had four of our six kids at home, and we were completely unprepared to deal with the panic that we felt, having been in the relative safety net of the military for our entire marriage. Neither of us slept. We cried, we prayed, we lit candles. We sniped at each other. *Why us? Did we not deserve a break?*

This began a recurring cycle for us. He would get a great job, inquire as to the stability and solvency of the company, receive glowing assurances, and within a few months, another layoff notice arrived. We would barely get caught up on past-due bills after robbing Peter to pay Paul before the next layoff happened. After a while, it became almost comical. I referred to him as Eric, Destroyer of Telecom Companies. He was the Typhoid Eric of Telecom.

As this progressed over the next two years or so, our reaction to the layoffs dramatically shifted. Toward the end of that experience, he would call me in the middle of the day and say, "Do you want to go out to dinner tonight?" I would ask, "You got laid off?" and he would cheerfully say, "You know it! Pick a restaurant!" We would take the last of our known income and blow it on an expensive dinner. Was it fiscally wise? Not at all. But at that dinner, we would count our blessings. We would toast one another. We would talk about what we wanted the next job to be and brainstorm for alternate ideas. Those dinners were an act of faith that the Universe would provide and that we were safe, even though we had no clue where we would get our rent money for the upcoming month; we were always so far behind on bills that there was no chance to establish savings or a security blanket. We were flying on faith and absolutely nothing else.

Our reaction transitioned from panic to confidence not by design, but due to exhaustion. We literally did not have the energy or emotional bandwidth to work up any more panic, so we laughed in the face of hardship. That is when we learned the true power of faith. When we met the disadvantage with calm assurance, another job came quickly and easily. Alternatives for income and resolutions for paying impossible bills appeared out of nowhere. Our relationship galvanized over those times of uncertainty that we turned into times of abundance, but, more importantly, we learned through trial and error what worked and what did not. We saw what created abundance despite all odds and what was a waste of energy.

Were we cursed? Was it a psychic attack? No and no. It was an economic downturn, and the way we approached it ultimately determined our outcome. It was not always easy, but if I stumbled, I had Eric to nudge me gently back onto the path of faith. He had me to do the same. Eventually, his series of jobs took him through enough levels of experience that he became an electrical contractor and owned his own business, which was an act of faith all its own. Our time of want and woe, those cycles of tragedy and triumph, gave us a tough schooling in effective crisis management.

Divorce, job loss, evictions, pregnancies, deaths, financial disadvantage, illness, injury, betrayal, and injustice are unfortunate—but very real—parts of life. My mother used to warn against "seeing demons behind clothes baskets," meaning that people often interpret normal life experiences as paranormal oppression. The fearful ones become paranoid to the point that they believe every inconvenience is a hex. For some (such as the drama-centric demographic I previously described), this is a thrill-seeking belief. They want to imagine that they are important enough that another person would spend time and energy working against them. They crave a good story to tell. The idea of being magically pursued feels exciting and evocative to those who want the thrill of being chased.

For the rest of us, it is a necessary cleanup operation; we must objectively evaluate what is going on, come up with a reasonable assessment, and take action to make things better. That action might be waiting for the wheel to turn and bring you up to the top again. Other times, you might need to find a trusted friend to help you remove energies that invaded your energetic field.

PART TWO

TYPES OF ATTACKS

CHAPTER THREE

INCIDENTAL ATTACKS

Some folks relish the idea of a good old-fashioned deliberate curse or hexing, and people in Hollywood make a lot of money using such drama as a focus of storytelling in TV and films. Many gothic novels center around family curses and personal hexing. It is a fascinating narrative, and how it plays out in real life is even more interesting.

Before we get into the excitement of those deliberate attacks, however, it is important that we explore something more common than, but just as destructive as, the deliberate attack: the incidental attack. An incidental attack occurs when there is no active attempt to curse, hex, cross, or affect the victim in any way. It may or may not come from someone else and might even come from within ourselves or from situations that occur in our lives. It may sound odd to consider the following experiences, so common in our society, as psychic attacks, but we must look at them from the perspective of the effect they have on the human energetic system.

The human energy matrix does not distinguish between internal and external stressors. It reacts to trauma as it occurs and incorporates a person's response to it into their overall spiritual wellness or breakdown. An attack that occurs incidentally without the intention to harm causes the same response patterns in the energetic system as attacks done intentionally. If someone deliberately shoots you, the gunshot wound damages your body. If someone is cleaning a gun and it goes off, accidentally shooting you, the gunshot wound damages your body. In either case, your physical body views the wound as an injury and responds the same way. Treatment of an incidental attack is the same as treatment of a deliberate attack (discussed in part IV), just as a doctor or surgeon would treat either of those gunshot wounds in the same fashion.

People use the words *curse* and *hex* interchangeably. In the southern United States, *crossing* might also get thrown into the mix. There are subtle differences in the three, but hex and curse are close enough in definition that there is no need to split hairs over the usage. The primary variance is that curses and hexes are deliberate, whereas crossings are usually incidental.

Crossings

A crossing is one form of incidental attack most often caused by strong emotional energy directed toward an individual. Crossings are, in my experience, far more common than curses and hexes combined. Like all psychic attacks, crossings can cause misfortune, psychic turbulence, and possibly even ill health.

Imagine that you have a boss who is emotionally volatile and known for erratic behavior. You come back from your lunch break to find a note on your desk saying that your boss wants you in their office *now*. How does that make you feel? Your breathing might speed up. Your stomach might lurch a bit. You might break into a sweat. Even if you are comfortable with confrontation, you are probably not looking forward to what is about to happen, especially if your job is vital to your financial security.

You might hesitate before you knock on the door. When you force yourself to go into the office, not knowing what waits for you there, think of how vulnerable you would feel. This person holds control over your livelihood, and maybe you have seen the after-math of some of their rampages. When you get into the office, the tension is so thick you could cut it with a knife. The boss launches into a rant and false accusations begin to fly. You're trying to keep up and part of you wants to jump to your own defense, but there is no room for you to speak. All you can do is take the wrath.

Your boss does not want to hear your side of any story and refuses to entertain any explanation. Imagine how your physical responses would escalate as the scene unfolds. Your skin tingles. You might begin to shake from the pumping adrenaline. Your heart pounds. You have trouble breathing. As soon as you leave, presumably with your job still hanging on by a thread, you slip out of the office and return to your desk. It will take a while for the physical symptoms to subside. In fact, they may intensify before they get better due to the release that comes when the immediate danger is gone.

You have absorbed a huge wave of unjust anger that was not yours to carry. You know you did not do what your boss accused you of; the boss has the story completely wrong. And yet, you can become physically ill from the emotional onslaught of their anger. When you see your boss over the next few weeks, you might feel the return of those symptoms, even if your boss acts like nothing ever happened. This type of outburst could have been the result of a hundred things that caused your boss to feel undermined or marginalized earlier that day: they might have learned their partner was leaving them; maybe they just had a similar encounter with *their* boss; their teenager could have been arrested. Regardless, this is an incidental psychic attack.

We never know what causes people to behave as they do, but when those around us—especially those with power over us—allow their emotions to take control of their behavior, everyone around them suffers. That roommate who is so passive-aggressive that you cannot find out what exactly they are angry about and yet they sulk around and look wounded? Yes, that can be an inadvertent psychic attack. The coworker who stares you down for no apparent reason, glaring at you from across the room? Yep, could be. Any of those situations can be just as damaging as someone who carefully draws cursing sigils, intently pushing pins into a poppet.

People are often careless with their feelings and their words, not realizing (or not caring) that these emotions carry destructive energy that can affect other people long after they themselves have forgotten the encounter. The victim may or may not know the person who crosses them and, interestingly, the sender may not know they have crossed the victim, which is why it is a form of incidental crossing.

Envy, rage, fear, and embarrassment are all intense energies that can create psychic trauma that causes an attack response. In any of these situations, the aggressor is not directly intending a psychic attack, but the effects are the same.

The Evil Eye

The evil eye is a crossing created by envy or jealousy. A person looks at what another person possesses with longing or with frustration that they do not have the same, and the energy of that envy manifests as illness and loss of vitality in the victim.

Jealous thoughts like "When is it my turn?" or "Must be nice!" are forms of the evil eye. The energy of jealousy or envy is a dark and malicious power. It is uncomfortable for the sender and the receiver, and even if the receiver never hears the words, there is power in the feeling generated by the sender who allows those emotions to flourish.

In Mexican culture, there is a fear of the evil eye, or *mal de ojo*, regarding children. Seeing a baby that makes you smile and think *What a beautiful baby!* is considered a form of envy. Unless the admirer touches the baby within minutes of the thought, many believe the child can become ill from the energy. Touching the baby humanizes the child and grounds the energy. Of course, most people are uncomfortable with strangers touching their baby, so this can get awkward. Many children wear bracelets or other amulets to repel the evil eye.

Friends or relatives may inadvertently cross a victim by comparing their living situations and perceiving an unjust imbalance in perceived reward and misfortune. Those who already think badly of the victim are even more subject to conveying negative energies toward them if they add jealousy into the mix.

Warnings against craving what rightfully belongs to another person pop up throughout history and many mainstream religions. The biblical Ten Commandments include the instruction that a person is not to covet their neighbor's spouse or possessions. World powers annihilate entire civilizations because they want the land or resources another country possesses. The obsessive desire for what belongs to another person—whether it is possessions, opportunity, love, or even good looks—rarely results in a positive outcome for the target of the jealousy or the one who feels it.

In Turkey, an amulet called a *Nazar* is a popular defense against the evil eye, and its use has permeated many cultures. The Nazar is a bead or amulet that looks like an eye and is usually a brightly colored blue. Artisans and jewelry makers incorporate its image into bracelets, amulets, and pendants. I have found the Nazar to be quite effective in warding off the evil eye.

Non-Magical Attack

I include the non-magical attack in the incidental portion of this book because in most cases of non-magical attack, the aggressor is unaware that they are being manipulative or harmful. Unlike the people who attempt to control others using spell work, these non-magical attackers may or may not wish to exact an outcome from the victim. In many cases, the aggressor is simply using their own conditioning and defensive mechanisms and does not realize these behaviors are contaminating the relationship and manifesting as trauma in the other person.

This relates back to the crossing, but a non-magical attack is more insidious and long-term. A crossing usually comes from a burst of negative energy that is sudden and intense; the non-magical attack is a slower burn that builds up over an extended period of time.

Non-magical attack is a frequent outcome of relationships that have an unhealthy dynamic. This can include codependency, a savior complex, narcissism, gaslighting, martyrdom, guilt-tripping, or other unhealthy interactions. Frequently, a person who is actively causing emotional and spiritual trauma in another person feels as though they are the victim and not only rejects any mention of accountability, but flips the personal narrative so that the victim is the one at fault. When your family teases you beyond the boundaries you try valiantly to defend, when your neighbor allows their dogs to dig up your yard after you repeatedly ask them not to, and when your history professor holds you accountable for assignments that are not in the class syllabus or mentioned in the curriculum, these are forms of psychic attack. Passive aggression is still a form of aggression that creates an imbalanced energy that can cause psychic trauma.

That is not to say that every time someone is mean to you, it is an incidental psychic attack. If that were the case, we would all be more contaminated than we are! What I'm saying is that in any of those cases, the energy could be strong enough to fester into psychic trauma under the right circumstances. When the emotional energy of a situation is sufficiently intense that it takes on a personality and intention of its own, it has crossed over into psychic attack.

Unfortunately, incidental psychic attacks are common in unhealthy relationships. There are many self-help books dedicated to identifying and managing the myriad forms of emotional abuse that happen in personal and professional relationships, and there are just as many reasons why people who are traumatized by others choose to remain in those relationships. There are times when a spiritual cleansing causes a client to have a moment of clarity when they recognize the dysfunction of their relationship and make plans to begin a new life, but that is quite rare.

The management of psychic attack discussed later in this book can be extremely effective in providing temporary relief for a person engaged in an ongoing traumatic relationship or even for a person recovering from abuse. Ultimately, however, I do not feel the victim can be made whole again until the source of the abuse is removed. In those cases, I feel as though I am cleaning the person up and then throwing them back into a mud puddle when they return to the influence of the boss, partner, friend, or family member who caused the trauma in the first place.

Incidental Infiltrates

Incidental infiltrates are different from a crossing where a person's emotional outburst or negative fuming takes on legs and goes after the victim. Incidental infiltrates are actual entities that feed on the energy of a human and usually go undetected until the victim rules out all possible medical explanations for their symptoms and goes to a spiritual healer for help.

There was a time when people found it hard to believe that we share our world with tiny organisms that can make us sick. Even after the invention of the microscope allowed us to see these tiny beings that are germs, it was hard to imagine that we could curb the spread of illness simply by washing our hands and covering our coughs and sneezes. Even *seeing* these little critters was often not enough to convince people that they could personally stop the spread of illnesses. And yet, it is so.

Similarly, it is hard for many people to fathom that we share our world with other entities, which in this case means energetic creatures that feed off personal energy flows. People speak freely of "psychic vampires," people who drain your energy intentionally or inadvertently, but most people do not consider that you can pick up entities from other people just like you do the germs that cause the common cold. These entities hang out in our bodies and can cause physical, mental, energetic, and even social maladies.

In my experience, it is rare to see someone who does not have entities in their energetic field unless they have frequent energetic cleansings. There are many types of entities in the world that, like ticks and other parasites, look for a warm, vibrant body. They hop from person to person, depleting the host of their vitality, good fortune, and clear thinking, and of their ability to effectively inter-relate with other people. They can cause brain fog, irritability, difficulty focusing, headaches, and malaise.

Imagine you are walking through a grocery store feeling fine. Then you pass by someone and suddenly feel heavy, tired, and uncomfortable. Your immediate thought might be *Wow, I must be coming down with something*. Meanwhile, the person who walked past you takes a deep breath, feels lighter, and has a sudden increase of clarity. They might even start to think the "flu" they have had for weeks has finally lifted. This is an example of how easily entities can switch hosts.

When you have a cold that you cannot shake or insomnia that supplements cannot touch, it may be from an energetic parasitic entity. The excitement of a lucky break or the exuberance of a great conversation with a dear friend is nectar to these beings, and they drain away at those experiences until you are unable to feel the buzz of joy from them. When you stop feeling excited over these delicious tidbits in life, you stop attracting them. Soon, the world feels gray and bleak and boring no matter what you do. If you cannot focus and are frequently irritated, it becomes harder to perform simple tasks. You are difficult to be around and likely are not at your best job performance. You forget how to be joyful and engaged and begin to pull back from people around you.

Once the entity has depleted your energetic resources it moves on to someone else, but this can take a while, and your quality of life suffers long before they leave. Meanwhile, this energetic parasite is satiated, happy, and satisfied inside you, absorbing your energy. If you have a strong constitution and healthy energetic field, you might carry an entity for years before it disengages in its search for a more vibrant host.

Although these types of infiltrations are not as insidious as a deliberate hex or curse or even an inadvertent crossing, their effect is still annoying at best and destructive at worst. They can interfere with cohesive thought processes so that your ability to perform simple tasks is compromised. Your hand-eye coordination might suffer and your memory may not be as sharp as it once was. Your ability to effectively empathize with others might change; your reactions may seem exaggerated or overly emotional. You may lack patience and compassion and become easily irritated, especially if you lose the ability to achieve restorative sleep.

These entities can also cause a change in your dream patterns so that nightmares, night terrors, or even sleep paralysis become a problem. Sleepwalking, sleep talking, and the inability to get comfortable enough to sleep may also occur. Some people have the sensation that they have bugs crawling under their skin or their arms and legs tingle as if circulation is cut off.

The treatment for this kind of attack is the same as it is for any other psychic attack: a spiritual cleansing. An effective cleansing will remove the entity and initiate the healing process so the client can quickly begin to rebuild their quality of life.

Bigotry and Discrimination as Psychic Attacks

In chapter 1, we discussed the energetic trauma caused by social media and political conflict. While we might want to imagine that people have evolved since the time of racially segregated schools and other forms of persecution against entire cultural demographics, what has instead happened is a dramatic polarization of societal perspective. Think of the posts you see on social media identifying groups of people as the cause for misery in the United States or even in the world. On one side, there are those who are so militant about social justice that they marginalize and reject people who want to have a learning conversation to correct their own misinformation. On the other side, there are unapologetic bigots who are no longer isolated to known hate groups but are often your own loved ones and associates, blasting their hatred and ignorance onto their preferred social media platform.

An unsettling number of Americans feel vindicated in their private and public persecution of "the other." It's so common in everyday life that it is easy to normalize this behavior. Think of the comments and posts that you scroll past to avoid conflict. Take a moment to mentally confront those dismissed words for what they really are: a blanket energetic attack on an entire group of people. Think about:

+ Immigrants, illegal or naturalized, who are accused of "stealing" jobs and told to "go back" to a different country.

+ Middle Eastern people who are branded as terrorists due to their presumed country of origin.

+ Native American people who suffer continued persecution in a country that their ancestors treated with dignity and reverence.

+ The LGBTQ+ population and anyone who does not fit into the cisnormative lifestyle, who are denigrated for wanting rights equal to other citizens.

+ African American people who fear police brutality and discrimination due to their ethnicity.

+ People with political viewpoints—or worse, no political viewpoint—who are blamed for the current world problems.

As you can imagine, this is only the tip of the iceberg, a small sampling of people enduring bigotry and biases every day, ranging from benign intolerance and general derisiveness to outright hatred and a genuine desire for their death. If you believe otherwise, I assure you that perspective comes from a position of tremendous privilege.

When people are targeted by this kind of intolerance—or worse, when the aggressors are motivated into action, fueled by the encouragement of their peers to purge the world of the mere presence of those who do not conform to their accepted standards—we all suffer.

For people who are part of targeted demographics, it is especially hard when family members and close acquaintances support, tolerate, or even endorse the behavior of these individuals. It is hard enough when people you do not know persecute you for not believing or living as they do, but when the beliefs of your loved ones cause you suffering, it is profoundly traumatic. And the spirit retains and reacts to trauma on an energetic level.

The negative energy launched at an entire culture by individuals or groups is a palpable evil that permeates the fabric of human existence. It changes and defines who we are as a species and creates a destructive force that requires the victim to take heroic measures to achieve any modicum of success or enjoy a quality of life that others take for granted. This is *precisely* what a curse does, and although the actions that create this kind of psychic attack are deliberate, it is incidental in that the aggressor is not usually working to magically curse the victim.

Haunted Items

Technically, this manner of incurring a psychic attack could go in both categories of incidental and deliberate attacks; however, because it is most commonly incidental, this seems the appropriate place to put it.

Just as we know that we can leave germs and other contamination on physical objects that can then transfer that contamination to another person, so too can we convey negative energy to one another by way of physical, tangible objects.

When you think of haunted items, you might imagine a spooky doll or a disturbing painting, but truly, almost anything can receive and transmit energy. It might be an item you pick up at a flea market or thrift store. Likewise, it could be something deliberately sent to a target after the aggressor infuses it with the energy of a curse. You might inherit a statue, piece of jewelry, or dish from someone in your family that has a family curse attached to it.

Possessions that play an integral role in traumatic experiences in your life can also convey negative energy, such as a wedding ring for a relationship that ended in betrayal and divorce or an object directly used to inflict harm on another person.

If you have symptoms of misfortune, low energy, headaches, or other signs of psychic attack such as those described in chapter 7, see if those symptoms began at the same time as the arrival of any object to the home that has an uneasy feeling to it.

Some things just *feel* off or uncomfortable to the touch, even for someone not attuned to psychometry. While it would make sense that if something in your home feels icky the best approach is to get rid of it, you have to be mindful of the accountability that comes with passing that energy on to the next person who picks it up. I recommend using sage to clear negative energy away from an item. You can also put it outside for the three nights of the new moon, allowing the dark of the moon energies to carry the negativity away and transmute it into positive energy. Washing an item with mugwort-infused water is also an effective clearing and cleaning process.

Why Do Incidental Attacks Matter?

It may be hard to believe, but a deliberate curse, hex, or other form of psychic attack is easier to manage than an incidental attack. With a deliberate attack, a person can usually tell approximately where the energy comes from and then be cleaned out. Setting up protective boundaries is easier for a victim of deliberate attack.

With an incidental attack, to paraphrase an old horror movie, *the call might be coming from inside the house.* The person's closest loved ones, their spiritual base, or even their own negative self-talk could create ongoing psychic trauma that results in discord, imbalance, and disruption in the victim's energetic field. If you have a mother who you dearly love but who is frequently condescending and judgmental, you might not be positioned to put her aside so you can move forward into living a life that is more supportive and uplifting. If you have adult children who disrespect you, do you really want to cut them out of your life forever? Rarely does a person leave their spouse for occasionally being mean to them, even if that emotional cruelty takes a toll and creates spiritual trauma. People frequently incur psychic abuse to avoid creating social or familial discord.

Although not all spiritual healers are of this mind, I give considerable weight to the idea that the behavior of others that creates trauma in your spirit constitutes a psychic attack. The word *psychic* comes from the Greek word *psychikos*, which means "of the soul."[2] We think of it in terms of the psyche, which is defined as the

---

2. *Merriam-Webster*, s.v. "psychic," accessed May 21, 2020, https://www.merriam-webster.com/dictionary/psychic.

totality of the human mind, including the conscious and unconscious. The maiden goddess Psyche was said to be the human soul in a divine form, and the Greek word *psȳchḗ* translates directly to "breath," which comes from *psȳchein*, which means "to breathe, hence, to live."[3]

A psychic attack, therefore, is an attack on the entire mental process, the soul, and a person's very life. To compartmentalize this broad scope of influence to encompass only the tiny box labeled "deliberate attacks" is to do a disservice to the people who endure incidental psychic trauma every day and have the symptoms to show for it.

3. Henry George Liddell and Robert Scott, *A Greek-English Lexicon: Based on the German Works of Francis Passow* (Salt Lake City, UT: Digitized by the Genealogical Society of Utah, 2009). https://openlibrary.org/works /OL2947300W/A_Greek-English_Lexicon.

CHAPTER FOUR

DELIBERATE ATTACKS

Now we've come to the part of the book most people want to know about: those intentional attacks where a Witch cackles over a stuffed and blood-spotted effigy while shoving pins into it and chanting in Latin. Or at least, that's what you might imagine a deliberate attack to look like.

Most deliberate attacks are either a curse or a hex. As previously mentioned, I often use the terms *curse* and *hex* interchangeably, and they are similar enough to allow for this interrelation when describing a psychic attack. There are, however, some subtle differences. While it is not essential for you to closely adhere to the distinction in your speech, it is good information to have.

Curses

A curse is usually long-term and may be multigenerational. Family curses tend to attack the prosperity of a family and its ability to expand and procreate. Historically, the firstborn son is a person of honor in a family, which makes them a frequent target for attack. The inability for women to become pregnant and ultimately

55

deliver a healthy baby that survives beyond the first year or depriving a family of the ability to flourish financially are also common leverages used in curse work. Another place for a curse to take hold is on the societal or cultural standing of a family. This means that the usual places for a curse to attack someone are via the reproductive system, in the cradle, or in the wallet.

Psalm 109 in the Holy Bible is one of the most aggressive printed curses in existence, and people are often more comfortable throwing it around believing that if words come from the Bible, the intention is somehow sanctified by God. This psalm is a profound curse involving everything from explosive diarrhea to death and obliteration of the enemy from the pages of time, as well as the annihilation of their genetic upline and their downline. It curses the enemy's children to be vagabonds and invokes the sins of his mother into full view, among other uniquely specific maladies. The detailed elaboration of those Bible verses effectively illustrates the far-reaching effects and specificity of a generational curse.

When I notice a pattern of repeating misfortune in a family line, I consider a generational curse. In the consideration of "nature versus nurture," we understand that some families pass on unhealthy behaviors due to the exposure to those traits at a formative age. This includes bad habits such as smoking, unhealthy eating, substance abuse, disrespect of one another, spousal abuse, elder abuse, and criminal behavior. This does not necessarily mean that they are cursed, even though they have a family history of unhealthy behavior that spans many generations.

Not all curses are generational or family curses. Some are carefully constructed, intensive psychic attacks intended to unfold in stages. Other curses are disguised as a simpler attack; this Trojan horse approach is common when professional spellcasters work on behalf of a client, and this is a more sophisticated attack.

Hexes

A hex is more personal, usually isolated to one person who has incurred the wrath of the sender. When a person is "casting against" someone, it is usually a hex. Binding a person to limit their influence, even defensively, is a form of hexing. In both curses and hexes, the action is deliberate and is usually infused with malicious intent or is a retaliatory response to a crime, real or imagined.

A hex is typically short-lived and will burn itself out once the sender stops feeding it energy, whereas a curse is energetically front-loaded and can renew itself, like a time-released medication. A generational or family curse can reactivate with every extension of the family tree and each renewed generation. Almost invariably, a hex is temporary and will eventually die out. Of course, the victim can be quite miserable during the duration of the hex, so removal is always desired over waiting it out.

There is an urban legend that says that for a curse or hex to work, the victim must buy into the idea that they are cursed. This expands to the theory of the power of suggestion that says that if a person believes they are cursed, they will manifest the symptoms of a curse when none is there, solely through the power of suggestion. In my practice, I have not found this to be true. I have had plenty of people come to me who believed they were cursed when I could find no evidence they had been. I have had even more people come to me with no thought that they were cursed and upon treatment, we found a curse or hex was present. The experiences I have had in treating people for maladies such as these do not support the belief that the victim's participation or willingness is a factor in the ability of a curse or hex to adversely affect them.

Demon Possession

An obscure form of cursing or hexing involves the conjuring of a demon or other entity to send to the victim. The entity then haunts or possesses the person, causing intense changes in personality and a profound loss of good fortune. The management strategies listed in this book may help alleviate some symptoms and can clear out lower-level demons or entities, but in most cases, assistance from a professional spiritual healer is needed for this type of attack.

Managing a demonic possession can be dangerous for all concerned and should never be attempted by an amateur. While this may sound concerning, the symptoms demonstrated in the case of demonic possession could never be confused for the ones we discuss here and label as psychic attack. Although this form of demonic possession is, by definition, an aggressive psychic attack, it is one that a person is unlikely to encounter and if they do, there will be no mistake about their inability to manage it. Do not get in over your head; if you are at all in doubt about your ability to manage an attack, consult a professional energy worker or spiritual leader.

Who Are the Psychic Attackers?

It oversimplifies the situation to say that only unscrupulous, hateful people use magic to attack someone else. In a person who is not sociopathic or homicidal, the desire to harm someone on a psychic level comes from the same strong emotions that would drive a person to cause physical harm. Those emotions are usually anger, fear, hurt, or frustration. A hex or curse could be considered a spiritual crime of passion: A person perceives a threat or a wrongdoing of some kind for which there seems to be no hope of justice, and they desperately want to balance the scales and recover some of that control that they feel was wrenched away from them.

If you had a loved one, spouse, child, or parent in imminent danger from another person, you would likely do everything in your power to help. If you know that someone is causing harm, you would likely feel compelled to stop them. At times when people feel powerless to employ practical means to stop the harm or if those means prove ineffectual, they might come to view an energetic attack as a more practical avenue for crisis management.

If someone affected your life in a negative way and you talked the situation to death, begging them to change whatever they are doing that is untenable, you would likely become extremely frustrated. The socially accepted resolutions did not work. Asking, pleading, and threatening did not work. Tough love did not work. When in that situation, a person might feel pushed to work on the situation from an energetic approach, especially when there is no smoking gun that indicts them or leaves them accountable for such a thing.

If someone you trust betrays you, the effect is quite visceral. You might question your judgment for allowing such a person to get close to you, and you would probably doubt universal ideas of balance and justice if you saw them thriving after doing you wrong. The anger created when someone hurts you in a devastating way and suffers no visible consequences may cause a person to take action they would not normally employ.

Before the world was so tightly interlinked, if you wanted to curse a person or use spell work to control their behavior, you had to know who in the village offered these services and how to contact them. You then sought that person out, usually under the cloak and secrecy of darkness, and secured their services. The average person likely had no clue how to curse someone, but they knew where to go if it needed to be done.

Many magical paths are tolerant toward cursing, hexing, and controlling someone through energetic means. Previously, the use of those techniques was limited to a handful, comparatively speaking. If you did not have the grimoire or know someone who knew someone who could do it, your options might be limited. Nowadays, I have witnessed hexing by practitioners of Pennsylvania Dutch (Deutsch) Powwow magic, Black Belt Hoodoo, New Orleans Hoodoo, Appalachian Granny Magic, and Brujeria, all of which are folk magic traditions that developed primarily in the United States. That does not even take into account the Holy Bible, which is rife with curses and a competent spell book for practitioners of any of those paths. Add to that the techniques and beliefs of magical practice in nearly every other country on Earth and you have an enormous body of punitive and manipulative magic.

In today's tightly connected global network, there is no longer any societal or geographical boundary to such information. A quick internet search will render many thousands of results, giving the seeker step-by-step instructions on how to launch a psychic attack. The information is out there for anyone who wants to learn and, short of checking browser history, there is no way anyone would know it was accessed and implemented.

Unfortunately, anytime we have someone in distress, there are people who will gladly take advantage of the victim's pain. I have had too many clients to count who came to me saying this or that spiritual healer told them they had a curse on them that they would remove for an enormous sum of money, usually in the thousands. It is profoundly sad that these opportunistic charlatans take advantage of people who are suffering, not to mention making legitimate healers look bad. This is itself a form of attack and adds to the trauma of someone who is suffering from a psychic attack.

These predators leverage fear to bilk people out of huge sums of money, knowing they will be long gone by the time their target realizes they were victimized yet again. If you find yourself in need of a spiritual healer, it is always good to work from personal recommendations.

In other times, everyone in a village knew whom to go to for this kind of care. There was no question. Now, unless you know someone who knows someone, it can be challenging to find a healer of integrity and skill. If you have a local metaphysical store, "Witch" shop, or even new age store, the people who work there are likely used to customers asking for recommendations for a competent healer. This will avail you much better than taking your chances with someone unknown and untested.

If you are forced by circumstances to find a healer or practical advice on a situation by gambling on an internet source, there are a few pointers I can offer. Mostly, the articles and books that show up in search engine results are somewhere between moderately safe and helpful. In my own research, I found few that gave me concern. You do, however, want to avoid some pitfalls that may not be obvious to the untrained eye.

Stay away from resources that blame the victim, using phrases such as "If you had not turned away from God, you would not be open to psychic attack." It is often easy to identify when a resource has an agenda other than helping someone heal, so read carefully and notice how you feel as you work through the information. If you feel hopeful, encouraged, and safe, read on. If you start to feel as if *you* have done something wrong, then the writer or healer is attempting to leverage your emotions to achieve their own goals.

Another warning sign is if you begin to feel fearful as you read the material you have accessed. Emotionally manipulative wording such as "The world is a dangerous place!" is a common tactic for those who wish to garner clients through panic rather than the ability to heal. A good healer or author will help you feel empowered rather than helpless and continually at risk in an energetically violent world.

Additionally, avoid healers or authors who directly disparage other practitioners. The purpose of a healing practice is to assist clients who are struggling, not to wage personal skirmishes. Those who outwardly attack other healers usually do not have the well-being of their clients as their primary motivation.

Another warning sign is when a healer insists that they are the only person qualified to help you. There are many excellent healers in the world and no one person holds the sole ability to heal a victim from their attack. In fact, victims can often heal themselves from an attack when they are carefully instructed how to do so. Many prefer to have a professional healer assist with their curative processes both for objectivity and to have the advantage of experienced eyes and hands on the situation.

When someone contacts me to commission spell work, I make it clear they could do the work themselves. I do not practice the upsell; I want my clients to know that what I am doing they could easily do for themselves. When they choose for me to do the work, sometimes it is because they do not feel competent to perform the work and want to take advantage of my decades of experience. Other times, it is a practical consideration because they do not have a place where they can safely burn candles or conduct spell work. More often, however, it is because they do not want anyone to know that they are involved with the magical manipulation of other people.

These cases are far more complicated than a client who comes to me looking for cleanup and healing after someone attacked them. A person who wants me to perform spell work for them that is ethically questionable or morally questionable is far more likely to mislead or outright lie to me. The ability to read people is crucial in discerning the true motivation of a person who wants to attack someone. Healing a person who suffered an attack is a far more elementary process.

Techniques for Psychic Attack

Once a person accepts the idea that they are the victim of a psychic attack, one of the first questions I get is "What exactly was done to me?" They want to know the actual mechanics someone went through to willfully inflict damage upon them. What candles did they use? Why did they do it? And of course, who did it?

Tracing a spell back to its owner is a complicated, heavily nuanced, and often flawed process, as we will discuss in chapter 13. Likewise, it is almost impossible to narrow down the specifics of what the attacker did. We can learn where the victim was attacked based on the symptoms they experience and certain diagnostic tricks. The effects of an attack are traceable and almost predictable once it is established that an attack took place.

A healer might intuitively feel that certain facts are correct, but those bits of information are only incidental to the situation. The first job at hand is to make the victim whole again and to get them to a place where they can actively work to reestablish the quality of life they want. With that as my focus during client care, I do not give much energy to finding out exactly how the psychic attack was created or who sent it. We can, however, speak in generalities about how these deliberate psychic attacks happen. Throughout the many magical paths that provide instruction for such attacks, there are often common or similar practices.

As previously stated, there are many spells throughout multiple paths that have the express purpose of bringing harm or chaos to the victim. The following techniques address the intentional inflic- tion of malice onto a person using magical means. Please note that these techniques do not include crossings in which the victim suf- fers due to the attacker hurling negative energy in their direction. In that case, the attacker probably does not imagine that their rage has any effect on the victim and the crossing is purely incidental.

Most people who go after someone aggressively using magic do it in a few predictable ways.

Personal Effects

In this type of spell work, the victim is identified by name and possi- bly by date of birth, photographs, personal possessions, hair, finger- nails, toenails, or body fluids like sweat, blood, saliva, or ejaculate. Facebook and other social media profiles are a wealth of informa- tion and resources for anyone wishing to inflict a psychic attack on another person.

DNA of the victim is the most precise way to target aggressive spell work toward the victim. A photograph is the second most effective means, followed by a person's name and birth date. The old fear that photography can capture the soul of a person is not that far off; I frequently use a photograph as a hook to connect to a client when I perform a remote healing or card reading because I can look directly into their eyes and connect to their spirit.

I know many casual magical practitioners who, sensing immi- nent betrayal by or departure of a significant other, quickly began canvassing hairbrushes, laundry baskets, and shower drains for ammunition so they were prepared if they needed it. The absence of a photo, personal information, or body leavings is not a deal-breaker to an effective attack, but they are a profound boost if the user has them. If you do not have those accessories, however, a person can direct a curse or hex just fine using identifiers like "the bitch who is sleeping with my husband" or "the owner of that dog that keeps digging up my iris bulbs." These identifiers are niceties that streamline and empower the spell work.

Candles

Candle magic is a common method of spiritual attack. The DUME (Death Unto My Enemies) candle is a popular tool found at most Hoodoo shops or botanicas. This candle invokes the power of Death and sends it to the person named on the candle. However, the sender loses all control over how Death will manifest in the person's life—it could be the death of their career, their good fortune, their parent, their pet, their child, or their own death. It is a brutal attack to send to someone and, unfortunately, it is a frequently used candle, as are other candles such as the Bitch Be Gone candle and the Destroy Everything candle.

Figure candles shaped like the male and female bodies are also used in psychic attack. Figure candles are used as effigies of those whom the sender wishes to harm, often with nails, pins, or needles stuck into the specific areas where the spell should focus.

Poppets

Poppets are small dolls made of felt, cloth, or wax. They are also used for effigy work. Poppets have an opening in the side or head where herbs, oils, personal effects, or slips of paper may be inserted.

The poppet is then closed and bound, buried, or otherwise compromised to convey the energy of the curse onto the victim.

Witch's Jar or Witch's Bottle

A Witch's jar or Witch's bottle is one of the easiest, most powerful, and most common curses I have encountered. The distinction between a Witch's jar and Witch's bottle appears to be regional, and while I was taught that the jar is a curse intended to be buried and the bottle is an ongoing spell that one keeps at the home, most people I know use the terms interchangeably.

This curse or hex is created by placing sharp objects like broken glass, rusted nails or pins, or thorns along with caustic powders like cayenne or sulfur. A poppet or other effigy dedicated to the victim or the victim's name and birth date on a piece of paper go into the container, followed by a sour fluid such as vinegar or, more commonly, the urine of the sender. This is a literal interpretation of the phrase "piss on 'em."

The sender then buries the jar or bottle in a place where it is unlikely to be disturbed, usually deep in a wooded area or in a cemetery. Vintage Witch's jars and bottles are frequently found in the foundations of buildings undergoing demolition, especially inside the cinder blocks. Burying a Witch's jar or bottle under the foundation of a building that is being constructed is a surefire way to leave it undisturbed for the lifetime of the sender and the victim. The emphasis on the security of the container comes from the belief that if the vessel is broken, the curse ends.

Dusts, Dirts, and Powders

Items such as Goofer Dust and graveyard dirt can also be used to attack another person. Goofer Dust works like an exterminator for people and is a yellowish, sulfur-based dust traditionally left in a place where the victim is sure to walk through it. This could be on their front doorstep, in their front yard, or near their vehicle. It may also be placed on office chairs, in the foot space under a desk, or even inside a person's shoes.

Graveyard dirt from the grave of a person known to be mentally ill, especially someone who was schizophrenic or had bipolar disorder, scattered near a living person for several days in a row or placed under their bed is thought to induce confusion and madness.

Most magical shops sell a variety of powders, usually made with a cornstarch base, imbued with the energy to confuse, hex, curse, maim, or otherwise harm another person. These come under many names, but their intention is clearly revealed in the photos on the package or by the name itself.

Entities

Ambitious spellcasters might summon an entity or demon to go after their victim, offering a piece of the person's hair, their body excretions, or a photo to identify the target. Entities are notoriously difficult to control and are usually either smarter or dumber than the person summoning them. This leads to any number of potential mishaps if the summoner is not well trained and perfectly adept at controlling what they invoke.

If the demon or entity is smarter than the summoner, they will usually find a way to exact a payment far beyond what the person wishes to pay. If the demon or entity is dumber than the summoner, they have trouble remembering what they are supposed to do when they get to the victim, and if the victim is experienced in such work, the dumber entity can easily be manipulated into returning to the original summoner to wreak havoc. Demonic psychic attack accounts for only a tiny sliver of all psychic attacks.

These are only a handful of the methods one person might use to attack another, but they are some of the most common. Knowing the method of psychic attack that was used is less important than identifying and treating the attack, which we will cover in subsequent chapters.

CHAPTER FIVE

CONTROLLING OTHERS THROUGH MAGIC

So far, we have discussed incidental attacks, which happen without the deliberate attempt to harm another person, and the deliberate attacks of hexing and cursing. But what about those times when the ambition of the sender is not necessarily to harm, but to control?

Easily more than three-fourths of the people who approach me to do magic on their behalf want work done that controls or alters the thoughts, emotions, or behaviors of other people. While these people may not consider what they want to do a psychic attack, there is no avoiding the fact that it most certainly is just that.

When you use energies to force someone to think, feel, or behave in a way that is not organic to them—or worse, in a way they actively *do not wish* to think, feel, or behave—it is a direct violation of their free will. When I inform the client of this, the reply is usually "I don't care. This is what needs to happen," or "It will ultimately be for the best."

Some people genuinely do not see anything wrong with breaking up the relationship of a couple if they believe the couple should not be together. Others are totally okay with casting a "Come to Me" spell on a person in a committed relationship. Some feel justified in forcing an adult child to get a job they do not want or forcing a spouse to stop philandering. Because in these people's minds, the justification is there; they do not consider what they are doing to be an attack. In their world, a violation of free will is nothing more than collateral damage to get what they want.

My mention of free will in this context is not as "Could you ...?," but "*Should* you ...?" Free will itself is neither an insignificant obstacle nor an insurmountable impediment to successful magical work. It is resistance that works for or against the energy put toward a goal. When I ask a client, "Do you understand that what you are proposing is a violation of this person's free will?" it is not to impart judgment on them from my own perspective. Instead, I want them to consider what they are suggesting from their own moral framework and to also understand how this affects the potential outcome.

To be successful, the power of what the client wants and how badly they want it must channel sufficient energy to overcome the power of how much the target does or does not want the intended outcome. If our work is successful and the target complies, we may then have to continue sending energy to the goal; otherwise, the energy from the first spell will wane and the target will default to their organic behaviors. The free will of a target does not negate the effectiveness of the work I do on behalf of a client, it just makes it more difficult to achieve and more complicated to maintain. I explain all of this to the client before they contract me to work on their behalf and often, they still wish to proceed.

If you think about it, most magical workings involve overriding the free will of another person. Want a raise? You must override the free will of the boss or the business owner who does not want to pay you more. Do you want a parking spot at a crowded department store? You must override the free will of everyone who also wants a good parking spot. Do you want it to rain so your garden grows better? You must override the free will of every bride and groom who wants an outside wedding that day and every family that wants to go camping that weekend.

Free will is a consideration, not an ultimate determinant, and it is one most of my clients are happy to dismiss outright, with or without my cautionary interjections. People do not like to be told no and they abhor rejection. It may be outside of a person's comprehension that someone genuinely would not want to be with them. They do not imagine that their ability to magically influence the thoughts, actions, or feelings of someone else could be outside of their moral right because they believe they know best, they know what they want to happen, and that is that.

The desire to use magic to control others usually comes from a strong set of emotions such as fear, anger, hurt, or frustration. Those emotions most generally arise in subjects related to love or money, but as the Bible says, "the greatest of these is love." [4] When money is the issue, I often mitigate the client's goals with encouragement toward a general money spell that brings them more income. I convince the client that rather than forcing their boss to give them a raise, we can work to make their own value shine through and draw a job to them where their skills and abilities are more appreciated. Money issues are easy to reframe into a less-invasive approach that does not force a reaction from someone else. If I attempt to do the same for a love circumstance, however,

---

4. 1 Corinthians 13:13 (New International Version).

most clients will have none of it. They want what they want. Of all the love-related situations people bring to me, these are the top six:

Bring Back My Ex-Lover

The overwhelming predominance of love magic I am asked to perform is to bring back someone from the past and to compel them to want to be with the client. Invariably, the people who beg me to get their ex-lover to return to them are A) ones who identify as female and B) in no way responsible for their partner being unhappy and leaving. Only a tiny fraction of clients who ask me to compel their ex to return are people who identify as male; this is almost exclusively a female ambition.

The story that comes with this request often includes tales of atrocities committed by the ex. When I ask why they would want someone like that back in their lives, they blink at me as if I have just sprouted seven extra heads. Their response is usually something along these lines: "Because I love them, of course. They are my soul mate, my twin flame, and I can't bear to be without them."

Meanwhile, my spirit guides are face-palming and whispering to me, "That person was *not* their soul mate."

If I suggest that we work to bring in a partner that loves and appreciates them, I am met with more blinks that form into a hard stare. "But I love *him*. I want to be with *him*."

It is telling that when I do choose to accept such a case, within a few months of their soul mate/twin flame/beloved coming back to them, the client is back asking me to do spell work to get rid of them. People break up for good reasons.

These clients have another frequent component of their stories: a tale of a seductress who bewitched their partner into leaving their happy, secure relationship. They are convinced their partner left them because the one who lured him away used "black magic" or had a "black Witch" helping them. And since in their mind there is no doubt that this is the case, they feel justified in using magic to break up the new relationship and compel the ex-lover to return to them. They do not see the obvious similarity in what they are alleging this unholy siren did and what they are asking me to do. They want to make sense of their partner rejecting them, which means they must relieve the ex of any accountability and put the blame on the seductress who stole him away, as well as any magical help she commissioned to that end.

A client will make this kind of request as a direct result of losing power in the relationship. Whether it happened yesterday or years ago, their partner wrenched the decisions about the continuation of the relationship out of their hands and they were given no choice in the matter. Working magic to bring back their ex gives them a sense of renewed control.

In most cases, I do not believe the client truly wants their partner back; they want to be the one to say if, when, and how the relationship ends. Sometimes they want to draw the ex-partner back into a relationship purely so they can dump them and force their partner to feel as abandoned as they did. This may be a conscious or subconscious motivation on the part of the client.

Compel This Person to Be with Me

This is much like the first situation and is a stalkerish sort of psychic attack. The client who asks me to do this for them may or may not know the person they wish to magically influence. It could be an ex-lover who strayed, as in the first scenario, or it could be someone they have never formally met that they see at work from time to time. It could be a person they dated once who did not call them back or, in some cases, it is a high school sweetheart they have not seen or contacted in twenty years. The underlying ambition is that there is a person who is not showing them attention, and they want to attract that person into a relationship.

Ideally, this is a situation where the target of the spell has unspoken or reticent affection and attraction for the client. In that case, we can clear away the obstacles that keep them from making their interest known and fan the flames of desire. In most cases, however, the client wants me to compel a person who has little or no interest in them and has made that position clear. These clients might believe that no means no … unless you have a "Come to Me" prayer candle you can light.

A major problem with compelling a person to be with you is the maintenance of the spell work you do. When you curse or hex a person, you do not have to work hard to keep the effect going. You send the curse or hex to them and let it sit in their energetic system and radiate discord, misfortune, and conflict. A compelling spell intended to change how a person thinks, feels, or acts must be reinforced on an ongoing basis or else the effects will begin to wane and the target's natural reactions will quickly resume.

People have the erroneous impression that you can light a candle to get someone to fall in love with you and then live happily ever after with your newly ripened and plucked soul mate. If the ideal situation described above is present and they already do have an interest but do not have the courage to make it known, sure, that can happen. But if you are generating feelings from nothing or, even worse, overriding negative feelings with positive feelings, then the energy will slow the minute the candle extinguishes and their organic responses, desires, and thoughts will return. This means you must continually light candles or cast spells to keep the target interested and attached if they truly have no interest in or attraction to the person.

How many candles or love spells does it take to get someone to fall in love with you? There is no set answer because there are so many variables; the target's genuine feelings toward the client is only one of the factors. There might be extenuating circumstances such as the target being married, having a different sexual orientation, having a past that they are ashamed of, or having a fear of commitment. They might have children to consider or a desire *not* to have children. Other obstacles like "no fraternization between employees" regulations or cultural opposition might come into play. Past situations like a restraining order or prior emotional abuse may keep the target from reaching out to the client. The target might have a hard and fast "no long-distance relationships" rule. Factors such as these will pile greater resistance onto any sort of "Come to Me" compelling spell work and could make it take longer or keep it from happening at all.

I tell my clients to think of their goal as a light bulb that requires X amount of batteries to turn it on (with X being unknowable). You do not know how much electricity the light bulb requires, so you have no idea how many batteries it will take to get it to turn on. You must keep adding batteries until you see light. If you are compelling someone to do something they don't want to do, feel something they don't want to feel, or think thoughts that are not their own, it takes a whole lot of batteries—and the energy does not last. It is also, to reiterate, a form of deliberate psychic attack.

I find it interesting that just as the "bring back my ex" work predominantly comes from clients who identify as female, "compel this person to be with me" work predominately comes from clients who identify as male.

Break Up Someone Else's Relationship

This work often goes in tandem with the first two situations, and it is one of the most difficult spells to enact since you have to simultaneously affect not one but *two* people who do not want to do, feel, or think what the client wants them to.

The clients who come to me with this request invariably presume intimate knowledge of the fitness of the relationship between the two people they want to break up. Some people do not even have a name and will instead specify, "Anyone my ex is currently seeing." In that case, they are asking me to potentially meddle in several relationships and affect multiple people.

Occasionally, a client wants to break up the relationship of someone who is genuinely abusive to their partner. This can be a person who is encouraging or forcing their partner into addictions or who harms them physically or emotionally. I also sometimes get parents—almost always mothers—who want their kids to break up with partners they deem inappropriate.

People are quite cavalier about meddling in the romantic relationships of others, and it happens more often than you would think, so if you find that you and your partner have a sudden rush of conflict that does not feel natural, it is reasonable to treat it as a psychic attack.

Get This Crazy Person Away from Me

I am sure you can guess that this often goes hand in hand with the second case, "compel this person to be with me." I frequently work with clients who need protection from stalkers or other invasive people. Of all these situations listed, protection is the easiest to manage. There are so many products to help with this that it is more of a matter of teaching the client how to use the items than of attempting to coerce a behavior in someone else.

One way to encourage someone to leave another person alone is to meditate in such a way that you can "profile" the target, much like a criminal investigator. Imagine what their payoff is for the target in chasing the person who wants them to go away, then send them a distraction—a way to fulfill that need without having to pursue anyone who does not wish to be pursued. What do they see in the person who does not want to be around them? What need does that person fill? What shiny situation could distract them from pursuing this person who wants relief from their attention?

I had an interesting situation in my practice where a woman came to me in tears over a man she dated several times who suddenly ghosted her. He refused to answer any communication and even moved without providing forwarding address information. She was devastated that he gave no reason for his abrupt change of interest and was heartbroken and confused because "things were going so well ... we were really connecting."

I made some suggestions and helped her choose some oils and candles that might give her insight as to why he left and open doors for his return. She was grateful and became a frequent customer for the next month or so.

This sort of thing was so common for my shop that I did not think much of it until a man came in and said he needed help getting rid of a stalker. He told me that he met a woman on a dating app and that on their second date, she had started talking about the two of them getting married and having children. He let her know that this was not his interest and she became hysterical, so he ended it with her since they obviously did not have the same goals in life.

Unwilling to take no for an answer, she began contacting him at work. She was messaging him incessantly, sending more than a hundred messages in a few hours' time. He said he did not want to go so far as to take out a restraining order, but he had to get some peace, so he moved into another apartment so she could not physically find him. When he handed me his phone to show me the text messages, I had to choke back my horror. It was the same name as the client I had helped pursue the man who dumped her!

This was a strong lesson that clients represent their circumstances to me in whatever way they feel will earn them the greatest favor, and they often believe their own narrative to the point that there is no room for any objective truth or self-awareness.

Change This Person into Someone They Are Not

Oh how quickly "We are so in sync that we finish each other's sentences" turns into "Stop interrupting me!" As time goes on in a relationship, it's common for people to want to change a fundamental character trait of a person they love. "I thought he would change as he matured," "They seemed so nice!," and "I thought I could live with it, but I just can't and I don't want to leave" are words I often hear from people who are dissatisfied with their spouses, roommates, or family members.

So many people want to change the people they love without having to do any heavy lifting to make it happen: "Make him more loving." "Make her more outgoing." "Make them less angry." In these cases, I usually recommend spell work to encourage peace and cooperation in relationships, which can help soothe both parties.

People are reluctant to take accountability for their choice in a partner or for any discord that tends to follow them around in life. It is always easier to blame other people. Most feel it should be obvious that how their partner behaves does not fit into social norms and should be changed, and they will vehemently defend that perspective.

When people become frustrated with others, they will sometimes turn to magic. Rarely do they assume any level of accountability themselves. These requests may sound like "Make my family be more peaceful," "Change my energy-draining friends into good people," or "Make my sister-in-law less gossipy." Again, actively controlling the choices and behaviors of the people around you is a form of psychic attack.

Lastly, the one I really hate to hear…

Use Magic to Kill This Person

This lands on my professional doorstep far more than I would like. Even once or twice is way too much. Yes, there are ordinary people out there who are comfortable using magic to kill another person. Can I do it? Sure, it can be done. But the trick is that when you invoke Death to a person, it can take many forms. It might be death of their career, death of their relationships, death of their prosperity, death of their loved ones, or, yes, even their own physical death. When you work with Death, Death has the final say in how the situation is managed and how Death will intervene. It is like making a deal with a high-level mafioso who is likely making other deals behind your back that you do not know about, yet those other deals directly impact the one you are making.

People you would least suspect—school principals, dentists, musicians, insurance adjusters, retailers—approach me with the fervent desire to kill someone else with magic, all of it fully justified in their minds, of course. What is worse is that they do not just want it to happen—they want a front row seat to see it. These are people who would never dream of pulling a gun on a person, poisoning someone's coffee, or even hiring a hit man to do the job for them. The distance of killing with magical energy is somehow more acceptable. To their minds, I should have no trouble doing it with one candle and for a single payment of thirty-five dollars. That would make me the cheapest hit man on earth!

Although it is possible, I believe it is rare that magic alone kills a person. In theory, it could happen, and I do know people who I feel were killed through the effect of sustained psychic attacks. For most aggressors who wish death upon someone who wronged them, the most they will get is conceptual invocation of Death into the victim's life. This brings the ending, or death, of prosperity, health, relationships, security, and so on.

This is a harsh and unforgiving curse to send to someone and I am frequently appalled by how cavalier people are about putting the idea onto the table. When we quickly and sometimes derisively dismiss the idea of a psychic attack as the cause of obvious symptoms, we must remember that this is what others see as legitimate conflict resolution, even to the point of killing off their adversary.

The amount of energy required to end someone's life is tremendous and exceeds what most people can manifest in their magical work. Wishing for someone's demise sends high levels of toxic energy in their direction so it will have an effect, but likely not the expected one. Those wishing for such an outcome should consider that invoking Death to resolve problems they have with someone resembles the invocation of concepts such as justice and karmic return. A person cannot come out of that kind of spell work without receiving some of the energy themselves.

People who would never dream of slapping another person, working to get them fired, or intentionally causing the breakup of a relationship in the mundane world get very excited about doing the same thing through magic. In their eyes, their hands do not get dirty and they have no accountability in the downfall of their victim. In fact, they are likely smiling at the victim every day in "real life" and acting as though they have no malice toward them. Controlling another person through magic is far more common than cursing, hexing, crossing, or any of the other types of attack.

CHAPTER SIX

SELF-CROSSING

Aside from what others might do to you to cause psychic trauma, unfortunately you must also consider what you do to yourself. Even the most evolved and enlightened of us are perfectly capable of effectively screwing up our own lives and creating untenable situations through our misguided choices.

In chapter 2, I put forth my observation that misfortunes happen in life and are not always caused by a curse or hex, despite what the more dramatic of us might like to believe. Sometimes you repeat the same unhealthy cycles in life because at your deepest core, you either do not realize you are causing the trauma through your choices or you do not want to change your life badly enough.

It is delicious and seductive to believe that outside forces cause the problems in your life rather than your own screwups. People love it when accountability is removed and when someone says, "It isn't your fault." There is no denying, however, that sometimes it *is* your fault that your life is a mess. Sometimes, we cross ourselves.

Why Jump to Psychic Attack?

So why are some people so quick to believe they are cursed? The most obvious clue that pushes people to decide they are under attack is the realization that they are not living the life they want to live. They experience symptoms or conditions that are painful, uncomfortable, and disappointing. For many people, blaming their misfortune on outside forces or unseen enemies is far easier than considering that perhaps the suboptimal life they are living is caused by their own choices. It takes strength and self-awareness to acknowledge such a thing.

As an example, someone close to me was having a run of bad romantic relationships. During one of our conversations, she wailed at me, "Why do all of the men I love turn out to be alcoholics?" My answer to her, "Because you pick them up in *bars*," was not well received, but it does perfectly illustrate my point.

People often do not want to know the truth, especially when it involves culpability on their part. Imagine what a relief it would have been for her if I had said, "Because you have a family curse that keeps you from finding happiness in love. Here, let's clean you out. Then the next man you meet will be your true soul mate."

After hearing my actual response to her dilemma, I would love to say that she paused and said, "You know, you're right! Why didn't I see it before?" Instead, she continued to look for love in all the wrong places and now, fifteen years later, she still does not have a satisfying, fulfilling romantic relationship. Her solution was not to change her behavior, but to stop asking me for romantic advice.

When you experience a series of challenging events (all at once or sequentially), emotional exhaustion keeps you from thinking clearly and turns you into that frog in the pot of water on the stove that keeps getting hotter and hotter. Whether someone is attacking you or not, when you are in a downward spiral it is difficult to figure out what to do. There are times when you are your own worst enemy and create negative outcomes, no matter how hard you try to make good choices. You owe it to yourself to be fearless in pursuit of the life you wish to live.

In my role as a life coach, I have helped literally thousands of people strategize their way out of some of the most difficult circumstances imaginable and go on to live joyful, fulfilled lives. It is not easy, but it is worth it. A bonus is that the more you clean up the manageable parts of your life, the easier it is to notice when a psychic attack sends things out of whack.

If your house is always a wreck with things strewn everywhere, drawers open and rifled through, and stuff pouring out of the closet, how can you tell if someone broke in? Likewise, the more you clean up your life, the easier it is to immediately know when you are under attack.

Uncrossing Your Life

What if your life is such a mess that you do not know where to begin? Trust me, you are not alone, and I have been there more than once myself. Have you heard the old joke "How do you eat an elephant?" The answer is "One bite at a time." Basically, you just get started. Here are some suggestions that can help almost anyone uncross themselves and banish ongoing misfortune.

Banish Complacency

If you are a functioning, rational adult and you wake up one morning with the moment of clarity that your life is not what you want, you have to admit at some point that you were complicit in letting your life become what it has. You do not, however, need to remain complicit one moment longer. I am not saying all changes happen overnight, but all changes *do* happen in your head before they happen in the outside world. Once you dedicate yourself to the changes, the Universe will rise up to help make those changes happen, provided they support your greatest good.

When you show your willingness to release what does not best serve you, the Universe says, "That's all I needed to hear" and gets busy. That does not mean you are off the hook as far as pulling your own weight and doing your part to make the necessary changes, but it does mean you will have Universal support in doing so. "As above, so below" in this case means that the Lord helps those who help themselves, and when your best future is on the line, wow— when you give a little, you get back a *lot*.

Stay Awake

Once you are awake and aware in your moment of clarity, do not go back to sleep. Journal about the changes you know are necessary. Talk to people who are loving and supporting. Keep the vibration high and stay on task. Truly banish that complacency that allowed you to be where you do not want to be.

Expect Setbacks

Overall, once you make the authentic decision to move forward, you will likely see a gradual or even sudden improvement. When you have an off day or you realize that you made choices that work against your goal, do not give up and do not fall into a pit of despair and self-loathing. Instead, understand that you thought and behaved a certain way for long time, long enough to get to where you are, and it is natural to relapse occasionally.

This is when you should reread your journal entries from when you were motivated and moving in the right direction to give yourself a pep talk. Do not let the setbacks get you down. Dust yourself off and immediately get back on the right track.

Do not expect everyone around you to support the changes you want to make. You might think that those who love you would be excited when you move forward, but sometimes they are the very ones benefiting from how you were before. If the changes you make inconvenience others, expect some pushback. Stay strong, stay firm, stay loving, and stick to your guns.

That brings us to ...

Banish Toxic People

Unfortunately, sometimes the people closest to you are the ones who keep you emotionally unhealthy and cause some of your incidental crossings. When you audit your life, it is important that you carefully assess everyone around you and the effect they have on your energy. One of my mentors told me that the best gauge of how a person impacts your energy is how you feel when you walk away from them. Do you feel happy? Uplifted? Encouraged? Or do you feel drained? Discouraged? Exhausted?

You are influenced by the people around you. My husband Eric says, "If you are the smartest person in the room, then you are in the wrong room." Are the people around you the ones you wish to emulate? We take on, validate, and encourage the behavior of people with our mere presence.

Keep the people around you who make you feel glad they are in your life after you have been with them. Don't rely on the glamour of memory. Spend time with people who make you feel proud and supported. If someone routinely causes you to feel embarrassed or as though you must apologize for their behavior, then they need to go.

What behaviors do you endorse in others through your complacency? Even if you wince or admonish someone when they misbehave, remaining close with them says you condone how they are in the world. Even the law acknowledges the complicity of a person who is present when an illegal act is committed: guilt by association. Energetically, the same goes for noncriminal behavior.

If you cringe at the way people around you treat others but believe they will never treat *you* that way, you are kidding yourself. If they gossip *to* you and *with* you, they will gossip *about* you. If they have a long list of people who have wronged them, eventually you will have a starring role on that list. Drama addicts, martyrs, users, takers, abusers, and guilt-trippers all willingly participate in unhealthy relationship dynamics. When someone repeatedly shows you their bad behavior, trust what you are seeing and get away.

Remove toxic people from your life when they negatively affect you to an untenable degree. When you feel your spirit suffering from their presence, you must honor yourself and them by letting those people go. You do not have to allow others to make you feel miserable and depleted, no matter who they are. This includes people who helped raise you, who did kind things for you, or who financed you in some way. You have the sovereign right to decide who gets to be in your life and influence the energy around you.

Be prepared, however, because people do not appreciate being banished. In a perfect world, you could intervene with your friends' destructive behaviors and explain to them exactly why you are uncomfortable, and that conversation could turn into a teachable moment. In most cases, however, you will be dealing with people who are set in their ways and have talked themselves into validating their own behavior, so they have a deflecting argument spring-loaded for such a conversation. More than likely, toxic people will turn things back on the accuser so that they become the victim. They are able to do this by having the same conversations with themselves enough times to come up with arguments that legitimize their choices.

If you have the time and emotional bandwidth to fight the good fight, then I am right there with you, applauding like mad. For myself, however, I have found that my energy is better invested elsewhere. You do not ever have to succumb to emotional blackmail and allow an abusive person to remain in your life. It is your choice and your power that allows someone the honor of being present for you.

If you choose to release someone, there is no need for a huge confrontation or blow up. Drama does not have to come into it. Most toxic people lose interest in those who are not feeding their needs. Use your knowledge by making yourself unavailable when a toxic person tries to engage with you. They want to gossip? Change the subject. They are rude to the waiter? Excuse yourself and leave. They want you to run endless errands for them? Make yourself unavailable. The less accessible you are to fulfill their needs, the faster they will lose interest all on their own and move on to someone whose currency in the world is over-giving.

For the toxic people whose presence you cannot eliminate, such as bosses, relatives, or neighbors, you can simply reestablish the distance between you. Back off and limit your availability, mentally pushing them to the outer circle of your attention. Be less available for text messages, phone calls, or in-person contact. Just say no—or say nothing at all.

The more you surround yourself with people you admire who uplift and support you, the more toxic people will fall by the way-side. And just in case no one else has ever said this to you, you are under no obligation to let others abuse you, whether they are your partner, your child, your parent, or your friend. No one is entitled to be in your life, no matter who that person is.

Banish Damaging Language

The way you speak greatly impacts how your brain processes the world and your experience in it. The Universe listens and affirms what you say. What you pay attention to is what the Universe will give you more of every single time. For this reason, you should avoid catastrophic, dramatic language: "This is killing me." "I am ruined." "This is absolutely the worst thing that could happen." "I have no choice." The more you solidify the negative aspects of any situation, the more power they will have over you.

Absolutes are also a way that you box yourself in and limit your ability to change your circumstances: "I can never love again." "You always hurt me." "I never get a break." "As soon as I have a win, I always lose everything." Each time you say "always" or "never," the Universe believes you and reinforces that statement.

You can turn your entire perspective around with the words you use to define your circumstances: "This hurts profoundly, but love is still out there for me when I have grieved enough." "This is really challenging, but I know the Universe has something amazing in store for me." "I have had some wins and losses, but every time I lose, I always win again." Each of these perspective changes shifts you from a position of being the victim to a position of power and faith.

Likewise, you should talk about what you want, *not* what you do not want. Life is like a garden. You do not go out into the garden and plant "not corn" or "not tomatoes." Again, the Universe hears and reinforces the nouns in your sentences. "I feel like I will always live in poverty" boils down to "poverty," and the Universe says, "I got your poverty right here!"

If you change the nouns in your sentences to what you want, you raise the vibration around you. "I am attracting abundance. Abundance is coming!" feels much different than "I don't understand why I am still so poor. I guess I will always be broke," and yet both of those sentences can apply to the same person with an overdrawn bank account.

Structure your sentences to focus on what you want to bring in, not what you want to leave behind. How often do you hear someone say, "I deserve ..." and then go on to state what they want to have happen in their life? It implies some sort of arbitrary entitlement. "I deserve to be happy." Well, apparently not, based on the evidence. "I deserve to be treated with respect." Do you? The word *deserve* sounds like a petulant child demanding what they want and cannot justify.

I am all for replacing *deserve* with the words *have earned*. To use the words "I have earned ..." you must evaluate whether, in fact, you have earned what you are asking to receive. Have you earned the right to be happy? Have you earned respect? *Earned* implies that you put in your time, did all the leg work, and now are entitled to the reward.

Choose the words you use carefully. Through simple changes, you can totally reconstruct the energy around your life that keeps you mired in dissatisfaction and frustration. You can build a life filled with joy and promise.

Banish Unhealthy Attachments

When I perform an energetic cleansing on someone, I frequently find hooks and attachments to the past. These usually come from toxic relationships and old traumas that the client never resolved. Many people live focused on the past, not facing toward the future. They define themselves and their current relationships based on atrocities committed by their family members, former partners, or other associates. Their narrative is not about what they have accomplished in life, but instead what others have done to them.

This mindset keeps the person from having any sort of present experiences because they are not plugged in to what is happening now. It also removes their own power and advantage in any set of circumstances. They are obsessed with past grievances. Everyday experiences are only significant for how they pertain to events of the past. Their current relationships mirror or are informed by their previous relationships. Likewise, they have no future except the fear of replicating those toxic relationships in new people they meet. This is a self-fulfilling prophecy. Because their focus is so strongly on those long-past relationships, they draw in the exact kind of energy they want so desperately to resist.

What most people fail to understand is that the energy required to hold on to grudges and fear from the past gives incredible power to the abusers. People feel the ties they have to others. Think about when someone breaks up with a partner and the one who was left waits and pines. Usually, their partner does not return, but the minute someone else catches their attention and they begin a new romance, the partner who left them suddenly comes back around again. Why?

The reason is that while the person who was abandoned waited, prayed, and cried, there was an active energy line between the two of them. The person who left got a payoff in knowing that they were missed, whether or not they consciously acknowledged it. As soon as that energy line dropped, the first partner felt the loss of connection and needed to reestablish contact.

It is the same with abusers. When you hate them, when you let those toxic experiences control your present and your future, you create an energy line to your abusers. This is the "hook" that mires you in the past. The cure for hate is not love, it is indifference. Hate is a known powerful force. Love is a known powerful force. Indifference is a painfully underrated powerful force that will kill off either love or hate.

I see fear in the eyes of clients when I tell them that the only way they can release the hold the past has on them is to forgive. They believe forgiveness must involve the abuser. They believe forgiveness condones what the abuser did. They believe forgiveness lets the abuser off the hook. What forgiveness actually does is allow the victim to dislodge the hook and walk away. Forgiveness is not freedom for the abuser—it is freedom for the victim.

Those you forgive do not ever have to know you forgave them. Forgiveness lets the energy line drop and deprives the abuser of any further power over the victim. You can frame your forgiveness however you choose. For example: "I hate that you were not able to love me and take care of me like a parent should. I hate that somehow in your life, you learned that abusing people is how to gain power. I am releasing you because I do not believe you have the capacity to be better than you were and that does not fit in my life. You cannot have further power over me."

When I remove hooks from the past for a client, I have them talk about the abuse while I run my hands over their body, looking for places that are especially hot or cold. This tells me where the hooks connect to them energetically. I then use a sacred blade and ritualistically cut the line that binds them to the abuser by pushing the edge of the knife blade along their body. I have them exhale forcefully as I do this to release the energy, then I push the blade of the knife against the energetic wound to cauterize it.

A person can also choose to release an abuser from their past by writing them a letter, detailing the effects the abuse had on them and their life, and then burning it. The person then says that as it burns, so does the attachment.

Sometimes I am called to treat a person who has a powerful attachment to the past not because they were abused, but because they were the abuser. Some people are unable to move past the guilt they feel over choices and behaviors from the past that harmed others. It is a horrible life sentence to feel you are not entitled to happiness because of the sins of the past. Sometimes, the person you must work the hardest to forgive is yourself.

Banish Petty Behaviors

If you have doubts about where to start cleaning up your side of the street, here are some suggestions that may or may not apply.

- **Gossiping:** Speaking ill of others not only puts more negativity out in the world, but it shows others that you must cut down other people and spread rumors to amplify your worth. It demonstrates untrustworthiness and a willingness to engage in bashing someone behind their back. It serves no positive purpose other than to bind together people who support one another in this vicious practice. Make it a goal of yours to never say something about anyone that you would not actually say to their face.

- **Chameleon Shifts:** Have you ever known someone who changes who they are based on the people they are around at the time? Do not be that person. Find your own truth, develop your own way of being, and stand firm in it. Do not weaken to emulate the people around you just to blend in and pursue acceptance. Instead, be the one other people want to emulate.

+ **Whining:** No one, absolutely no one, enjoys a complainer or those who belabor a difficult situation by ongoing whining. There is no greater wet blanket than the person who evokes the response of "We are *all* hungry! We are *all* tired!"

+ **Interrupting:** This is the height of disrespect, and people do it more often than they realize. Interrupting someone else sends the message "Forget what you were saying. What I have to say is more important!"

+ **Competing:** Life is not a contest. The only competition you should have is to be a better person than you were before. When you compare your life, your successes, and your losses to those around you, it robs each person of their own experience.

+ **Resenting:** This is common for people who get their power and define their worth through martyrdom. Resentment comes from refusing to embrace your own power in a situation. A mentor of mine used to say, "Never agree to do something you are going to later resent." Just say no and save the other person from enduring your seething resentment.

+ **Humiliation Humor:** Humor at the expense of someone else is not funny; it is mean. It's yet another form of cutting others down to make yourself feel bigger. Unfortunately, it is common today, and it is far more tolerated than it ever should be. I promise you that if you participate in humiliation humor, you will hurt someone. Choose not to participate and see how that impacts others' behavior.

Reclaim Your Power

Taking positive steps toward wholeness can require healing and even grieving. Removing the effects of a psychic attack dredges up unexpected emotional fallout. And for all the good it does, it puts you face-to-face with some of the internal demons you might wish to ignore.

When recovering from psychic attack (and when getting your life in order in general), it is essential that you step into your own power and take responsibility for your choices and outcomes. The challenge is that when you accept accountability for your outcomes, you have no one to blame but yourself for your circumstances. The good news is that you then have the power to change whatever is not working in your life.

Yes, people might harm you, but how you respond to that harm is completely within your control. You decide how far you let that abuse knock you down and how long you stay there.

While some of what we discussed in this chapter may not sound like anything related to a psychic attack, what happens in the energetic field of a person who condones, participates in, or is the victim of some of the behaviors described here is very similar to the impact of a psychic attack. Exposure to concentrated negativity is the instigating and destructive force, whether it comes from petty behavior, unhealthy attachments, or a full-force curse.

PART THREE

IDENTIFYING AN ATTACK

───────◆───────

CHAPTER SEVEN

IS THIS AN ATTACK?

Recognizing and verifying a psychic attack is a tricky undertaking since the symptoms mimic medical conditions, substance abuse, and simple bad luck. This ambiguity of diagnosis allows curses, hexes, and crosses to persist, affecting prosperity and happiness, while hiding in plain sight, disguised as ordinary conditions. In most cases, it is the sheer persistence of the effects that causes the victim to seek help.

Since you now know that hexes, curses, crossings, and incidental attacks can all create the same effects and appear as common misfortune and life derailment to the untrained eye, how can one tell which form of psychic attack they are suffering from?

Fortunately, the treatment is the same for any of those circumstances, so you really do not need to know what kind of attack it was, who sent it, or how it was done. You only need to know how to effectively manage it. The only true benefit to knowing any of those other bits of information is that it could possibly help prevent a recurrence.

In my practice, I am on the front line, going to battle with energies every day on behalf of my clients. This makes me a prime target for hexing, cursing, crossing, entity infiltration, and all manner of attacks, so I am well positioned to describe to someone what a psychic attack feels like, having experienced plenty of them myself.

Most energy workers have sufficient experience working with their own energetic field that they quickly notice when something is awry. There are techniques anyone can use to shield themselves from incoming energies, but those methods get in the way of effectively feeling a client's energy. For myself, I need to be present and plugged in to the energy to manipulate it the way I want to, which means that I must be unshielded when I step into the arena. Anything else feels as comical and ineffective as trying to do battle while trapped inside a gigantic hamster ball or while wearing oven mitts.

Energy workers often network to help one another. There are four energy workers who have their practices in my shop and we all will reach out to one another and say, "I think I picked something up. Can you clean me?" If your vocation puts you in the energy field of another person, you are subject to any contaminants that might be in there. Physical healers such as acupuncturists and chiropractors are quite vulnerable to attack. If you are a healer, I encourage you to establish a support system that allows for a trained set of eyes and hands to work on you when the situation calls for it.

I cannot count the number of times I have caught a psychic attack, whether deliberate or incidental. When this happens, I call one of my apprentices to come clean me out using the exact procedures described in this book. It is much like being a zookeeper who expects they will get bitten from time to time.

What Does an Attack Feel Like?

We will discuss at length the list of symptoms that often accompany a psychic attack, but people often ask me what it *feels* like as opposed to what it *looks* like. If you are familiar with your organic energy, it will be easier for you to feel foreign energy. Regular meditation can help a person discover what is their organic energy and what is foreign to them, regardless of whether someone sent them the foreign energy or they picked it up in the world incidentally.

Because I have endured many magical attacks—both from my involvement and presence in a client's energetic field and from the counterattacks of those who want the attack to remain in place—I can quickly recognize the feeling of being affected by intrusive magic. To me, most psychic attacks feel pretty much the same: a generalized feeling of hopelessness, fear, frustration, and, sometimes, panic.

Psychic attacks feel like everything you are doing to improve your life is actually setting you back several paces, and no matter how hard you try, you never catch a break. It feels as though life is punching you in the face repeatedly and you are losing everything that you trusted and held dear. It is as if the Universe has you by the forearms and is whacking you in the head with your own hands while saying, "Stop hitting yourself! Stop hitting yourself!"

Psychic attack is like waking up to find your house on fire and being forced to quickly decide whether to put out the fire or run. Sometimes, it is intense enough that you just want to lie down in the fire and let it consume you because resisting it seems too daunting. Everywhere you turn, a new misfortune or obstacle appears. Even the strongest, most confident people who fall under psychic attack may feel scared, violated, disempowered, and vulnerable.

If allowed to fester, psychic attack can reach the point where you wake up after another restless night's sleep and think, *I wonder what will go wrong today.* Eventually, you watch helplessly as assured opportunities dry up. Your relationships suffer because no matter how carefully you try to express yourself to the people you care about, you say the wrong things and it results in tension. Every drop of pleasure dries up and there are no safe ports for you in the storm. Even those who want to comfort and reassure you end up saying words that feel empty or inadvertently cause hurt.

Unless a person is given to high drama and victimization, it may take a while to recognize that what they are experiencing is energetic rather than situational. The victim could sense that something feels off but might not begin to put all the pieces together until someone else expresses concern. Sometimes a person close to the victim is the first to observe that they are not quite being themselves and are acting out of character. The person who points out a behavior change may not consider that a curse, hex, or crossing is to blame; they may only notice that something is wrong. Other times, the person may think of psychic attack, although it can be challenging to broach the topic of psychic attack.

It is easier to see personality shifts from the outside if the person knows the victim's usual moods and behaviors. People are not always quick to notice the subtle changes in themselves and can easily write them off.

Specific Symptoms

There are certain symptoms that I look for to indicate psychic attack. Among them are emotional and mental changes that are atypical for the client and have no obvious cause. The following symptoms are signals that a person might be under psychic attack *if the person is not normally given to these behaviors*:

+ Depression
+ A desire to self-harm
+ Feelings of helplessness, hopelessness, and worthlessness
+ Fear
+ Paranoia
+ Feelings of doom
+ Feeling powerless
+ Extreme loss of confidence and loss of feelings of security
+ The sudden onset of victim mentality

If a normally upbeat person's beloved father dies, their dog runs away, and their spouse leaves them, it is reasonable that they could be depressed. If a person has a long history of clinical depression, they may be cycling through another down time. If, however, a person is not usually given to bouts of depression and they suddenly develop a desire to self-harm or begin feeling that life is horrible and they no longer have a will to live, a psychic attack may be the cause.

Most people who routinely experience various forms of psychic attack notice a specific symptom that they develop when they are under attack. My own tell is the last symptom listed, the onset of victim mentality. My organic personality does not engage in victim-thinking, and when I begin to hear words coming out of my mouth and thoughts moving through my head that are from a victim perspective, I immediately know that I have picked up an energetic contaminant.

Rarely will a victim of psychic attack experience the entire list of symptoms. An objective evaluation of the list of additional symptoms that manifest during a psychic attack shows that a cold, flu, chemical imbalance, substance abuse, or other physical maladies could cause the same reactions. This is how most psychic attacks are effectively explained away, and thus never properly managed.

Because so many of the symptoms of psychic attack are indicative of routine medical issues that are easily treated, the victim may go through multiple rounds of testing and treatment, only to find that the symptoms do not resolve or quickly return. This may result in a medical doctor determining that the patient's symptoms are psychosomatic and have no legitimate basis, which further delays the treatment process and adds to the patient's anxiety and frustration.

Severe, Unshakable Fatigue

This may manifest as chronic insomnia that leaves the victim exhausted and yet unable to achieve any kind of restorative sleep. Alternatively, it could also present as excessive sleeping for many hours at a time or at odd times during the day. The victim may feel depleted, confused, disoriented, or unable to maintain focus. This otherworldly, displaced feeling interferes with cognitive function and can make it difficult to complete even simple tasks.

Another manifestation of this symptom is that the victim appears to sleep normally without obvious disruption but remains exhausted upon waking and never gains energy throughout the day.

Extreme Anxiety or Panic Attacks

Our ancestors were finely attuned to the energy around them and needed to be in order to survive. The ability to detect any threat around them kept them alive, and we have not lost that innate, primal alert system that tells us when we are at risk.

When you are under psychic attack, your higher self knows and reacts, putting the energetic system on full alert. This is one reason why victims have difficulty sleeping. Unfortunately, your conscious self is not conditioned to effectively interpret signals such as these and only understands that it sees no obvious reason for the heightened anxiety. The dissonance this creates in the mind, body, and spirit intensifies the feelings of panic and anxiety.

Symptoms that fall under this category include heart palpitations, extreme weakness in all of the body or parts of the body, vertigo and dizziness, tingling or numbness in the hands and fingers, a sense of terror or impending doom, clammy skin, profuse sweating, chills, chest pains, difficulty breathing, and feeling as if your body is out of control.

Nightmares

Often these dreams are of someone, especially an unseen nemesis, chasing or trying to kill the victim. The nightmares are usually quite vivid and remain in the victim's memory after they wake up. Night terrors, where a person wakes up in the middle of the dream and appears lucid yet is still locked into the dream, may occur, as may sleep paralysis, where the victim is awake and cognizant but unable to move.

Dream time is one of the portals your higher self uses to communicate with you. Unfortunately, it does so with symbolism, and we often take our dreams literally rather than as allegory. The feeling that you are under threat may manifest in your dream time faster than it hits your conscious thoughts, resulting in nightmares. Invariably, the higher self knows you are under psychic attack before your conscious self does and tries to warn you, but unfortunately, those selves speak different languages.

These panic and sleep disorder reactions are a spin-off of the "fight, flight, or freeze" response generated by the amygdala during times of crisis and threat. During a psychic attack, your conscious mind does not see any discernible threat and sends the message throughout your energetic system that all is well and you can stand down from red alert. Your subconscious, however, knows good and well that something is very wrong and is ringing all the warning bells, forcing the energetic system into hypervigilance.

During waking hours, we can usually talk ourselves off the ledge of panic, but at night, we are defenseless without the reassurance of placating thoughts, so the subconscious has a greater degree of control and uses that time to scream that something is wrong. Your system is flooded by stress hormones and your entire body reacts.

Inexplicable Coldness or Heat
This may present in one part of the body or throughout the entire body. Your body systems are a physiological and energetic wonder and more often than you realize, you have a physical reaction to an event occurring on a mental or spiritual level. This intricate trinity of health and life experience—the mind, body, and spirit—harmonizes in such a way that when one system is compromised on any level, the other systems react. When your energetic flow gets interrupted by congested toxic energies or other blockages, that part of the body may become colder or even warmer than the surrounding areas as the energy rushes to the traumatized area.

When the victim of a psychic attack is in a house or other building, there may be inexplicable cold and hot spots throughout the area, indicating places of dense energy externalizing from the victim. It would make sense that if a curse, hex, entity, or other infiltrate is lodged in the person's energetic system it would stay there, but just like a sneeze or cough can carry germs into the air, the aura of a person, which extends for several inches around the body, can also carry the toxic energies.

Continuing with the comparison to germs, a person who is under psychic attack can leave traces of the attack in areas they frequent, such as bed linens, workstations, and vehicle interiors. This can cause unusual hot or cold pockets in those places.

Severe Headaches

Headaches often manifest from fatigue, anxiety, or stress resulting from the crises a psychic attack can produce. In my practice, I have noticed that one of the first things a person who is in crisis forgets is to drink adequate amounts of water, so headaches might also develop due to dehydration.

On an energetic level, a person who is under psychic attack is processing energy and impulses that do not belong to them and that on its own can cause headaches, especially in the base of the skull near the cervical spine, radiating upward toward the top of the head.

A favorite place for hexes and curses to set up shop is in the seven chakras of the energetic field: the root chakra, the sacral chakra, the solar plexus chakra, the heart chakra, the throat chakra, the third eye chakra, and the crown chakra. Another frequent target is the base of the skull. If the attack centers anywhere from the shoulders up, it could cause head pain.

Other Severe, Localized Pain

In addition to headaches, the victim may feel pain, sharp or dull, in the chest, solar plexus, stomach, or intestinal area. The solar plexus chakra is your place of personal power and the sacral chakra governs your passion, motivation, and the reproductive organs. These are prime targets for curses, spells, and hexes to take hold, and physical symptoms may manifest in those areas if the attack centers directly on these power points.

If the attack targets relationships, the victim may have chest pains or shortness of breath. If the person's self-confidence or passion is at risk, they may have stomach or intestinal pains. Women may experience uterine cramps or menstrual abnormalities. I have even seen long-menopausal women experience a menstrual period while under psychic attack. Erectile dysfunction is also common in men when they are attacked, especially if the root chakra is targeted.

Shaking and Trembling

The primal instincts we discussed in the section on anxiety and panic attacks can cause rushes of adrenaline as the "fight, flight, or freeze" response engages. This is the same response that causes people who are intensely frightened or excited to tremble.

Psychic attack ignites these feelings of hypervigilance and even though you see no sign of threat on the outside, the energetic system reacts to release the adrenaline through shaking. The victim may also tremble from lack of restorative sleep and overall exhaustion.

Animals Behaving Strangely

Animals are sensitive to energetic shifts, particularly those that are threatening. This is especially noticeable when a pet is closely bonded with its beloved human and feels protective of them. If you fall victim to a psychic attack, animals around you may begin to behave out of character. Some may be clingier and needier, hovering around you as if you are ill. Others may pace, resist affection when they were otherwise loving, or even refuse to eat or go certain places in the home where they were previously comfortable.

Chances are good that your furry friend will sense something is amiss before you do, so pay attention to the signals they send and trust what you see. If you notice your pets behaving strangely, scan yourself for other signs of psychic turbulence or foreign energies.

Sudden Bad Luck

A series of unexpected, inexplicable, and seemingly unrelated health, financial, and/or relationship problems is, in my experience, the most common manifestation of a psychic attack. As mentioned before, yes, sometimes a person has a run of bad luck that is not the result of anything other than life course correction or motivation from the Universe to do something different from what they are doing. In some cases, however, a person's life going sideways can be traced back to when they cut ties with an especially volatile person, broke up with an obsessive partner, or had an otherwise negative interaction with someone.

I sometimes ask my clients, "When is the last time you remember feeling good about your life? When things were mostly good?" When they are in a relaxed, receptive spiritual space and can objectively look back on their history and follow the trail of destruction, sometimes they can identify an exact moment when the misfortune began. This may lead to an awareness of what event sparked the start of their problems and give us a better idea of how to effectively manage their cleansing and healing process.

Outward Appearances

After years of working with victims of psychic attack, I have developed a reliable sense for recognizing the type of attack a client is experiencing by their appearance and the feel of their energetic field. When I am training students and apprentices, one of the things I ask them to do when we are working with a client is to make notes of what they pick up from the client *before* we conduct the interview and the client describes their symptoms. The ability to work intuitively is a true blessing in these cases, but the inability to do so does not affect a person's capacity to help a victim. I work to cultivate these sensitivities in my students for their own benefit as well as for the benefit of their future clients.

When someone meets a psychic or other intuitive healer, they often expect that the person is reading them, causing them to feel exposed and vulnerable. Others actively invite the examination, eagerly asking, "What are you picking up? Do you get anything from me?" Some will even test us, saying things like "No, you tell *me*" when we ask how their day is going or how they are feeling.

Contrary to popular belief, psychics and intuitives are not "on" all the time. Just as a plumber does not whip out a tool bag and start repairing your sink when you have them over for drinks, psychics and intuitives usually shut down their abilities when they are not working and only open up shop when the situation calls for it.

Sometimes, I will be in a crowded room or elevator and sense that someone next to me is under attack. Instinctively, I want to ease away, but instead, I usually send out healing energy to them. Since they have not invited me to remove the infiltrate, it is not my place to invade their energetic field and start working on them or even to lean in like a co-conspirator and say, "Hey, buddy, is that an entity in your pocket or are you just happy to see me?"

In some reality shows, a medium or psychic will accost a stranger and tell them that a relative has a message for them or that they have spirits around them. This is the absolute height of arrogance and imposition and is far outside of the realm of professional behavior and discretion. Real mediums, psychics, and intuitives of integrity do not do that.

Long ago, when I worked in an Air Force hospital, a few of the ward nurses knew me well and would discreetly ask me to come visit a patient and "do the thing." This usually happened when they had a patient who was not responding to conventional treatment. I would go in and visit with the patient, usually under the premise of something relating to the administrative job I did in the hospital, and steer the conversation toward how they were feeling and what they experienced just before they were admitted to the hospital.

This was many years before I was formally trained as an energetic healer. I was doing what felt natural for me to do. I quickly learned that if I could gain the patient's trust enough that I could get them to share their experience with me, all I had to do was find a way to casually touch their arm, brush back their hair, or physically connect with them in some way and I could pull what I then saw as darkness out of them. I would pull the energy away and toss it to the floor, then touch them again and pull more energy away and toss it to the floor. Sometimes it was domestic assault; sometimes it was post-traumatic stress disorder or childhood trauma triggered by a recent event.

Without the benefit of direct training, I did not yet consider the ethical concepts of energetic privacy or whether it was an invasion for me to manipulate someone's energy without their knowledge or consent. To my mind, if the room, the person, and the world had less darkness when I left it than it did when I walked in, I was doing the right thing. Like in so many other areas of life, as we become older and more experienced, our perspective shifts.

Fortunately, I never had a patient think I was making a pass at them or accuse me of inappropriate behavior. Usually, they were grateful for the company and the physical gesture of kindness and, almost always, their condition began to immediately improve.

When I look back now, I can see how those years of working in the hospital and the trust the nurses showed me prepared me for what I now do. Sometimes when I interview a client, I will ask if I can hold their hand, or I will casually touch their arm or knee in a comforting way as they speak. This helps me sense what is going on inside them.

During the interview portion of treatment, I also take extensive notes, partly because I am working between the worlds at that time and I want to make sure I am tracking what the client actually says in addition to the information I receive intuitively from them and from my spirit guides. There have been many times that I wrote down a bullet point about a client during the intake interview only to have them later say they never told me that. It can be difficult for me to recall whether information was spoken aloud or whether it came to me intuitively. Taking notes helps to anchor me in the "real" world and stay rooted in the experience while I process information from what the client says out loud as well as what I pick up from them in other ways.

Psychic attack is sensory. It has a smell, a low vibration that you can hear and feel if you attune to it, a dulling to the person's aura that you can see, and a sour, almost metallic taste that comes into my mouth when I am around it. You can feel the warm and cool places on the victim's body. You can sense the condensed energies bottlenecked in their lymphatic areas and the blocked areas where no energy flows. You can see that there is no sparkle of life or light in their eyes. Their face looks unusually slack and their skin tone is not vibrant or warm.

The victim of an intense or long-term psychic attack exudes fear, hopelessness, and pain as if it comes out of their skin pores. Their speech may be manic and scattered or slow and disjointed. They may tuck their appendages into their torso as if guarding their midsection, reluctant to unfold their bodies. They may have muscle tics and startle easily at unexpected sounds or sudden movements. The victims of psychic attack often *look* sick, which again makes it easy to presume a physical malady.

Understand that most rational people do not jump to the idea that they are under psychic attack. That consideration usually comes after ruling out multiple alternative causes for their symptoms and misfortune. Because it is not the first thought to come to a person's mind, by the time they seek out care, the attack is often years or even decades underway.

When you work with a victim of psychic attack, whether it is on a professional level or not, it is crucial that you treat them with dignity. It is hard enough to deal with the effects of the attack, but to also have to discuss the attack with others and work through the subsequent emotions in front of them is even more traumatic, especially for those who are not used to having "woo-woo" conversations. For many, the idea of a psychic attack is uncharted and highly suspicious territory, and it can be a challenge to get the victim to relax and trust you to handle their situation. For this reason, it is essential that a person who is under psychic attack (or suspects they might be) is treated with the utmost respect, compassion, and care.

PART FOUR

---◆---

MANAGING
THE ATTACK

CHAPTER EIGHT

WHAT CAN I DO?

Considering psychic attack by definition and through the qualifiers established in previous chapters, it is easy to see that most people will experience an attack (likely multiple attacks) throughout their lives. You must sweep your floors, wash your dishes, and get your teeth cleaned and, likewise, you must regularly clean out your energetic system. When you suspect that you are under active attack, it is even more essential that you have a complete energetic cleansing to remove the contaminants.

When you get to the critical point of seriously considering the idea that you are under psychic attack, it is important that you respond quickly, always remembering that if you are *not* under attack and treat the symptoms as if you are, you will not do any damage. If anything, the removal of negative energies around you, including stress and anxiety, could cause you to have greater clarity about your circumstances and provide better insight for how to manage your difficulties.

What follows is a technique I have used for decades for managing both psychic attack and general life cleanup. Whether removing a curse or banishing toxic people and unhealthy patterns from your life, this is a solid framework for structuring out your approach.

IOB Techniques

For years, I have used what I call the IOB method of problem-solving, and it applies beautifully to the management of psychic attacks of all kinds and also to the life strategy issues discussed in chapter 2. IOB stands for Identify, Objectify, and Banish. You can use IOB on almost any task that requires organized management.

1. **Identify:** List symptoms, determine the threat level, and name the problem.
2. **Objectify:** Lose emotion, come up with a plan, and go into management mode.
3. **Banish:** Remove anything that does not support your goal.

Identify the problem, objectify the problem, and banish the problem. Here's an example:

1. **Identify:** Victim has ongoing misfortune, malaise, and thoughts of self-harm that may be a psychic attack.
2. **Objectify:** I set up a sacred space and cleanse the victim.
3. **Banish:** We do an energetic cleansing to remove the attack, then reparations toward healing begin.

Identify

First, identify the problem by establishing a list of facts and symptoms. What exactly is happening, in the simplest of terms?

If needed, use divination such as pendulum work or tarot readings to discern between psychic attack, poor life choices, or a combination of the two. Cards such as the Devil, the Tower, the Three of Swords, Five of Swords, Seven of Swords, Eight of Swords, Nine of Swords, Ten of Swords, Five of Cups, Five of Wands, Nine of Wands, and Five of Pentacles tend to show up during psychic attacks.

Identify the problem. Give it a name. Write it down. Say it aloud to make it more real. Write in a journal in a stream of consciousness fashion if you cannot put your finger on the actual issue. What needs to change? What feels out of place and off-kilter?

Talk to a trusted adviser who knows you well and who will give you a solid answer on why they feel your life is off the rails. Do not talk the situation to death. Do not confide in nine or ten different trusted friends, going through folks until you get the answer you want. Find one or two people who will speak frankly with you and who love you enough to want you to be successful.

You do not have to be wise at this point. You do not have to have a solution—not even one thought of how to fix things. You only need to fearlessly move forward, willing to turn over every rock and look in every shadow for the true source of your unhappiness. Be painfully honest with yourself and identify how you feel. Experience the emotions running through you and give them a name. Bookmark them for later use.

When you are brainstorming, use words like "I think ..." and "I feel ..." and "I believe ..." not "You never ..." or "You always ..." or "But you ..." Identify ... don't *you*dentify. This exercise is about your situation and how to best manage it. That involves stepping into your power and assuming responsibility for how things are. The challenges another adult faces in life come second to your challenges for the purposes of the identifying phase.

You can use tools such as the All Seeing Eye candle to help you dig out the truth. This may take some time to process, so be prepared for some thoughtful, bold investigative work into yourself and your life. Do not fear the emotions you go through during this time. Let them flow. Emotions are like weather: they pass, even if it is a particularly bad storm. Emotions are like water over rocks, water over rocks, water over rocks. This is the time to experience any fear, anger, guilt, or another emotion you have about a possible attack.

As most of you are likely aware, it is easy to identify glaring problems and immediate solutions—provided the person you are evaluating is someone else. As illustrated earlier in this chapter, objectivity is a valuable tool, but rarely can it be used effectively on ourselves. That is why an outside pair of eyes is always a great asset to the identification and healing process.

Identifying the attack is a tricky process. It must be approached with an open mind and open eyes. The sense of urgency to fix what is wrong can work against you, especially if circumstances are worsening rapidly for the victim. The good news is that once the identification process is completed, the treatment goes quickly. As stated earlier in this book, if you move forward into the treatment part of the process prematurely or without determining in advance if an actual attack occurred, that is perfectly fine. The practices that follow in the next chapters pose no threat at all to a person who is not under attack and can promote healing of non-attack maladies as well, so you can only do good with them.

Identification and confirmation of an attack is more for the benefit of knowing what you are dealing with rather than determining the method of treatment. What you want are results! You want the victim's vitality and vibrancy to return, their bad luck to turn to good, and their road to success to blow wide open and be free of obstacles. You want to get them breathing again, relieve the tension and anxiety they feel, and give them hope for a brighter future.

Sometimes all the victim needs is for someone to listen and care without judgment or criticism. It is the spiritual healer's place, and a true friend's place, to hold that space for them. I keep at least two boxes of tissues in my healing room because young or old, male or female, big and burly or small and frail, the tears will inevitably come. A coworker once called me the Barbara Walters of healers because my clients always cried at some point during the intake interview.

When you go through this identification process with a client in the healing room, you track their emotional readiness to enter the treatment phase. The interview begins to wind down energetically on its own, and you can feel when it is time to transition from conversation to action. That is when the management of the situation fully comes into play.

Do not get stuck in this phase. Experience your emotions and collect your underlying problem identification statement, such as "I believe I was psychically attacked" or "I need to make better friends"—whatever statement feels the most organic and correct to you after you have worked through an evaluation of the situation and your emotions about it is likely the correct one. When you have come up with an assessment that you believe to be accurate, it is time to dry your eyes, wash your face, and move on to the next phase.

Objectify
Once you have identified the problems and how you feel about them, your next move is to objectify the situation, meaning to

remove all emotion, especially fear or panic, and get to work. To accomplish this, you must plan and act, not sit and contemplate. *Now* you must be wise, clever, crafty, self-aware, shrewd, honest, and ruthless as you think about how you can solve the problem.

The transition into objectification is its own process and is an essential step to effective management of a psychic attack or other problem. You should not move forward if you still feel afraid, angry, sad, or otherwise controlled by your emotions. Remember that for best results, you should find a neutral position from which to continue, and objectivity is how you do it. Once you enter the objectification phase, you need to put on your grown-up pants, get real with yourself, and decide on a plan of attack.

To get to the necessary level of objectivity, it helps to imagine what you would tell a friend if they came to you with the same problem. What good advice would you give them? Show yourself the same compassion you would offer to someone you love who told you they were in the same situation, but at the same time, be as honest and forthright as you would be to someone who trusted your input and desperately needed assistance.

Go deeper and, like a war general, come up with a strategy for how to manage the problem. Your plans do not have to be reasonable or make sense right away. Keep throwing out ideas until you find one that seems plausible. Even the most ludicrous ideas may have substance when you break them down to their smallest components.

Think of the dynamics of a battlefield. The warrior who is in the heat of battle focuses only on swinging the sword and staying alive. There is nothing in that moment other than instinct, training, and fighting. Slay one enemy and two more advance. The warrior cannot strategize or objectify beyond the moment or think outside of the immediate conflict.

That responsibility goes to the general who is on the hill away from the battle, observing it from a distance. The general can see if another wave of enemy troops is advancing toward the battleground. They can tell which side is prevailing and which is losing. The warrior does not know if they are fighting the final enemy combatant or if fifty more are behind them; they are just swinging the sword and trying to survive. The warrior is identifying, the general is objectifying.

As with the identifying phase, it is essential that you avoid getting stuck in the objectifying phase. Analysis can lead to paralysis, and if you think the problem to death trying to find a management strategy, you never reach the place of true crisis management.

Come up with a plan of attack and move forward with confidence.

Banish

After you objectify, move on to banishing. In the case of psychic attack, you banish any energy that does not belong to you so that you return to your own normal energetic baseline. Banish any entities, attachments, psychic turbulence, or other disruptive influences. Banish any hooks to past traumas and unhealthy relationships.

What you cannot banish, unfortunately, is the damage already done by the intrusive energies. You can prevent further damage from occurring, but simply removing the problem rarely fixes existing or past problems. For instance, if you banish the curse that caused your marriage to fail, removing the curse will not automatically bring back your spouse. If a hex caused you to lose your job and your home, those do not immediately come back to you. What removing the negative influence will do is clear the path to creating new and better circumstances for your life. Taking away the cause of the problem can improve damaged communications and strengthen failing connections.

Once you complete the objectifying phase, you will know or at least have a good idea of what to banish. If you go through the identify and objectify phases and the conclusion is that a psychic attack is likely, then move on to the banishment of that influence in your life. If you get through those phases and are still unsure about the validity of an attack, using the techniques that follow in subsequent chapters will produce no ill effects if there is no actual attack and may help with the stress and emotional fallout of other causes of your symptoms.

Self-Cleansing

There are many methods an individual can use to manage cleanup themselves, including bath products specifically made to purify, uncross, and spiritually cleanse, as well as Uncrossing candles, Reversing candles, and stones that drain away negativity or return it to its sender.

Protection products are also quite useful, but it is important to consider that amulets, candles, and other items intended to offer protection from psychic attack are not spiritual cleansers—they are protectors. So while they are just as important as the spiritual cleaning items, their function is entirely different.

When you suspect that you are under attack, taking self-cleansing measures right away can help alleviate symptoms and reduce the impact of the attack. To completely remove the cause of the attack and ensure a purified energetic system free from any sign of the attack, I fully recommend a spiritual cleansing that someone else performs on the victim. Just like tickling yourself, is it difficult to spiritually cleanse yourself. There is something about the union of two spirits working together on the effort that creates a synergistic effect, amplifying the cleansing process.

Because what happens inside of you feels familiar, it is hard for you to be objective about what you experience. Having another set of eyes on you, especially if that person has any talent or experience for following and managing energy movement, is incalculably helpful. Whenever possible, I try to use two additional apprentices during a spiritual cleansing so that there are three of us working on the client at once. Many times what one of us did not pick up on, one of the other two did, giving us a multifaceted operation that covers more territory than one person alone can manage, even if that one person is well trained.

For this reason, seriously…

Call for Backup

I highly recommend, whenever possible, that the victim seek out someone they can trust to assist them throughout the clearing and cleansing process. Ideally, this is a person with experience working with energetic systems who can intuitively follow the flow of energy. In a pinch, however, anyone who is supportive, calm, and open-minded can effectively assist. I have trained partners, neighbors, and friends with no healing experience to go through the process of spiritual cleansing, and they achieve good results almost immediately. The more people practice the techniques, the better the results will be.

Some healers, such as myself, are trained to conduct spiritual cleansings remotely, using proxy vessels in place of the victim. This is another option, but be sure to carefully investigate before giving money to a healer you do not know. There are many charlatans out there who will charge you hundreds or even thousands of dollars for the service. Most genuine healers are modest in their fee scale. Intuitive spiritual healing is *not* one of the fields where you "get what you pay for." Some of the most expensive healers out there are frauds, so follow your instincts carefully and do not give anyone money or credit card information until you have interacted with them and gotten a feel for their energy.

Most professional healers *will* charge for their services because of the energy exchange process. Reiki, for instance, traditionally requires a payment of some kind, although not necessarily money, to balance the energy exchange of the healing. Even though healers channel divine energy rather than using their own, I can tell you that healing a person is exhausting! Receiving an offering in return balances out the energy and keeps the practitioner from completely depleting their energetic resources.

One of the reasons using a professional energetic healer is desirable is that often your loved ones' concern for you gets in the way of unbiased healing, but a professional remains objective. Choose carefully when you bring someone else into the management and healing process. A good, experienced healer will have worked with similar cases frequently enough that they are not fearful or reticent about digging deep and finding each part, piece, and strand of the attack.

If you cannot get to a professional who specializes in spiritual cleansing, the next best thing is to have a trusted friend help you. Choose wisely. It should be someone not given to panic or doubt who can calmly and methodically handle the situation. Pick someone who can remain calm and supportive during a crisis and provide the comforting, confident presence you need at such a time. Obviously, you should choose a support person who will not balk at the idea of psychic attack, or you will end up teaching an entire lesson on the subject while you are under energetic siege.

Banish All Fear

I cannot stress enough that fear and panic will cause you to act rashly in any situation, but none more so than when you suspect a psychic attack. You need objective, deliberate action after you get over the initial emotional reaction. There is plenty of time to react and contemplate later. Treating a psychic attack requires a fearless approach of systematic detection, cleansing, and protecting. Both the victim and the healer must carefully guard and restrain their emotions, remaining neutral and calm. Approaching from a position of fear or panic intensifies reactions and feeds energy into the curse or hex, so a balanced, assertive perspective is necessary.

It is natural to feel afraid when you think you are under attack, and you certainly may feel afraid when your energies are out of whack and you experience bizarre symptoms. There are plenty of fear factors at work in a psychic attack. Unfortunately, the energy of most psychic attacks becomes stronger when fear is present. The activation of the fight/flight/freeze response when you are under attack puts your energetic system into high alert, and alarms sound throughout your mind, body, and spirit. You will notice that most of the specific symptoms listed in chapter 7 are stress-related symptoms that are a result of our natural instincts.

To get away from the science for a while and instead speak colloquially, psychic attacks feed on fear and get bigger, more powerful, and more destructive as the fear grows. Because energetic systems extend beyond the physical body to include the aura, a "bubble" of personal space, and intuitive scanning, the energy of your own psychic attack can pick up on the fear of people around you and absorb that as well.

If you think about it, anger and fear feel very similar in the body. People have the same responses to each: pulse quickens, breath changes, and there is a rush of adrenaline. With anger and with fear, the fight/flight/freeze response flies into action. Psychic attack feeds on anger just as easily as it feeds on fear, so when you transition from identifying the problem into actively managing the attack, you must banish your anger as well as your fear. You do not want the energy of the attack growing while you are trying to mitigate it, or else your efforts are as effective as trying to sweep a dirt floor. When you begin to work on the attack to clear it out and negate its ability to further damage the victim, you do so from a balanced, neutral approach. Your entire focus is on the victim, not on the sender, and your emotions must be controlled and level.

Even though psychic attack may have originated from malice, it is still only energy, and energy is malleable. All energy is neutral until it passes through the filter of intention. Take, for example, the energy in the form of electricity that runs through wires in the walls of your house. It has no emotion; it is neither good nor bad. People assign those human attributes to energy based on what it does. Energy can give you light for your home, cook your food, and activate your electronic entertainment devices. It can also electrocute you, burn down your house, or short-circuit your television. The goodness or badness attributed to the energy comes from how it affects our lives, not from an innate moral character of the energy itself.

Energy does what influencing factors tell it to do based on a complicated process of generation, conduction, and resistance. The energy that comes to us in a psychic attack is energy doing what it was told to do. Even if the push of the attack was negative, such as a crossing that comes from an outburst of anger, the energy itself is still just energy. The flavor of it derives from the emotion behind it.

Just like electrical energy, psychic energy is manageable and manipulatable. You can ground it, redirect it, and change it. The effective management of the energy of a psychic attack involves relocating the energy out of the client's energetic system and either grounding it or returning it to its original sender. When I went into hospital rooms and pulled darkness off of a patient and dropped it to the floor, I was removing and grounding energy that negatively affected a client.

There are techniques to purify and transmute the energy of the attack so that it helps the victim rather than causing harm. You can use sound, for instance, to reprogram the vibration of the energy. These seem like complex achievements, but they are really quite simple. You can use a three-tone chime and go from the largest bar to the smallest to raise the vibration of the energy, or chime from the smallest bar to the largest to lower the vibration. You can use a drum to stabilize energy. The sound of a rattle builds up energy. As with electricity, you must know what you want the energy to do instead of what it is currently doing.

In the case of an incidental entity, you simply move the entity from the client's energetic field to a different place where it cannot cause harm. Even though the entity itself is only energy, the effect it has on the client is negative, and, therefore, it must be rerouted (moved), transmuted, or grounded. The negative effect is why it is thought of as an energetic contamination.

When you manage psychic attack—either your own or someone else's—do not presume there is something to fear. Healers use terms like *demons*, *entities*, and *negative energies*, which sound scarier than they actually are. The idea that someone would intentionally launch a psychic attack on another person is frightening to consider, but it is equally sobering to imagine that someone is so emotionally out of control that they inadvertently conveyed an energetic attack through their outburst or seething. Fear the people who send attacks, but do not fear the energy. When you are managing psychic attack, you are engaging the energy, not the people. Dealing with the people can come afterward.

Stages of Response to Psychic Attack

In 1969, Swiss-American psychiatrist Elisabeth Kübler-Ross identified five stages of grief in her seminal book, *On Death and Dying.*[5] The five stages she posited are denial, anger, bargaining, depression, and acceptance. In a later work with grief expert David Kessler, she expanded that model to include other experiences of loss such as divorce, loss of employment, incarceration, addiction, infertility, and rejection.

In my practice, I see that most victims of psychic attack go through the same process, often within an hour's time of sitting on my consulting couch. At first they deny that psychic attack could be the cause of their problem, although many go through the denial process before they reach out to me. Once they become convinced of the attack, they get angry and want a cleansing. On the heels of the cleansing, they want revenge, after which they move on to bargaining, usually under the guidance of a professional healer. This usually sounds like "Fine, then we won't kill them. We will just return to them the energy they sent to me." Depression comes after they realize that removing the curse, hex, crossing, or entity is not going to undo the damage that was done by the attack but will only keep further damage from occurring. There is more work to do to achieve wholeness. Acceptance comes sometime later, when they begin having positive experiences and find themselves once more in a position of safety where they are free to pick up the pieces and craft the life they want to live.

By the time most people come to me for help, they are already well into the anger stage and will sometimes forcefully demand that I share the name of the person who did this to them and then launch a return attack. What I tell them is that I am a healer. If an

---

5. Elisabeth Kübler-Ross, *On Death and Dying* (London: Tavistock, 1989), 7.

emergency room doctor has a patient with a gunshot wound on his examination table, the doctor does not leave the patient to go looking for the person who shot them. Instead, the doctor treats the wound and makes sure the patient is safe. I am like an energetic surgeon. I use diagnostic tools and intuitive guidance to go into the energetic system of the afflicted person and find what is causing the problem, then I remove it. I provide aftercare instructions to make certain the victim stays safe, especially during the first month or so after treatment when they are more vulnerable to reattack.

CHAPTER NINE

PREPARING THE HEALING AREA

Psychic contamination, whether deliberate or incidental, is treated as dirt and filth picked up by the victim. Like energy, dirt is not inherently evil, but that doesn't mean we want it on our clothes or skin, and we certainly don't want it inside us. For the most part, psychic contamination is managed the same way a dirty house is cleaned: find the mess, clean it up, then try to prevent or quickly remedy further contamination. From here forward, the book presumes the victim found someone they can trust to help them perform the spiritual cleansing.

When you provide care for a person under psychic attack, you must do so in a sacred space conducive to effective energy manipulation. While this might sound lofty, it really is about setting a standard for energetic care. You would not dress a wound in a dirty cellar or with filthy hands; provide a level of hygiene when you work with a person's energy. Start by cleaning and preparing the space where the cleansing and healing will take place.

Cleaning the Working Area

Every energy worker has their own way to cleanse their healing area, and none of these ways is right or wrong. If the reader's inclination is to suggest "Couldn't you use ..." when reading the following suggestions, the answer is very likely "Yes. Yes, you could." This is not a comprehensive exploration of all the ways to cleanse and clear a sacred space, which could easily fill a book on its own. These are the most effective techniques I have found, and they are ones I use in my practice.

White sage is a common tool used to purify an area and is a valuable part of the process. Consider that different surfaces respond best to different types of cleaning depending on the use and density of the surface. Porous structures, such as feathers, fibers, and cloth, respond well to smoke and sprays. Denser materials like the altar surface, floors, and tools often require washes to release trapped negative energies.

Smudging

Smudging is the act of using the smoke of smoldering herbs—or, in the case of palo santo, wood—to purify the air. You can use white sage, sage brush, sweetgrass, cedar, juniper, or palo santo to perform a complete energetic cleanse of the area where you will treat the victim. If breathing issues or other restrictions prohibit the use of smoke, use a spray designed to energetically cleanse.

Smudging removes toxic and negative energies from the air around you. Hold fire to the herb or palo santo until it begins to smoke or *cherry* (having a strong red-orange glow to the surface) or place it on a hot charcoal intended for incense or hookahs. Move the smoking herb around the room you wish to purify, starting in an upper corner and carefully covering the entire surface of the room from top to bottom, ending in the same place where you began.

Sacred Sprays

Sacred sprays are commercially or personally prepared products used to cleanse and bless people, tools, and working spaces. Sprays are a wonderful compromise between smoke and washes. They are not as complicated or time-consuming to use as washes, and they are more penetrating than smoke.

Most nonaerosol sprays have an alcohol base, usually vodka, which is then infused with essential oils to create a specific effect. Some also have small stones in the bottle to further empower the spray. The alcohol base causes sprays to dry quickly rather than add dampness to the receiving item. You can use sprays on yourself, tools, altar cloths, carpet, draperies, and furniture. Be sure to check if a spray is non-caustic, fabric safe, and pet-friendly before use.

Sacred Washes

Smoke and sacred sprays cleanse the air, but I recommend going a step further and using products such as Four Thieves Vinegar and Chinese Wash to purify the structural area where you will work.

Four Thieves Vinegar and Chinese Wash are traditional Hoodoo products that, when used together, cleanse and bless the structure of a home in the same way that sage purifies the air. Most botanicas and magic shops that specialize in Conjure products carry some form of Four Thieves Vinegar and Chinese Wash. You can also make the products yourself using recipes easily obtainable on the internet. The beauty of Hoodoo products such as Four Thieves Vinegar and Chinese Wash is that there is a long list of acceptable substitutions, so acquiring the necessary ingredients is rarely a complicated process.

Four Thieves Vinegar smells like meat marinade, and you know you have an authentic product when you see a piece of garlic at the bottom of the container. Chinese Wash has a castile soap base that other ingredients are added to, much like in the preparation of Four Thieves Vinegar. Like Four Thieves Vinegar, Chinese Wash has a "tell" for whether it is authentic, and that is the presence of three broomstraws inside the bottle. The broomstraws must be from an unused broom, so I keep a straw whisk broom on hand and harvest my straws from it when I make my own Chinese Wash.

You can use Four Thieves Vinegar and Chinese Wash straight from the bottle or dilute them with hot water. The power of the product remains consistent even in its diluted state. The heat from the water seems to wake up the properties of the products even further. The usual dilution when using the product as a floor wash or cleanser is two tablespoons per gallon of hot water.

To use either product undiluted, pour it onto an unused sponge in the shape of a cross. Wipe the sponge across the surface you wish to cleanse and then load the sponge with product again as needed. Alternately, if you dilute the product, you can dip the sponge into a bucket or bowl of the mixture and wipe down the surface. I use the product straight if I am cleansing doorjambs and window frames, but I dilute it for washing floors or countertops.

Use the Four Thieves Vinegar first, then follow immediately with Chinese Wash, using the same sponge and the same process for each. After you finish, rinse out the sponge; you can use it for future spiritual cleansing of your home. Make sure to keep it separate from your everyday sponges. Do not use your spiritual cleansing sponge for mundane chores, and do not use your mundane sponge for spiritual cleansing.

When you have cleaned and prepared the working area, the next step is to clean the healer.

Cleaning the Healer

A ritual bath or shower puts you into a sacred mindset and removes any toxic energies that could contaminate the process. It aligns you with your divine powers and connects you to your higher self to hear the messages those powers relay to you.

There are many bath and shower products you can use to cleanse yourself for psychic battle. In your spiritual bath, use purifying and protecting agents such as rosemary, citrus, dragon's blood, sage, lemongrass, spearmint, or peppermint. You can use commercial bath products with these scents if you choose those with natural oil components. Whenever possible, use bath products prepared by a qualified and experienced energy worker. The influence of personal energy added to the manufacturing process is especially valuable when working on defensive magical techniques.

Take time to steep in the water, letting it absorb any residual fear, doubt, or pessimism. Let the ritual bath or shower purify you to be a vessel for divine energy that you will channel to the victim to remove the contaminant and purify them. Connect with your higher power and allow divinity to flow through you and guide you.

This step of spiritually cleansing is vital. You cannot effectively clean another person if you are not clean yourself, and connecting with whatever divine force is sacred to you stabilizes and empowers you for the cleaning process that is to come.

Healers should wear clothing that is easy to move around in and that does not get in the way. Long, flowing sleeves, for instance, can be dangerous to wear around fire and should be avoided. You should wear clothing that allows you to lift your arms all the way up and to stoop down easily. Some healers feel better connected to spirit if they work barefoot. Avoid wearing heavy colognes or strongly scented perfumes and oils.

Set Up a Healing Area

You have cleansed and readied yourself as well as the air and underlying structure where you will conduct the healing. Now it is time to turn your attention toward the deeper magical work. The way your healing space looks is based entirely on functionality, personal preference, and visual stimulation. What is magical to you? To the person you are healing?

This may sound like overthinking the process of spiritually cleansing a person, but it is essential that both parties, healer and victim, feel as though they are in a sacred, protected space for the work that is to come. Taking the time to effectively prepare the area helps everyone involved feel greater spiritual support and confidence during the coming work.

Consider what visual prompts create the necessary atmosphere of peace, healing, and confidence. Fresh flowers symbolize a new beginning. Stones, especially black ones, are effective at absorbing negative energy. Himalayan salt lamps help cleanse the air, boost your mood, and aid in restful sleep. Copal is the traditional incense to burn during a spiritual cleansing, but any incense that lifts your energy and does not negatively impact the client will work. Candles around the room lend energy and ambiance. You may wish to include statuary to represent gods, goddesses, angels, saints, the Blessed Mother, Jesus, or other protective forces. Your divine figures should have a place in the process, and your energetic connection with them is intensified by representations of them.

Many spiritual healings take place in a kitchen or outside in nature, so do not feel pressured to create a temple to work within sacred space. Sacred space is defined by what feels sacred to *you*. It should put you in touch with the higher powers you will access to effectively complete the cleansing.

Necessary Tools

Assemble all your supplies ahead of time. You do not want to leave the client and come back because you forgot an essential tool. For the techniques described here, you will need the following tools:

A Chair

Unless the victim has physical challenges, they will likely stand in an upright position for the cleansing. As the healing progresses, they may begin to feel faint or fatigued as their energy field is rearranged, so having a chair nearby allows them to rest and feel more supported if needed.

A Pendulum

The pendulum is used to evaluate the activity and response of the seven primary chakras. If you do not have a pendulum, there is no need to rush out and purchase one. You need a hanging pendant with a little weight to it, so a chain or corded stone or amulet are all good options. Your pendulum must be able to swing freely when you hold the chain or cord between your thumb and forefinger. A ring tied onto a string will work just fine if it has enough weight.

White Sage or Smudging Spray

I prefer to use white sage whenever possible, but if the victim is sensitive to white sage or the use of smoke is contraindicated, a cleansing spray works. Other purification herbs such as cedar, sagebrush, or lavender will work fine as well. These are used to clean the aura of the victim and, in the case of burning herbs, to detect areas of concentrated energy in the body.

Jar of Water

For this, you need a clean half-pint jar with a lid that is filled two-thirds of the way with water. It is best if the jar has smooth sides without engravings, labels, or embellishments because you will be looking inside of it later on.

Two Raw, Unbroken Eggs

The eggs should be at room temperature. At my shop, if we have several cleansings in a day and run out of room-temperature eggs, we healers pull them from the refrigerator and wear them in our bras to warm them up. Before we use the eggs on clients, we cleanse and reconsecrate the egg to make sure our own psychic flotsam and jetsam does not stay in the egg meant for the client.

The color of the eggshell is irrelevant. It does not have to be an organic or grass-fed egg. The eggs I use for cleansings come from the local Walmart in a five-dozen pack. They stay in the refrigerator until they are needed, keeping out only four or five at a time.

I recommend using two eggs in case the first one breaks during the cleansing, which happens occasionally.

Sacred Sprays

You can use Florida Water, Cut & Clear, Fiery Wall of Protection, rose water, holy water, or any other type of purifying spray you have on hand. I do not recommend using colognes or commercial air fresheners due to the high chemical content in them.

To make your own spray, fill a spray bottle with water or vodka (preferred). The vodka can be plain or flavored. Add a stone or two that you like (you will get it back unharmed when the spray is gone) and a few drops of your favorite essential oils, then shake well. I use a citrine stone, but amethyst, jasper, quartz, and obsidian also lend good energy to your mixture. Make sure your stone is water safe to preserve its integrity. Selenite, for instance, is a powerful stone, but over time it will dissolve in water. There are many different essential oils with properties that are purifying, protective, or empowering. Research the magical properties of various essential oils and find the combination that best suits your goals and your fragrance preferences.

Broom, Wing, or Branches

You may use a soft hand broom, a large preserved bird's wing (such as a pheasant), or three leafy branches from a tree or bush. The hand broom should not have been used for any other purpose; mine is from Thailand and has long, soft bristles. Be sure to check your local and state restrictions regarding the keeping and use of bird and animal parts.

If you use freshly cut branches, be sure to leave an offering for the tree in payment for what you took. Dimes are the traditional offering. Make sure the branches are leafy and have no thorns or burs since they will be used to sweep the client. I use bay laurel, which grows easily in California. You can also use newly cut lavender, mugwort, lemongrass, or even flowers with longer stems such as marigolds.

Black Stones
Collect medium-sized black stones of any type. Each one should fit comfortably in the palm of your hand. The black stones I use are dark agates pulled from the river nearby. You can use basalt stones, obsidian, tourmaline, or any other dark-colored stone, even if it has striations of different colors running through it.

Hand Drum and Tom (Optional)
This is used as an additional measure to solidify the work you do on the victim.

The folk traditions that use these types of cleansing do not treat them as a perfect science, nor should you. Folk traditionalists literally use what is available in their kitchen cupboard in the art of substitution, the ingenious magical process that it is. These instructions are simply the foundation for how to perform the cleansing, and adaptation is expected when necessary.

Create the Sacred Space
Your sacred space should look like an invisible bubble around you, allowing enough space for you to move around the room as needed. You can bubble the room you are in, your house, the area in the woods where you are practicing, your sacred temple, or wherever you happen to be. I have a room dedicated to healing.

Within that room, I have a carpet where the client stands or sits while I work on them. The carpet is a primary cleansing area, and the room is the secondary protected space.

Your sacred space is a shield that protects you from incoming energy, both positive and negative. For now, you must eliminate all outside energy that is not divine in nature and focus exclusively on the affected person and what is going on with them. Because they need your exclusive attention while you work on them, make sure that all cell phones are off, children and pets are managed for at least sixty to ninety minutes, and other distractions are minimized.

If you are not sure how to create a sacred space, once you have cleansed the area, here is one method. Stand in the center of the space and imagine a brilliant ball of white light that starts at your solar plexus and moves forward into the room. It is dense and intense and constantly growing. Imagine that the ball of white light pushes outward and purifies everything it touches. See it reaching the areas of the space you wish to define as sacred and stopping its growth at that point. Your skin may tingle a bit as it grows and encompasses the area. See an impenetrable shell forming around the white light that rejects all incoming energy. *Pew pew pew.* The energy bounces right off it, keeping all within the white light safe and secure. This is a shield, so when you hear someone talking about the importance of shielding for empaths and other sensitive people, you now know that they are referring to being in this kind of spiritually protected place.

Now that you have prepared your area and established your shielding, you are within your sacred space. It is important to remember that shields—such as the white light protection you just created—are not a one-way boundary. Not only does a shield keep out energies that are not your own, but you also cannot send energy *outward* when the shield is in place. You are contained within the white light, just as everything else is isolated outside the white light. Your energy is blocked from moving outward, just as other energy is blocked from entering. This means that any work you do to send energy away from the victim must happen after you drop the shield, including returning the curse or other negative energies to the sender.

Checking Your Intention

A true spiritual cleansing goes far deeper than what a ritual bath or simple smudging can provide. Ideally, a professional spiritual healer performs the cleansing. If it comes to it, anyone can do it, provided they are open-minded and sensitive to the movement of energy. If you are unable to find someone suitable to assist with the spiritual cleansing, you may wish to seek out a professional healer who can work remotely.

Management of psychic attack is a spiritual, intuitive, and thoughtful process. To assist the victim of an attack with their cleansing is a sacred task, and those who are asked to do so should feel honored. I am frequently astounded by the emotions and experiences my clients share with me. For some of my clients, it is the first time they have told anyone the things they tell me in the confidentiality of the healing space. I am humbled and honored that they give their trust to me in such a way.

Honor that trust by giving your best to the healing process and doing all you can to make sure the victim is restored to wholeness again. This seems like a weighty task, but in most cases, you can remove a psychic attack and start the process of healing with careful attention, an open mind, and a good spiritual connection.

CHAPTER TEN

THE INITIAL EXAM

When you agree to assist in an energetic cleansing and healing, you undertake a sacred mission to help the person who may or may not be under attack to clear away contaminants in their energy field that block them from achieving success. This is not a lifelong contract. When you agree to perform a spiritual cleansing, you are under no obligation to act as counselor, energy worker, or support crew for this person in perpetuity. You get to decide the terms and assist as you feel prepared and able to do so.

Unfortunately, there are some people who will take advantage of the spiritual cleansing to appease needy parts of their personality. It is up to you as the healer to maintain clear vision to know when you are helping and when you are enabling. The healer can take up the gauntlet on behalf of the victim and allow them to rest and receive healing, but eventually and ultimately, the victim must take responsibility for their own circumstances and make any necessary changes to the framework of their lives to encourage their wellness and protect them from future attacks.

Do not rob the person you are healing of their life lesson and opportunity for self-empowerment by taking over their lives and guiding their every step from the cleaning onward. There is a gentle balance to the dynamic between healer and victim that is the responsibility for the healer to maintain, since it is possible that the victim is under undue duress due to the attack.

In the spiritual cleansing, you banish whatever negative influences are causing the victim's troubles, whether they come from within or not. When you enter a client's energetic field, you must always do so with the knowledge that there could be multiple issues or different issues than what you are expecting. You should be prepared to handle anything at this point.

In chapter 8, I mentioned that you must banish all fear from the healing space. Some may feel that I am leading untrained novices into a potential encounter with hellish demons or angry spirits possessing the victim. That is an understandable concern for those who have not previously worked in the field. Rest assured that cases of demonic possession manifest quite differently from psychic attack, with a specific set of symptoms that could never be confused with a curse, hex, crossing, incidental entity infiltration, or any of the other conditions covered in this book.

The chance of encountering an incidental or accidental demon possession "in the wild" is slim to none. You would likely never encounter such a thing unless you went into business as a professional healer. If you did encounter a demonic possession, you would have no doubt about what is going on and would immediately know if you were in over your head. Demonic possession does not sneak up on either the victim or the healer. It takes hard work to be possessed by a demon, and it is even harder work to get rid of it.

The scope of this book covers various forms of psychic attack. You do not need to fear that the person you spiritually cleanse using the techniques described here has any demons hiding in them that could cause you concern or threat. Granted, some curses and hexes are more intense than others and can take a great deal of effort to completely remove, but using these methods repeatedly can be quite effective at doing so, provided the victim does not reengage the environment that caused the contamination. There are always victims who return to the same unhealthy relationships that crossed them before.

Likewise, there are always angry, determined, vengeful people who will curse and hex and curse again, sending a new attack as soon as you get the previous one cleaned up. Protection tools, like those discussed in chapter 13, help prevent this from happening, but the energy can sometimes slip through even the strongest protection field. Multiple cleansings are often—and in fact, usually—required, so when you undertake the sacred task of assisting with a cleansing, deeply consider how involved you want to be in the process.

The Human Energetic System

To best understand how the spiritual cleansing works, you must have a basic understanding of the human energetic anatomy and functions.

The energetic system consists of the seven primary chakras, which work as tiny hearts, pumping out energy specific to their scope of influence within the spiritual body. The meridians carry that energy throughout the body and into the aura, just as blood vessels carry the blood pumped by the heart within the circulatory system.

The lymph node areas and other key points of the body process out toxic energies, just as we sweat, urinate, and exhale to remove waste from the body. The energetic system is every bit as much of a miracle as physiological human anatomy. For most people, the energetic system is an efficient, well-oiled machine.

Interestingly, the primary areas of toxic energy release—the lymphatic areas under the jawline, the underarms, the pelvis, and the feet—also correspond to where some of the most disagreeable smells emit from the body: the breath (jawline), the armpits (underarm), the genitals and bottom (pelvis), and the feet. Toxic energies definitely leave their mark when they exit!

By the time you invite the victim into your sacred space (referred to in this book as the *working area*) and begin your initial evaluation, you have likely already discussed their symptoms with them as well as any theories about what caused their condition. This happens during the identification and objectification phases. Because you have a strong working knowledge of what is going on with the client, you can speculate as to which chakras are most likely affected by their situation. The following bulleted list may be helpful.

+ The first chakra is the **root chakra**. Located at the tailbone, it relates to issues of safety, self-identity, and home.

+ The second chakra is the **sacral chakra**. Located in the lower abdomen and lower back, it relates to passion and emotion.

+ The third chakra is the **solar plexus chakra**. Located at the central abdomen and the mid back, it relates to personal power.

+ The fourth chakra is the **heart chakra**. Located near the sternum and shoulder blades, it relates to relationships.

+ The fifth chakra is the **throat chakra**. Located in the neck, it relates to effective communication.

+ The sixth chakra is the **third eye chakra**. Located between the eyebrows, it relates to wisdom and self-reflection.

+ The seventh chakra is the **crown chakra**. Located at the top of the head, it relates to an individual's connection with the divine.

Consider each symptom the victim experiences that causes them to believe they are under psychic attack and anticipate which chakras are likely affected. If a curse, hex, crossing, or infiltrate manifests as relationship difficulties, expect dense energies and blockages in the heart chakra and possibly the throat chakra. If a curse, hex, crossing, or infiltrate manifests as misfortune and poverty, expect dense energies and blockages in the root chakra and the solar plexus chakra. If it manifests as infertility or sexual dysfunction, expect issues in the root, sacral, and solar plexus chakras. And so on.

It's interesting to note that, in my experience, men usually react to psychic attack in their root chakra. I was taught that people with male reproductive organs respond to sexual trauma or misfortune in the root chakra and people with female reproductive organs respond in the sacral chakra, although there are schools of thought with perfectly legitimate arguments to the contrary. This makes sense to me because for much of history, men were traditionally responsible for curating the safety and security (root chakra) of the home, and women were the emotional support (sacral chakra) of the home.

People who are known for their ability to heal are common targets for psychic attack due to their frequent exposure to the energetic systems of others. Attacks against healers most often manifest in the solar plexus chakra, the third eye chakra, or the crown chakra. This blocks the healer's ability to access spirit and interrupts their spiritual flow.

Spiritual Cleansing

My intention in this section is to address the person conducting the cleansing, guiding them through the process that I use with my own clients.

As I stated when outlining the steps to cleanse the working area, the techniques that follow are the ones I use, many of which I learned from my mentors. This is not to say that they are the only techniques. Practices from folk magic to new age healing have countless modalities for treating psychic attack and healing the human energetic systems. In this book I share the procedures that work best for me and that I have found to be the most universally effective.

The mechanics of the step-by-step process are easy to teach to anyone. The intuitive tracking and management of energy in another person's body takes talent and practice, so the level of effective cleaning that an inexperienced person can manage is incredibly varied.

The spiritual cleansing that I do with my clients happens in phases. A full cleansing has the following:

1. The Initial Evaluation: Chakra and Energy Check
2. The Initial Evaluation: Sage Bath
3. The Egg Cleansing

4. The Sweeping

5. The Blessing

The Initial Evaluation: Chakra and Energy Check

Make any adjustments needed for comfortable room temperature; a room that is too hot or too cold can be distracting to the healing process. Once you and your sacred space are ready, invite the victim to come in. Wherever they are standing, you should have room to move all around them with free access to their body and to your tools.

Point out the chair that is available to the victim if they feel faint or weak as the cleansing progresses, or if they are physically unable to stand for the cleansing and healing. Otherwise, they will likely stand for up to an hour while you work on them. Then ask the victim to remove their glasses (if applicable) and any electrical devices they are wearing like watches, fitness trackers, phones, etc. These can disrupt energy readings. The victim may leave on their jewelry, unless you feel that the jewelry is interrupting energy flow, which sometimes happens. The metal of pocketknives will also sometimes block energy movement. If the victim's hair is tied back, they should let it down to allow energy to flow unrestricted. In most cases, I have the victim take off their shoes, but they may leave on their socks. The victim should be wearing comfortable clothing that allows free movement and is not too thick. Some sweats and flannels are hard to cleanse through because of the thickness of the fabric.

Encourage the victim to take a few deep breaths in and out to help them relax. Tell them to ground themselves firmly by standing on all four corners of the feet. Reassure the victim that they are in a safe space and that you will take good care of them. Tell them to let you know at any time if they need you to stop what you are doing. If you wish, lead them through a brief meditation to help them become even more grounded, centered, and receptive. Two phrases I like to tell my clients are "Relax and let me do all the work" and "Just relax, receive, and release."

As the victim is settling in, I make certain that I have a solid connection to my own divine energies and that I can feel the divinity flowing through my body, especially into my hands. I slow my thoughts, casting away any thoughts that do not concern the person in front of me. When you are cleansing someone, your focus must be singular, so remember to silence any cell phones and make sure there is no chance for outside distraction. When I am confident that I am in a calm, sacred place, I start to work on the victim.

First hold the pendulum in front of each of the victim's chakra points, beginning with the root chakra, and observe the motion of the pendulum. Hold the pendulum steady between your thumb and forefinger (or wrapped around your forefinger) so that it is suspended and able to move freely. When you hold the pendulum in front of a chakra, watch for pendulum movement that does not come from you. If the pendulum remains still, this means the chakra is blocked. If the pendulum swings wildly, the chakra is hyperactive and is locked in a fight or flight response. Both blocked or hyperactive chakras can indicate a trauma response.

If there is a gentle swing to the pendulum, the chakra is firing normally. However, a chakra that reacts within normal limits does not guarantee that there is no curse, crossing, or trauma. A professional level curse may be programmed to avoid affecting the chakras, which helps it continue working undetected since some healers only check for chakra imbalance. The chakra check alerts you to obvious places you should pay special attention to when conducting the full energetic cleanse, but it is only part of the diagnostic process.

If the client seems anxious or appears to have manic energies, give them a dark stone to hold in each hand and invite them to release what they are feeling into the stones. They can hold the stone for as much of the cleansing/healing as they wish. You can also press the stone against the base of the skull, the forehead, or at lymph node areas to pull chaotic energies away from the body. My favorite dark stones to use for a cleansing are basalt massage stones; I favor them for their cool, smooth surface texture. (If you use the dark stones during the healing, be sure to clap them sharply against one another afterward to release the energies and cleanse the stones.)

If you are sensitive to energy movement, lightly run your hands over the victim's body, leaving maybe an inch of space between your hands and their skin or clothing, and note where energy feels denser or less dense. As you perform this scan, pay attention to any thoughts or impressions that go through your mind. Sometimes odd, disconnected thoughts will slip in, such as *He needs to drink more water* or *There is an old injury here.* Areas where there is little or no energy flow may have old injuries or may have been surgical sites. Above all, completely trust the intuitive insights you receive.

Trusting your intuition may take time. If you aren't totally comfortable sharing impressions you get with the victim, try giving a disclaimer up front, such as, "I am new at this, so I am just going to say whatever comes into my head. If it does not feel applicable, don't overthink it." This gives you and the victim an open door to accept or discard any intuitive messages you receive. After you have done this sort of cleansing many times, you will become more confident in what you are feeling and can better sort out what is an intuitive message and what is an unrelated, stray thought. If your focus is isolated to the person in front of you and to the divine energy flowing through you, you can always trust the intuitive prompts that come to you.

The Initial Evaluation: Sage Bath

The sage bath is an important part of the initial exam, both for its diagnostic acumen and the curative and cleansing powers of the sage itself.

Once I have noted the condition of all chakras and completed the initial evaluation, I begin cleansing with smoke. If, for whatever reason, you are not using smoke for this part of the cleansing, lightly mist sacred spray over the areas that felt dense or uncomfortable in the first part of your initial evaluation. Whenever possible, I recommend using sage for its amazing ability to react to, identify, and clear out areas of condensed or blocked energy.

Move a smoldering sage bundle all over the victim's body, watching where the smoke thins and where it grows denser. This shows me where the toxic energies are collecting in the body's energetic system. The smoke will thicken and intensify around toxic energy condensation to identify places that need greater attention during the egg cleansing that follows.

The most common areas where dense energies collect are in the lymph node areas (under the jawline, underarms, and the pelvis), as well as the base of the skull, the hands, the knees, and the bottoms of the feet. The kidney area in the lower back is another place that activates dense sage smoke if the person is not drinking enough water or has a systemic infection. Thicker smoke and dense energies at the base of the skull often indicate headaches or difficulty sleeping.

Pay attention to smoke that gathers at the knees. This may indicate a person who is acquiescing to the will of another, as in "bending the knee" and succumbing to bullying or intimidation to do something they do not want to do. Dense energy and heavy smoke at the feet shows up when someone is not walking the path they know they should follow. Although pain in these areas may also cause the sage smoke to billow, the pain is often indicative of an underlying spiritual conflict.

As you move the sage stick over the person's body, gently inform them that you may be touching them "in a familiar way" as you push your fingers into the areas mentioned above, feeling for energetic density and movement. Feel for areas where the air seems tighter above the body part and where the smoke billows more. Areas of dense energy may feel hotter or colder to your touch than the rest of the body. Sometimes I use my fingers to pluck out energy that feels out of place in the victim or is foreign to their system and then drop it to the floor to neutralize the energy.

Because the egg cleansing is where you can see objective results from your cleansing process, it is easy to want to rush through the initial exam to get to the exciting part. I cannot stress enough the importance of the initial exam to relax the victim, to familiarize the healer with the energy of the victim, and to identify areas of concern. Take your time and work carefully on the victim's body, trusting what you feel and see.

When the sage stick begins to go out, or when you intuitively feel that you have done all you can do with the smoke, it is time to move on to the egg cleansing. Because the egg cleansing is such a detailed part of the cleansing process, the following chapter is solely dedicated to it.

CHAPTER ELEVEN

THE EGG CLEANSING

Of all the cleansing and healing techniques mentioned in this book, the egg cleansing is the most important not only for its cleansing attributes, but also because of what the egg tells you when you break it into a jar of water.

Eggs are used in many folk traditions to cleanse impurities out of people and are especially effective at removing curses, hexes, crossings, infiltrates, and nearly every other form of psychic attack from a victim. People who are familiar with the Hoodoo tradition of egg rolling to remove negative energies should note that this is a slightly different practice.

In this case, instead of rolling the egg down the body, you hold the egg still while aggressively scrubbing the victim with it from the crown of their head to their feet. While egg rolling is similar in that its purpose is to remove negative energy, the technique I use is not quite the same.

What Does It Do?

The egg cleansing removes energies from the victim that do not belong to them, such as curses, hexes, crossings, entities, infiltrates, and other negative contaminations sent by someone else, whether intentionally or incidentally. It also removes past spiritual trauma and hooks from old relationships that the victim is having difficulty recovering from. The egg cleansing is both a curative in that it removes these contaminants and a diagnostic tool as it informs you of what was troubling the victim before the cleansing.

An egg cleansing does not leave a victim in perfect condition because, as mentioned before, a spiritual cleansing does not undo all damage caused by these energies. It does, however, considerably lighten the load the victim carries, and it clears away psychic turbulence and debris that keeps them from progressing by locking them into past traumas. The most common remark I hear after a cleansing is "I feel cleaner and lighter."

How Does It Work?

An egg cleansing, by tradition, works based on the idea that an egg is a living cell. You can temporarily convey the essence of the victim into the yolk and then rub the unbroken egg over the victim's body, convincing the contaminants inside that the egg is the person. This may sound ludicrous in the light of modern science, but it is a long-held belief. And hey, it works! I teach it to my students and use it almost daily in my practice.

For the egg to work effectively, I have found that it must be room temperature or warmer. A cold egg does not absorb negative energy as well as a warm one. If the egg is cold, I put it in a bowl of warm water or in my bra until it is warm enough to get the job done. As mentioned in chapter 9, if you warm up an egg using your body, make sure to cleanse and reconsecrate it before using it on the victim.

How to Do It

Make sure you have all the necessary tools from chapter 9. Begin by squirting a bit of sacred spray into the jar of water. This charges the water, changing it from simple water into blessed water. Next, spray the egg itself until it is damp all over. Hold the egg for a moment until it feels comfortable in your hand. During this time, ask the egg to open and receive the energy that is about to flow into it. Ask that divine powers (for me, it is Goddess) guide your hands, your words, and your intuitive flow to best serve the victim.

Ask the victim to blow on the egg hard, as if they are blowing out a birthday candle that has a big flame. Like a sneeze, it is difficult to describe the feeling of the victim's energy conveying into the egg, but trust me, you just feel it. I sometimes have a client blow two or even three times onto the egg until I feel the energy go into it.

Once the victim's energy is solidly in the egg, begin to scrub them down with it, visualizing that the egg is pulling out any darkness, negativity, or other energy that does not belong to them. Although you should not hurt the victim, this is not a gentle rub down. I tell my clients I will mess up their hair, and I do as I deeply scrub against their scalp, down their face, under their jawline, into the base of their skull, and down their neck. From there, it is across the shoulders, down the back, into the small of the back, along the ribs, all through the collarbones, down the chest, along the lateral muscles, and into the abdomen.

Yes, this tickles quite a bit. My husband, who is usually a stoic-looking "get off my lawn" kind of guy, giggles like a schoolgirl when he gets a cleansing because it tickles like mad. Another point to make here is that when you perform a spiritual cleansing, it is normal for the victim to laugh strangely, cry, cough, hiccup, tremble, or show other signs of release. As the negative energies unlock and begin to leave the body, the victim will often undergo a surge of adrenaline, and it releases through these behaviors.

As you rub the egg over the person, it often gets heavier. When passed over areas of dense negative energy in the body, the egg may start to make a knocking sound inside the shell. Sometimes the egg sweats. I have even seen eggs break out in goosebumps.

Continue aggressively scrubbing the victim's body with the egg, paying close attention to the areas previously mentioned: the base of the skull, under the jawline, underarms, across the groin area, and the small of the back, as well as any chakra points that registered on the pendulum as hyperactive or blocked and any congested areas that the sage smoke identified. Sometimes I press the egg against the affected area and ask the client to inhale and exhale deeply, pushing energy into the egg.

Take your time with this part of the process. Be as methodical and careful as you can. Don't be afraid of getting into the person's pubic lymphatic area, where the legs join the torso. Press the egg up their thighs as far as you can go while still maintaining your integrity and theirs. A victim should not ever feel violated by a cleansing, nor should you push beyond areas where you feel uncomfortable. Continue to keep the channel of communication open during this process and do the best you can.

Respray the egg from time to time as you intuitively feel the need to. The egg does not need to be sloppily wet to effectively cleanse, but the sacred spray does create a more dynamic connection between the victim and the egg. If you begin to feel the drawing energy from the egg and victim start to wane, give the egg another spray and pick up where you left off.

If, by chance, the egg should break because it is dropped or because it gets too full of energy, do not despair. Clean up the broken egg as best as you can, spray the second egg, have the person blow on it, and then pick up where you left off. Fortunately, it is rare to lose an egg, but it does occasionally happen.

After you finish scrubbing the entire body with the egg, take a moment and step back, viewing the victim as if you are scanning their energy field. Look for areas that appear to need attention and go back over them again.

When you are confident that you have done all you can do with the egg, break the egg into the jar of blessed water and close the lid tightly. Observe the egg as it resolves. At first, you might only see the yolk in the water, but as you watch, the egg white will start to form shapes in relation to the yolk.

Interpreting the Egg

My students go through an intensive study of what the different formations of the egg mean and how to manage the treatment of a client whose cleansing shows those shapes. For the purpose of this book, I will keep the information simple, but if you check out my YouTube channel, you can see actual photos of the different egg shapes that are discussed below.[6]

Sometimes the egg yolk breaks apart when you drop it into the water or separates out into individual segments. In this case, the person is in extreme distress and may need professional medical or mental health management. When I see this, I will sometimes

---

6. Visit www.youtube.com/katrinarasbold.

perform a second egg cleansing with the idea that one egg was not enough to pick up all that we needed to remove. Use your instincts to make a judgment call on whether this is necessary. I have had some clients who required three or four eggs before they were cleansed to my satisfaction, meaning that there were no longer concerning or critical markers in the egg indicating that the client might be at continued risk, such as the yolk that breaks apart when it enters the water.

Usually the yolk will be intact. Each healer has their own interpretation of the appearance of the egg. Each aspect of the egg in relation to the water and the egg white to the yolk means something. I learned most of my interpretations from my mentors, but some I have added from my own experience.

Skeptics think egg yolk variation is simply chance. They will point out that when you crack an egg into a pan to cook it for eating, it can have different properties. That is true, just as when you burn candles for mundane purposes, they can burn in different ways. The question you must ask yourself in either case is why did this specific egg or candle turn out this way? For whatever divinely driven reason, you chose this egg and/or candle. You did so because it had a message to convey to you. When you reach up to the divine power for assistance with a cleansing, you must accept that everything that happens in the sacred space is a message for you to interpret. Do not discount the divine messages you receive.

Egg Messages

In the following egg readings, you will see that I mention primary or secondary entities. This does not designate a level of Hell from which they came, but is instead relevant to the entity's ability to create discord in the victim. It suggests the entity's overall impact and level of aggression toward the victim.

A primary entity has teeth, so to speak, and is usually more vicious. They create greater discord and disruption to the victim's quality of life and they are generated by other people to do just that. High levels of hatred and jealousy may create a primary entity as well, so they do not come only from deliberate attacks, although that is the most common cause.

A secondary entity is usually an incidental infiltration that is mostly unobtrusive but can cause symptoms such as ongoing fatigue, generalized malaise, or a series of misfortunes. They are the ones you can pick up like a virus as they jump from person to person.

As you go through the following interpretations, remember that in each one, the yolk represents the person who received the cleansing. Whatever is in the jar with the yolk believes that the yolk *is* the victim due to the energy conveyed by breathing on the egg at the beginning of the cleansing. Interpret everything inside the jar relative to the yolk, and speak of the yolk as though it is the victim.

Be sure to read the egg as soon as you cap the jar, watching it for a few minutes as it develops. Things can change quickly inside an egg jar, and you want to be able to see whatever messages are there for you.

MURKY WATER

When you put the egg into the jar of blessed water, the water should be clean and clear. If the water becomes murky and appears dense and clouded once the egg goes in, this tells you that the negative energies from around the person were removed by the cleansing. This means energy vampires and users are slowly bleeding the life out of the victim. This may be an intentional energy drain, or it could be a person who is so needy that there is no possibility that anyone can ever fill them up. It could also be that the victim is around people who have a chronic negative outlook or a fearful, doom-and-gloom approach to life—or perhaps it is the victim that is this way.

VEIL OVER THE YOLK

A veil over the yolk means the person is not practicing good self-care and that they are confused and conflicted over a situation. A veil on the yolk is common since most people who undergo psychic attack stop taking care of themselves as soon as the depression and misfortune hits. Sadly, good self-care habits are fragile and give way quickly in the case of an attack.

CHILD GRIEF FORMATION

A pronounced white tail at the end of the yolk, usually in a curlicue shape, often indicates unresolved grief from the loss of a child through miscarriage, abortion, child death, custody issues, or gender reassignment, or grief for children the person fears they will never have. It could represent the death of a sibling at an early age or the separation of a parent or close relative from a young child.

In American society, fathers are rarely given room to grieve children lost to miscarriage or abortion as attention often centers on the mother. I see child grief formation in men quite often, likely for this reason. Likewise, people often treat women who choose to terminate their pregnancies as if they are not entitled to grieve the loss of their child. Women who miscarry are told "It is only a bundle of cells," "It is good it happened early on," "If it had lived, it likely would have been deformed," or "You can always have more." All of these statements dismiss the actual grief of the child loss, and this repressed mourning can show up in a child grief formation in the egg, indicating attachments and traumas that the victim carries around related to the experience.

WHITE STREAKS OR SPECKS ON THE YOLK

Specks or streaks of white on the egg yolk identify old scars and traumas that continue to haunt the person. Almost everyone has some sort of old trauma, but the ones that show up in the egg are life-altering, spirit-crushing traumas. These are the events that shaped the victim and influenced their current relationships and worldview, including how they feel about themselves. The victim may or may not know what these traumas are and, if they do know, they may not be ready to talk about them.

Like tarot readings, an egg cleansing often reveals situations that are deeply personal and take a person by surprise when they surface. It is important that you do not force the victim to share or explore the possible reasons for these representations in the egg unless they wish to do so. Give them space and allow them to speak if they wish, but do not push them beyond their comfort zone.

The white areas reveal circumstances the victim will need to address at some point in time if they are to embrace wholeness.

BLOODY OR BLACKENED AREAS ON THE YOLK

Black, red, or bloody-looking areas on the yolk indicate hatred or jealousy from someone close to them. The bloodiness or blackness can extend into the water in extreme cases. I have worked with eggs where the water looked completely bloody or black to the point that the yolk was barely visible. This usually happens in cases of full-blown, deliberate attacks.

Sometimes a bloody or blackened yolk indicates the use of blood magic in the sending of a curse or the wish for a person's death or injury.

Darkened Areas on the Yolk

A dark shadow around the yolk means the victim is causing some of their crossing themselves, likely through negative thinking and a self-punishing outlook. If a person feels that they deserve to be punished, hated, tortured, or attacked, they will draw the energy to them that will do exactly that.

When you seek a dark shadow directly on or around the yolk, ask gentle, leading questions to discern the person's level of self-esteem. The dark shadow (which is different from the murky water mentioned previously) indicates an extreme level of self-loathing in the victim that may contribute to an actual psychic attack—or create one if none exists.

Low-Lying Yellow Water

A strong yellow cast on the bottom of the jar indicates that the person is not drinking enough water and that the kidneys are struggling as a result. In this case, you likely felt concentrated energy in or around the lower back. The sage smoke may also have intensified in this area. You may have felt condensed energy around the bladder area, just above the pubic bone. Remind them that to effectively purge toxins from their system, they need to drink extra water. This does not include vitamin water or other sweetened drinks. Lemon water or water infused with mint or ginger is fine.

Clear, Formed Bubbles

Tiny, clear, pearl-like bubbles floating in or on the water represent spirit guides providing divine assistance from the other side of the veil. These bubbles could be ancestors, loved ones who have passed, saints, angels, or any other entities who lend support from the beyond.

It is important to note that these helpers from another plane are not now trapped in the jar; the bubbles are representatives of those energies, like placeholders to show they are there and working for the person. I often see these bubbles congregating over, within, and onto other formations that indicate aggressive actions against the victim, such as the reaper formation and the fortress formation.

FORTRESS FORMATION

A jagged formation that circles the yolk on more than half of its perimeter is a fortress formation. These structures look like ice or crystal walls around the yolk and create at least a partial boundary between it and anything else going on in the jar. The fortress formation means the victim experienced trauma so severe that they now isolate from others. They fear attachment, connection with people, or attention from others and may separate themselves from personal contact. They build walls in their relationships and do not let others get close to them.

These are defense mechanisms created by the past trauma and, most of the time, this does not reflect the victim's actual desires. It is possible that due to cognitive dissonance, the victim may not realize they are creating distance with others since this is typically an unconscious reaction.

REAPER/SPECTRAL FORMATION

A reaper or spectral formation is a large, looming shape that hovers over the yolk, often taking on the appearance of a grim reaper, a beast, or another imposing apparition. It sometimes appears several minutes after leaving the egg to rest and will often quickly break away, so pay careful attention to the egg for a few minutes after you add it to the water and cap the jar.

A reaper formation is a primary entity that was attached to the victim, sent to cause disruption and grief in their life. These entities may be sent by someone wishing harm to the person in the form of a hex or crossing. It is possible to pick up a primary entity incidentally, but it is rare to do so.

Entities such as these may be in the person's body for decades without them knowing. The effects include marked loss of vitality, ongoing malaise and fatigue, an inability to connect to others in a meaningful way, an inability to sustain good fortune, and difficultly sleeping, as well as physical maladies. In extreme cases, the victim may experience a series of deaths of loved ones, including pets and people, especially those who are vulnerable due to illness and age.

Secondary entities are usually free-floating in the jar and look like tiny ghosts that are just dancing through the water. They may also look like small spikes or bumps on the bottom of the jar.

SENTINEL FORMATION

Sentinel entities are thin spikes that stand apart from the yolk with clear bubbles on top that create the impression of a head. Sentinel entities are ones sent to a person to observe and track the person's behavior, status, and even their thoughts and intentions, much like energetic spies.

CURSES

A large bubble attached to the yolk at one side that grows while the egg resolves in the jar usually represents a secondary curse deliberately sent to the victim. I have even seen a reaper formation holding one of the bubbles that represents a curse, seeming to flaunt that they are part and parcel with one another. In that case, it was a curse sent along with a disruptive entity.

The bubble may also indicate emotional baggage a person is carrying from past trauma that has manifested into a curse.

Parachute Formation

When the egg white grows dense and takes on a parachute formation on one side of the yolk, it usually represents a stronger curse sent by someone who wishes the victim ill will. This is most often a deliberate curse. Rarely, it could be an inadvertent crossing where a person felt profound envy or anger toward the victim.

Primary Vortices

A generational curse shows in the egg jar as a structure with a bubble on the top and a funnel shape that reaches down to the yolk or near the yolk. This is called a primary vortex and looks like an iridescent funnel cloud extending downward from the bubble to the yolk. It shimmers and moves when you touch the jar. The bubbles atop a primary vortex are usually approximately the size of a pencil eraser or a small marble or gumball, but I have seen them as large as a plum or bigger than the yolk itself, even. These bubbles are usually opaque with a murky but transparent whitish appearance. In rare cases, the vortex may open and extend over the entire yolk.

After the Egg Reading

Share what you see in the egg with the person you just cleansed and talk with them about what it means. Keep in mind that what you see in the egg yolk after you break it into the jar is not what *is* wrong with the victim—it is what *was* wrong with the victim before the cleansing. I often tell my clients, "What was wrong with you now lives in a jar on my altar." You have literally removed the offending attack from the victim and captured it in the jar.

Again, to be clear, the spirit guide bubbles in the jar do not indicate that a person's spirit guides are trapped in the jar with the entities. Just as the yolk represents the person you are cleansing, the bubbles represent the spirit guide, but neither are actually in the jar. The infiltrates, however, *are* actually in the jar.

The active components inside the jar will eventually die off, which can take anywhere from a few minutes to several days. When I am confident that there is no longer any activity in the jar, I dispose of the contents. This is covered more extensively in chapter 12.

CHAPTER TWELVE

---✦---

FLYING SOLO

The advice given in part IV of this book presumes that you have someone—a friend, a relative, or a professional healer that you trust—who can assist you with the process of removing the toxicity of a psychic attack from your energetic system. This book is admittedly biased toward the idea of finding a partner to work with you, based on my own experience. Time and again I have seen how difficult it is to fully remove all residue of an attack, and I have watched as people have tried and failed to do it on their own, even seasoned professionals.

After all my years of working with energy, I would never attempt to remove a curse, hex, or crossing from myself without help. This is akin to treating yourself when you're sick or injured. It would be difficult to treat yourself because you are ill and your energy reserves are low, but also because you are likely not a professional health care provider. Therefore, in cases of suspected psychic attack, going to a professional energy worker is always best. Most competent energy workers are trained to cleanse and heal people from a distance and can do so just as effectively as they can with the person right in front of them.

From my own perspective as a healer, I feel there are advantages for me when I work remotely on a client. I can move a proxy vessel (I use a teddy bear) in ways that I cannot move a human being. I can access and treat areas of their body that are too private to dig into in person. I can lift the proxy vessel in one hand and easily move the sage stick under, over, and around, following the smoke to find the areas of condensation. When doing remote healing, I get to choose the incense, sprays, and oils I enjoy because I don't have to worry about client allergies or sensitivities. I can also wait until the energy feels right to do the work rather than sticking to a scheduled appointment.

There are times when a sickness or injury is a medical emergency and requires an actual physician to provide care, and there are times when energetic emergencies require a professional energy worker to provide care. Psychic attack is one of those times.

In the absence of a trained professional, the next solution is an extra set of eyes and hands, preferably attached to someone who is *not* currently under psychic attack. An objective person who is not under attack is far better at observing personality changes, following the smoke of a sage stick, or accessing the victim's body to scrub it down with an egg than the victim is. Having a person assist with the treatment allows the victim to be still and focus on releasing the curse, hex, or other infiltrate, as well as focusing on receiving the healing energy. Receiving healing energy is tremendous work when you are under attack.

If, however, you truly have no one else who can reasonably assist you, there are techniques you can use to mitigate the symptoms of the attack. If the attack is weak, you may even be able to remove it completely using these suggestions. Treating the symptoms of an attack is better than ignoring an attack and allowing the effects to continue or worsen.

To repeat the warning from the beginning of this book, if you have physical symptoms from an attack that interfere with your quality of life, consult a professional medical caregiver. If you have mental health issues from an attack that interfere with your quality of life, please seek treatment from a trained and competent mental health professional. Do not allow yourself to live in misery because someone else cannot or will not control their energy.

The next part of this chapter covers ways to banish psychic attack or mitigate the symptoms of the attack if you are unable to turn to someone else for help.

Necessary Tools

Once you determine that psychic attack is a possible or likely cause for what you are experiencing, there are steps you can follow to help mitigate the symptoms and possibly remove the attack. Ultimately, you would ideally seek help from a professional energetic healer, but these suggestions will ease the symptoms until you can get assistance and, again, may even work on their own.

Keep in mind that fear feeds a psychic attack, so the first step is to shake off any essence of fear you may have. Step into your empowerment. This can be difficult to do if the attack has been going on for a long time and your energy reserves are low, but imagine that you are the biggest, baddest force around. Take deep breaths and pull yourself upright. Stand tall. Put your fists on your hips and push out your chest, lifting your chin. Say, "This can no longer hurt me. I am now fully in charge of myself." Banish fear and doubt and boldly move forward.

Now it's time to get to work. First, cleanse your living area as described in chapter 9. This removes any toxic energies from the environment and reduces the chance of recontamination. Then gather your necessary supplies.

Candles

It is always best if you use a candle specifically intended to manage psychic attacks. There are several different kinds, but gravitate toward candles with names like Spell Breaker, Cast Out Evil, or Uncrossing. Stay away from candles with names like DUME (Death Unto My Enemies), Destroy Everything, and other revenge energies. Your attention should be on healing and cleansing yourself, not on harming others.

If you have no way to obtain this type of candle, you can use a plain, white, glass-encased prayer candle. It does not matter if the candle is scented or unscented (unless you are sensitive to smells or do not care for the candle's scent). This candle will burn for approximately three to five days if you let it burn continuously, so the protection of the cleansing ritual will continue.

You will also need seven tea light candles, one for each chakra, and a lighter or box of matches.

Stones

Black or dark stones absorb negativity, and blue stones provide peaceful, healing energy. The stone I most use for protection and to eliminate negativity is black tourmaline. You can also use obsidian, onyx, or even dark-colored agate. Sodalite and lapis lazuli promote tranquility and healing. Blue kyanite repels evil. If you think you were deliberately cursed, fluorite cloaks the aura and makes it easier for you to fly under the radar for a short time.

Recommendations given here are merely suggestions. Choose at least four stones that feel right to you. Let your intuition guide you in your selection. They can even be stones from your yard, garden, or driveway.

Incense

I recommend temple incenses such as frankincense and copal. Dragon's blood incense is protective and works great for exorcism because of its effect on toxic energy. Lemongrass is a purificant. Rue drives out evil.

If you do not care for incense or cannot use it, you can skip this step. If you can tolerate the incense, it adds an additional level of purification and protection to the process. You will burn your chosen incense as you conduct your self-cleansing ritual.

A Cooking Pot with a Lid

You will cook the infusion for the uncrossing bath in this. It should hold at least a quart of liquid.

A Larger Pot to Contain the Final Bath Infusion

Your final bath infusion will be just over a gallon, so choose a large container that you can carry. This could be a bucket, a pitcher, or a large pan like a tamale steamer.

A Place to Bathe

You need a place to take your ritual bath. It does not have to be a bathtub; a shower stall will work just fine.

Bath Infusion

Gather at least one gallon of water to infuse with other ingredients. Rainwater is best, purified water is second best, and tap water is acceptable but the least desirable. Then choose three or more of the following herbs, roots, and resins:

+ Dried rosemary
+ Dried sage
+ Powdered dragon's blood resin
+ Calamus
+ Powdered calamus root
+ Dried rue
+ Ground patchouli leaves
+ Dried lemongrass
+ Three whole bay leaves

Written Affirmation

Write the following affirmation down on paper, focusing on each word as you write it:

"I am cleansed of all that is harmful, baneful, and not organic to my own energy. I am uncrossed. I am clean. No further harm or inconvenience may come to me. My power is my own once more. I am free. I am blessed. I am safe."

A Raw, Unbroken Egg, Still in the Shell, at Room Temperature

It does not matter if the shell is white, brown, or another color. The egg does not have to be farm fresh, but it should not have gone bad. You can tell if an egg is rotten by dropping it into a container of water. If the egg is bad, it will float.

A Pint-Sized Jar with a Screw-On Lid

Fill the jar half full of water. The jar should have smooth sides and no label so you can easily see inside.

Sacred Spray

If you do not have Florida Water or any other sacred spray, you can substitute by choosing a healing essential oil such as eucalyptus, lavender, rosemary, or citrus to use instead. I will explain how to use the essential oil during the egg cleansing section.

A Clean Cloth

This cloth doesn't have to be anything fancy; you can use a washcloth, cloth diaper, or dish towel. Just make sure it is clean before using it.

Making the Bath Infusion

To make the infusion, remove approximately four cups of water from the gallon of water and put it into the pot. Add your chosen herbs, roots, and/or resins to the pot of water. Heat until the water boils. Allow it to boil for three minutes, then put a lid on the pot and remove it from the heat. Let the infusion steep for at least two hours.

Once the infusion has steeped and cooled, strain out all solid ingredients and discard them, keeping only the concentrated liquid. Just before you begin your cleansing ritual bath, pour the rest of the gallon of water into your carrying container and add the concentrated uncrossing infusion, stirring well. Bring it into the area where you will take your ritual bath and leave it for later use. Put the paper with the words of affirmation somewhere nearby.

Getting Clean: The Process

It is important that you are not interrupted during this ritual and that your self-cleansing has your entire focus. The best time for a cleansing to happen is at midnight between Saturday and Sunday, preferably during the three days of the new moon (the day before, the day of the new moon, or the day after). Should these two periods of time line up together, it is an especially favorable time, but do not hold off on healing to wait for that to occur.

Have your tools assembled and your infusion ready before you start the ritual.

Call In Your Team

When you are ready to begin, invite any divine assistance you wish to invoke. This can include God, Goddess, Blessed Mother, saints (Saint Germain and Saint Michael are especially good choices), archangels (Raphael and Gabriel are good choices), ancestors, spirit guides, or any other helpers from beyond the veil.

Set Up the Healing Area

Leave the bath items in the bathing area and bring the candles, egg, and water jar into the healing space. Bring your sacred spray or essential oil with you as well. Find a comfortable place to sit. This can be on the floor, on a pillow or folded blanket, or on a chair. You will be here for several minutes, so make certain your position is sustainable.

Place the seven tea lights in a circle around you. Place the primary candle—the large, white, glass-encased candle or the Uncrossing type of candle—inside the circle with you. Then light the first tea light and say, "This candle makes clean and pure my first chakra so that I feel safe."

Light the second tea light and say, "This candle makes clean and pure my second chakra so that my passion drives me to my own greatest good."

Light the third tea light and say, "This candle makes clean and pure my third chakra so that my personal power is my own once more."

Light the fourth tea light and say, "This candle makes clean and pure my fourth chakra so that I may love well and be loved in return."

Light the fifth tea light and say, "This candle makes clean and pure my fifth chakra so that I may speak my truth and hear the truth from others."

Light the sixth tea light and say, "This candle makes clean and pure my sixth chakra so that I may know my own inner wisdom."

Light the seventh tea light and say, "This candle makes clean and pure my seventh chakra so that I may hear the will and wisdom of the divine."

Light the primary candle and say, "I bless this candle to remove the toxic energies that are within me."

Sit in the circle of candles for a few minutes, feeling their power and your safety. Nothing can harm you within this circle.

The Egg Cleansing

Spray three squirts of sacred spray into the jar of water or place three drops of your chosen essential oil into the jar of water. The water is now blessed and ready to receive the egg.

If you are using sacred spray, spray some directly onto the egg. Cup the egg with both hands. Firmly blow on the egg as if you are blowing out a birthday candle. Visualize that any negative energy in or around you is beginning to drain into the egg.

Touch the egg to each of your seven chakras, beginning with your root chakra and working your way up to crown. Hold the egg at each chakra location for a few minutes, visualizing that any negative contaminants, unhealthy attachments, and toxic energies are draining into the egg. When it feels appropriate, move to the next chakra.

After you finish holding the egg to your chakras, place it at the base of your skull and hold it there for a while, letting any toxic energies move into it. Place the egg under your jawline on one side, then the other side. Continue to visualize any negative energies moving into the egg as you press it against the underarm area, one side at a time. Press the egg against the front of your pelvis, where your leg joins your torso, on each side. Finally, rub the egg along the bottom of each foot.

Once you have used the egg on each of these areas, focus on your body and see if any of the cleansed areas feel different. If necessary, go back to any areas that need further cleansing and gently press the egg against the area. You can rub the area with the egg if you wish, continuing to visualize negativity and toxins being absorbed into the egg.

When you feel confident that you have cleared all you can with the egg, crack the egg and let it fall into the jar's blessed water.

Retain the eggshell. After the cleansing, you can crush it and place it outside your front door for protection.

Cap the jar and observe the egg to see how it develops. It may take several minutes for the egg to fully finalize. To read the contents of the jar, compare what you see to the information in chapter 11, then set the egg jar aside.

You may leave the tea lights burning in their protective containers until they self-extinguish or extinguish them yourself if it is safer to do so. Pick up your primary candle and take it into the bathing area for the next part of the self-cleansing process.

The Uncrossing Bath

Your bathing area should be a bathtub or shower stall. You need to soak as much of your body as you can in the uncrossing bath you created. Place the primary candle in a safe place in your bathing area, preferably where you can see it since it has an open flame.

There are two ways to take the uncrossing bath; both are equally effective.

TECHNIQUE #1

Fill the bathtub about one-third of the way, using water that is slightly warmer than you would ordinarily use. Pour the entire contents of the container of uncrossing bath infusion into the water. Get in the bath when the temperature is comfortable enough for you to do so, then fill the tub the rest of the way.

Immerse as much of your body as you can into the bathwater and steep yourself for at least twenty minutes.

While you are in the bath, focus on releasing the toxins and negative energies attached to your energetic system. When you feel that you have released all that you can, carefully step backward out of the bathtub so that you are facing the water during your exit. Open the bathtub drain and watch the water disappear, taking your negative energy with it. As the water drains, read aloud the words of affirmation you wrote down:

"I am cleansed of all that is harmful, baneful, and not organic to my own energy. I am uncrossed. I am clean. No further harm or inconvenience may come to me. My power is my own once more. I am free. I am blessed. I am safe."

Technique #2

Get into the tub or shower stall while it is empty, making sure you have access to the uncrossing bath infusion water.

Put a clean cloth into the infused water and let it absorb the water. Take the cloth out and lay it on or near the side of the tub or shower, somewhere you can easily get to it later. Do not wring out the cloth.

Turn on the shower, letting the water flow over you at a comfortable temperature. When you are ready, pick up the container of uncrossing bath infusion, close your eyes, and slowly begin to pour it over your body. Pour from your head down if you feel comfortable doing so, allowing the infused water to cover your entire body. If you are uncomfortable pouring the infusion over your head, pour it onto your body from the neck down. The warm water from the shower should make the temperature of the infused water more bearable.

After you empty the container, pick up the soaked washcloth you set aside and gently wash any areas missed while pouring the infusion.

When you feel that you have washed all parts of your body with the infusion, finish rinsing off with the water from the shower. Then turn off the shower and exit by carefully stepping backward out of the stall or tub. As the water drains, read aloud the words of affirmation you wrote down:

"I am cleansed of all that is harmful, baneful, and not organic to my own energy. I am uncrossed. I am clean. No further harm or inconvenience may come to me. My power is my own once more. I am free. I am blessed. I am safe."

After the Uncrossing Bath

Dry yourself, put on comfortable clothing, and try to sleep. Remember that this ritual is best done starting at midnight between Saturday and Sunday and ideally within the three-day span of the new moon. Sleeping immediately after the cleansing allows you to wake up in a whole new world, free from psychic attack and feeling healed and refreshed. When you wake up, read the words of affirmation aloud again.

Make sure you blow out the glass-encased candle before falling asleep. If you prefer, you may allow the glass-encased prayer candle to continue burning until it burns itself out (provided that you feel safe doing so and that the candle is in a firesafe location). This can take hours or days, depending on the candle. Be cautious around fire; you should always keep a close eye on an open flame.

It is common to feel a drop in energy after negativity is removed from your energetic system. Your entire being has been locked in fight or flight because of psychic attack, and when the energy of the attack leaves, your mind, body, and spirit all suddenly relax. People also sometimes feel dizzy or nauseous during or after a cleansing as their energy attempts to recalibrate.

PART FIVE

HEALING AFTER PSYCHIC ATTACK

CHAPTER THIRTEEN

———✦———

AFTER THE HEALING

Once you have read the contents of the egg jar, carefully move your hands around the victim's aura once again, feeling for areas that are warmer or cooler than normal body temperature. When you remove a component from the energetic field, the body registers a vacancy and responds. This may initially result in coolness and then warmth as the energy rushes to the affected area.

If a part of the body seems reactive, cup your hands over it and imagine that you are flooding the area with healing energy, flowing from your crown chakra out through your hands. The victim may feel warmth or a tingling sensation as you convey healing energy to them. Check in with them to see how they are feeling and have them note any unusual pain or sensation. Usually, they will tell you that they feel quite good.

Then it is time to finalize the healing process with an energetic cleansing. Receiving an energetic cleansing can be a transcendent experience regardless of whether a psychic attack was present. Some recipients even spiritually leave their bodies and disconnect from what is happening during a cleansing. It is common to feel a wave of euphoria as the healing occurs. Sweeping and blessing the victim re-grounds them in their physical form and helps stabilize their energetic field after psychic surgery.

Sweeping and Blessing

To finalize the cleansing, I do a brisk sweeping. I use a pheasant wing sprayed down with Florida Water, Fiery Wall of Protection spray, or another sacred spray. Some healers use the branches from a bush. Some use flowers such as long-stemmed marigolds. Be sure to inspect the branches carefully to make sure any leaves are soft and supple and that no thorns are present; the sweeping should feel invigorating rather than like a beating. You may also use the soft hand broom mentioned in chapter 9 if you spray the bristles with sacred spray.

This sweeping should be vigorous, as it is intended to brush away any remaining impurities. As with the sage and the egg, start at the top of the head and sweep downward, vigorously brushing off any residual psychic debris or negativity. This refreshes the victim and brings them back into their body, effectively grounding them. This sweeping is the primary reason why you should ask the victim to remove their glasses at the start of the cleansing—anything that is not well attached can go flying during this part of the process.

Once the sweeping is finished, have the victim take several deep breaths and check their chakra responses again. Since the entire energetic system just had an overhaul, the responses may be different. Ideally, at this point, you want all previously blocked or hyperactive chakras working normally, so the pendulum should have a gentle swaying motion at each of the seven chakra points. If the pendulum still moves wildly or is perfectly still, cup your hands over the area of the chakra a few inches from the victim's body and imagine that you are sending pure, sacred, healing energy to the area. You may also relight the sage stick and cleanse the area with smoke again. Continue this until you get a normal pendulum reading for the chakra.

After I finish rechecking the chakras, I use sacred spray to bless and consecrate the person, sealing the work we have done. You may also anoint the person with holy water or sacred oils to bless them after the work is done. This completes the cleansing and blessing process.

In most cases, the person begins to feel better shortly after the spiritual cleansing or possibly even during it. The cleansing removes the attack and any unhealthy attachments so that normal energetic function resumes. A gradual recalibration process occurs over the next few days, but right away, the person feels lighter and cleaner and will likely sleep very well that night. As previously mentioned, this may not last long if the victim returns to a toxic environment after the cleansing.

Do not forget to pull in your bubble of sacred space once your work is completed. You can do this with or without the victim present. Take in a deep breath, raise your arms upward, and feel the white light begin to pour into your hands from all around you. Once it is all drawn in, drop your hands to your sides and release the white light into the earth beneath you, thanking it for its protection.

The Recuperation Period

It is rational to think that if a person has an energetic infiltrate like a curse, hex, crossing, entity, past attachment, or other issue, removing the problem would be the cure-all. In truth, it is just the beginning. Now the true healing begins!

During the cleansing or immediately after, the victim may feel slightly disoriented, dizzy, or spacey. People are used to certain energy flows and components and when those change—even if they contained unhealthy components—it is natural to respond to the shift.

Offer the person you just cleansed some tea, juice, or something to pep them up a bit if needed. Some just want water—*lots* of water. Washing their hands in cool water, holding dark stones, and eating a non-sugary food can help ground any excess energy. The victim may want to sit for a little while, put their head back, and let their energy readjust. Some are excited, energized, and very chatty. Taking the time to be responsive to the victim's needs after the cleansing is an important part of the healer's participation in the process.

If the cleansing is extensive, the victim may have purging symptoms such as nausea, vomiting, sweating, or diarrhea over the next few days. This is most common if there was a heavy level of contamination or if they had the curse or hex with them for a long time. The purging process may even happen twelve to twenty-four hours after the cleansing.

The body recognizes that something that was incorporated into the system was abruptly removed—even though it was a contaminant—so the mind, body, and spirit go into high alert. When pulling out the infiltrates, other scraps of negativity may fall away. The body rejects those free-floating radical bad things, and they must come out somehow! As an energetic healer, I try to clear out as much as possible while working with the victim's system, but what I shake loose is not always visible in the initial cleanup and can release later, after the person is away from my care. Flu-like symptoms are the body's attempt to rid itself of remaining toxins.

At best, a person feels clean, light, and energetic after a cleansing. Most people sleep very well the night after they have their cleansing, but in the days that follow, there may be sleep disturbances. Once remnants of the attack are removed from a person's system, messages sent by their spirit guides that were blocked by the curse, hex, crossing, or entity come flooding in. The conscious mind may be too distracted to accept and interpret those signals, but the unconscious mind is wide open during sleep. The effects of this can range from strange dreams to waking visions or disturbing memories that surface without warning. This is especially true if the victim's egg reading pointed to spirit guides attempting to help from the other side of the veil. It is usually a matter of adjusting to the pathways now opened to a person's higher self and spirit guides. The psychic chatter is likely to wane after the initial recovery period, and the sleep disturbances usually resolve themselves.

The newly cleansed person may be more emotional than usual, responding to experiences to a greater degree than others feel they should. Remember that for some people, their fight/flight/ freeze response was in full activation for weeks, months, or even years. Without that response fueling them, they may feel a loss of energy when the constant flow of adrenaline is no longer pumping through them.

The person may feel fatigued and sleep an unusual amount, or they may feel more activated and plugged in so that it is difficult for them to wind down and sleep. In either case, this is the body adjusting to a change in energy flow. Within a few days, the person will adapt to a new normal without the hindrances they had before and sleep patterns will normalize.

After a physical surgery, patients are not expected to come out of the operating room ready to take on the world. There is an understandable rehabilitation time. Recovering from psychic attack is the same. It is essential that the victim prepare for intense self-care, rest, and comfort strategies during the days immediately following the cleansing. They should drink plenty of fluids, rest, eat foods they love, spend time alone or with people who help them thrive, meditate, and reflect.

It is reasonable to think that an entire catalog of treatments for the various maladies we have discussed would live in these pages, but truly, a spiritual cleansing is the best treatment for psychic attack. Uncrossing baths, candles, and other items are helpful, but they are akin to putting a bandage on a deep wound. Eventually, a cleansing needs to occur for full healing to take place.

Ideally, people have frequent spiritual cleansings so that incidental infiltrates and attacks do not sneak up on them. If you take time to work with your own energy via meditation, you quickly become familiar with it, which helps you identify foreign energy faster. Again, infiltrations are not always insidious or malicious— sometimes they are the result of being in the wrong place at the wrong time. Infiltrations may even be past traumas that you thought were long healed; they may reactivate for further attention because you are ready to learn lessons from them. Receiving these experiences with grace and acceptance allows you to grow and learn more about who you are and why difficult experiences happened the way they did.

Regular energetic cleansings not only remove infiltrates, they also keep your chakras clean and dispel dense energies as they accumulate. Like a visit to the dentist, you should not wait until you are in pain to seek help. Instead, once the pain starts, you should address it immediately.

Disposing of the Egg

If someone sends energy to another person in the form of a psychic attack, where does the energy go after it is taken out of the victim? From my observations, the energy remains contained in the jar of blessed water with the egg until it changes form.

Leave the egg contents in the jar until everything dies off. It is easy to see when the elements captured in the egg and subsequently released into the jar of water expire. Usually, they will disconnect from the yolk and float to the surface of the water or collapse over the yolk and appear dead. When the infiltrates first go into the water, they have a shimmery, iridescent appearance and move easily when the jar is touched; sometimes they even move of their own accord. Once they die off, the component that was the white of the egg does not move, even when jiggling the jar. This dying off process may happen quickly, within an hour or so, or it may take several days.

I call it "dying off" because it takes on the appearance of neutrality and surrender. What was once glimmering and active in the jar turns from an opalescent, gossamer color to a pale white opaqueness. It no longer hovers over the yolk, which it believed to be the victim, but instead breaks away. If what was in the jar looked alive initially, it will now look quite dead.

When you open the jar to dispose of the egg, it often feels like it has been sealed shut. It is often harder to open than it should be. I use two-part canning jar lids and the ring separates easily, but the lid often remains attached to the jar and must sometimes be pried off. You can talk about gasses that build up as an egg breaks down in water, but that does not explain why some egg jars are easier to open than others because by that theory, all eggs should behave the same way in water.

When I take off the lid, there is a whooshing sound. I have learned to shield myself and the immediate area from the energies that could emerge before I remove the lid. I do that by envisioning that the room I am in is a steel-lined safe room that nothing can penetrate.

I then flush the egg and the water down the toilet, starting the flush first and then dropping the egg into the moving water. By tradition, the egg should be released into a moving body of water, and flushing is exactly that. If the toilet is connected to a septic system, the energy remains contained within the septic tank. If the toilet is part of a sewage system, the egg eventually finds its way to open waters. Regardless, it is carried away by moving water. Some healers prefer to bury the egg away from the client in a place where it will not be disturbed.

Either way, the egg will eventually make its way underground, putting layers of dirt between the victim and the energy that was in the egg. The egg ultimately does what an egg that was in a jar of water for a few days would do if you flushed it. The energy, however, gets neutralized by the dirt around it. The energy disperses into the ground, where it can cause no harm. The egg truly always was just an egg; it became the vehicle for the energy that was in the person just as the jar became the containment system.

I prefer to release the egg out of the presence of the victim. Even if it has been several days since the cleansing, there could still be remnants of the energy in the jar that might find their way back to the victim if they are present; after all, they are the familiar host.

The Risk of Re-Infiltration

By the time a person seeks help for psychic attack, the curse, crossing, entity, or hex has usually been there for a while, mostly due to the natural inclination to dismiss the idea of an attack. At that point, the effects probably feel uncomfortable but familiar to the victim; removing a psychic attack may feel invasive. Once it is gone, the victim sometimes feels a sense of longing or unease in its absence, much like when a decayed tooth is removed. The victim might understand it was not good for them, but once it is gone, things feel odd and a bit off—something is missing.

Nature abhors a vacuum, and when a person notices the absence of something, they will usually work to replace it (consciously or subconsciously). This means that people who truly experienced a psychic attack and then had it removed from them may inadvertently draw the curse back or pull in something that feels similar to it. In its own way, this creates wholeness since the person registers a vacancy in their energy. Because of this tendency, victims are vulnerable to re-infiltration.

Another danger is the very real likelihood of a subsequent attack. I have admittedly angered people enough that once I am clean and free of their attack, they reload their psychic guns and fire again. If the psychic attack was a deliberate curse or hex and the person who sent it is still living, they will probably notice, especially if they have experience tracking energy movement. It is the consensus of the healers I have worked with over the years that when you remove magical work from a victim, the attacker feels the energy release and fall. It feels like standing on the edge of a cliff holding a rope with someone hanging onto the other end and then suddenly feeling the rope go slack.

When an attacker recognizes that their spell work is no longer hooked into the victim—or better yet, comes back to them with a "return to sender" stamp on it—the usual approach is to reattack. Sometimes this occurs within the first twenty-four hours and other times it takes years for the attacker to figure out that their spell work is no longer active. The timing of the attacker's response depends on how obsessively focused they are on the victim and how many distractions they have in their lives.

For the most part, setting up effective protective energy around the victim is enough to ward off future attacks and keep the person safe. I will discuss some of those protective devices in chapter 14.

Recontamination

In addition to repeated attacks and the tendency to draw in similar energy, there are also victims that return to the same toxic environment or influences that damaged them in the first place. If you cleanse a person of the anger they feel from an abusive relationship and they go right back to the abuser, they will quickly become contaminated again. If they work in a hostile environment, you can burn candles and use other energetic tools to attempt to mitigate the negative feelings, but it is likely they will still undergo exposure and become recontaminated. If they surround themselves with people who take advantage of them, say hurtful things, and cause them to feel minimized but refuse to distance themselves from those people, they will likely become recontaminated.

I recently explained this to a client by telling her that I could clean her up and dress her in her finest dress, but if she went out and jumped in a mud puddle, the cleansing would no longer matter. Even if I thoroughly cleansed her, if she got back into that mud puddle, she would be just as dirty as before.

The victim receives some temporary respite from the toxic energies you remove, but once they reexpose themselves to the negative influences that previously harmed them, they will quickly revert to their attacked state unless they make significant life changes. Ideally, the victim will take advantage of the clarity and strength brought on by the cleansing to make changes that remove or reduce negative influences in their life. A victim's intense resolve to stay strong and not be influenced by toxic forces is pretty much useless—over time, even the best resolutions wear down if nothing on the outside changes to meet the needs of the inside.

CHAPTER FOURTEEN

PROTECTION AND RETRIBUTION

Because of the threat of recontamination or a subsequent attack, some cases require that the victim work aggressively to protect themselves from incoming energies. As with shielding, protection methods may restrict outward-flowing energy as they work to keep incoming energy at bay. Protection techniques need not be invasive or complicated to be effective. The following are some simple techniques that help ward off subsequent attack and change the energy of a space to complement the new energy flowing inside the victim.

Protection

You can usually thwart the threat of subsequent attacks and recontamination by employing strong energetic protection around the person. I give my clients protective amulets to carry and have them use sprays and baths to increase the protective energy around them. Protective candles, oils, and boundary products such as red brick dust and graveyard dirt are effective at warding off further attacks.

A popular protective amulet is a mojo bag containing stones, herbs, oils, and charms enchanted to provide protection to the victim. Stones such as malachite, black tourmaline, and obsidian are protective and can deflect psychic attacks. According to legend, malachite will break in half if the owner is under threat. (And yes, I have seen this happen in real life!) Another option is the aquatic Asian plant *Trapa bicornis*, which has a pod that invariably takes on the shape of a demon head, called a "bat pod" or "demon pod." These convey strong protection energies and are also very effective amulets to carry, especially when regularly polished with protective oil blends such as Run Devil Run or Fiery Wall of Protection. Carry the devil pod or protective mojo bag in your pocket, keep it in your car, or slip it into your pillowcase at night.

In my experience, most attacks are one-time hits. It is rare that a person is malicious enough to invest energy and attention into continued attacks. It does happen, though, and for that reason, you must stay vigilant after you relieve a victim of a heavy attack. You must also look for signs of re-infiltration or recontamination.

To effectively protect someone from psychic attack, look at where the potential victim spends their time. If they drive on a regular basis, protect their car. If they spend their days in an office, protect their desk area or cubicle. If they sleep at home or spend a lot of time there, protect the home. Offer to protect the places most occupied by the victim and then effectively protect all those areas.

For the at-risk victim, I recommend that they completely cleanse their house, then lay a protective grid around the home. (I will explain how to do this later in the chapter.) Sprays such as Fiery Wall of Protection and Florida Water can help keep the personal energies of the victim clean and protected. Hanging a Nazar amulet by the front door can help ward off negative energies.

When someone suffers a psychic attack, the air around them feels different and toxic, as if the energy of the attack exudes from that person's pores and breath. This contaminates bed linens, furniture, the physical structure of a home, and the air in it. When someone gets sick, their environment get sick. Psychic attack or energetic illness pervades into the victim's environment, and part of the healing process involves removing all traces of the energy of the attack from the places where they spend most of their time.

The ritual of cleansing and protecting the home is empowering and rewarding. When facing any type of psychic attack, it is normal to feel vulnerable and violated. Taking steps to cleanse and protect the home brings the power back to the victim and lets them take aggressive action to protect themselves. A proper cleansing infuses the home with a sense of peace and joy that is felt immediately. This is one of the few times that you do not have to wait to feel the magic at work for you.

Cleansing the Home

There are some differences between cleansing the home where a person has lived while under psychic attack and preparing an area to conduct an energetic cleansing as described in chapter 9, but the processes are very similar. The following techniques apply to houses, condos, apartments, or even rented rooms. Modify as needed.

I recommend cleansing when there are as few people in the home as possible. When I cleanse a home, I like as few active personal energies around as I can manage. This also eliminates the need to explain what you are doing to others, which can sometimes be embarrassing or uncomfortable.

You will need:

+ Four Thieves Vinegar
+ Chinese Wash
+ An unused sponge
+ White sage, cedar, sweet grass, sagebrush, or palo santo. If you absolutely cannot burn items to cleanse the air, Florida Water or smudging spray will suffice, but smoke is always better
+ A plate, shell, or other vessel to catch any cinders that fall
+ Three candles, one of each of the following colors: white, black, and your favorite color. These can be tapers, votives, columns, or jar candles, but in each case, you should devote the entire candle to the cleansing of the home and not use it for anything else. It does not matter if the candles are scented or unscented unless you have a negative reaction to scented candles. The color is what is integral to the process
+ Matches or a lighter

Four Thieves Vinegar and Chinese Wash are easily available online or in most botanicas and witchy shops. They are also quite simple to make yourself, and there are many recipes to be found online. Using authentic Four Thieves Vinegar and Chinese Wash that you purchase or make yourself is ideal, but if you are for some reason unable to obtain these products, you can substitute plain vinegar for Four Thieves Vinegar and liquid soap for Chinese Wash. You will not achieve a result on par with using the correct products, but it is better than nothing, and your intention will give the substitution a good boost.

When winter is over and the weather is mild enough to leave your doors and windows open, this brings a new and refreshing energy into the home. Use that sensation of freshness and change if you can. Cleansing can be done anytime of the year, so don't let cold weather deter you. However, weather permitting, open as many doors and windows as possible before starting to cleanse. This creates a flow of air and energy throughout the home.

Use the Four Thieves Vinegar and Chinese Wash exactly as described in chapter 9. Pour the product onto the sponge in a cross shape and wipe it directly onto doorjambs, windowsills, kitchen counters, and any other primary locations in the home. Four Thieves Vinegar comes first, followed by Chinese Wash.

If you have non-carpeted floors, put two tablespoons of Four Thieves Vinegar into a gallon of very hot water and use it to mop your floors. Dump the water, then put two tablespoons of Chinese Wash into a gallon of very hot water and mop your floors again. As you mop, imagine that you are removing the filth of the attack and making your home new again, essentially reclaiming it.

Once you complete the Four Thieves Vinegar and Chinese Wash cleanse, it is time to cleanse the air with sage, cedar, sweet grass, sagebrush, or palo santo. If the home has more than one story, start on the top floor. This includes attic space and upper crawl spaces if they are accessible. If the home is single story, start at either side of the front door. Some people will tell you that you must always cleanse in a clockwise direction, but I have not found this to be necessary at all. Move in the direction that feels most natural to you.

Light the white sage or other herb and make sure it is blazing well, then blow on the flame so that the smoke billows. With extreme focus, begin to "paint" the walls of the home with the smoke. Move the smoking herb up and down the walls, making sure to cover every section from ceiling to floor. Relight the herb as necessary. Remember to hold the plate or shell under your smoking herb to catch any burning product that falls. If you'd like, use a feather or fan to help waft the smoke across the walls.

Pay close attention to areas that feel dense, stale, or cold. These are often in closets, bathrooms, underneath the bed, or in places where furniture sits in the corner of the room, leaving an empty space behind it. Spend extra time at any areas of egress such as windows, doors, dryer vents, and heating and cooling vents. Continue wafting smoke until you have cleansed the entire house. If your house is single storied, you will end where you began. If the smoldering herb goes out while you are cleansing, simply relight it. A single sage stick is almost always sufficient to cleanse an entire house several times.

Next, find the area that you consider to be the heart of your home. This could be the fireplace, the kitchen island where people gather, the dresser in your bedroom, or another special place. Find a flat surface and set your three candles down. Light the black candle to absorb any further negativity. Light the white candle to imbue the home with purity. Light the candle of your favorite color to bless the home with your own energy. Then say, "This home is cleansed of all negativity and blessed with all that supports my greatest good. So be it."

Once you conclude the cleansing, allow the three candles to burn down until they self-extinguish, provided that you can safely do so. If the candle goes out and cannot be relit, then it has done its job and can be discarded. If the candle goes out on its own or you extinguish it for safety, it may be used again later to cleanse and bless the home. After the cleansing, it is time to set protective boundaries around the home.

Setting Boundaries Using a Power Grid

Once the cleansing with Four Thieves Vinegar, Chinese Wash, and protective herbs is completed as described above and the candles are burning, lay down a power grid to fully protect the home from outside energies. Imagine that you are creating a solid boundary to block out any who wish to harm the people and pets inside. To do this, you can build a fence made of energy, channeled through physical items.

Use iron nails or railroad spikes for the fence posts, placing one at each of the four corners surrounding the property you wish to protect, and drive them deeply into the ground so that the top is flush with the ground's surface. If you use nails, they do not have to be brand new or perfectly straight, but they should be made of iron. If you live in an apartment or communal home, you have a few options. You can lay the spike or nail in the inside corners of the home or you can follow the previous steps to protect the entire property, including those not involved in the attack.

Once the iron spikes or nails are in place, sprinkle a small amount of brick dust or black salt from one nail or spike to the next until you have drawn an entire boundary from nail to nail around the area you wish to protect. Brick dust is the dust from red clay bricks and black salt is a Hoodoo blend of components geared toward protection. You can purchase either of these items online or from any local botanica or magic shop. The brick dust or black salt acts as the fence boards with the nails or spikes providing anchorage at the corners.

You can also lay black salt or brick dust around the home itself, scattered over the thresholds and across the windowsills where energy can enter. If a threshold plate is removable, I recommend unscrewing the screws holding the plate in place and putting the brick dust or black salt under the threshold, then replacing the plate once again. This keeps routine sweeping and cleaning from disturbing the substance, which will continue to protect you just fine from underneath the plate. As you lay the black salt or brick dust, envision that it is an impenetrable boundary that none who wish ill to the inhabitants inside can cross.

Once all the brick dust and black salt is in place, close your eyes and visualize where the nails or spikes are located. See them glowing with activation. The energy of the iron at the four corners spreads through the brick dust or black salt, creating a power grid to protect your home.

Other Crafty Techniques

You can place small mirrors (like those inside makeup compacts) on the outside of your home, reflecting away from the building. The mirrors do not have to be visible; they can be behind bushes or lawn decorations. Arrange the mirrors in such a way that they do not encounter direct sunlight to avoid reflecting light into the eyes of nearby drivers or overheating grass or foliage in the area. I suggest three mirrors on each side of the home to represent mind, body, and spirit, the avenues of threefold law.

You can also place cat's eye shell or peacock tail feathers throughout the home. These act as guardians that watch over the protection grid and identify anything that tries to get through. Cat's eye shells are the shells of a small sea snail that look like the eye of a cat. I have a friend who wears peacock feathers in her hair with the "eyes" facing behind her so she can see if anyone is following her.

If you spend a lot of time in your car, a small wand tucked into the glove compartment provides protective energy.

Should You Seek Retribution?

When I validate a victim's fear that they have been cursed, most people immediately want to know who cursed them and if the curse was sent to them by a professional Witch. Truly, knowing who sent the curse does not matter. It does not change the effect or the treatment. All three of my mentors were unanimous in their opinion on this, and I heartily agree.

Knowing who sent the curse could change the diagnostic approach because professional Witches often structure their spell so that a more insidious attack lies hidden under what appears to be a minor attack. This is a sophisticated maneuver that I rarely see, but just in case, when I work on a client that may be cursed, I dig deeply and check carefully.

As soon as the confirmation of an attack comes forth, you can almost see the gears turning and smell the smoke coming out of the victim's ears as they sift through their mental files to figure out who might have done such a thing to them. Some people have immediate ideas on the identity of their attacker: "Was it my ex-sister-in-law? It was her, wasn't it? I should have known. She always was shady." In my experience, I often see more energy going into identifying the culprit than in rebuilding life after a psychic attack.

When I treat someone for any form of psychic attack, I do not offer the service of discovering who is responsible for the attack. There are several reasons why I do not do this:

It's Easy to Be Wrong

Tracing a psychic attack back to its sender is one of the most difficult magical tasks a person can do. In some cases, the victim can look back through guided meditation to when their symptoms began and notice conflicts or traumas that occurred around that time, but it's almost impossible to know for certain. Occasionally, the person who attacked the victim will brag about what they have done, and that eliminates the guesswork.

Where Does It End?

In some cases, there may be multiple directions from which the attack originates. If a person has a rough month and manages to irritate several people in their world as a result, there may be multiple incidental crossings.

As with the Newtonian laws, if you have multiple sources of energy working toward one common target, the effect will be bigger. That being the case, if you create negative responses in ten different people, it creates a strong negative force aimed directly at you. Do you really want to launch a retaliatory attack against all the people who thought negative things about the victim?

If you are thinking about retaliating, there are so many layers to consider:

+ If someone is angry enough to hire a professional energy worker to curse you, do you go after the energy worker who did the work or only the person who hired them? Or both?

+ If someone plans to curse you and talks to your mutual friend about it and the mutual friend says, "I agree. Their behavior is unforgivable and I think you should curse them," do you go after the mutual friend as well?

+ What about the shop owner who sold the attacker the tools to do the spell work? Or the YouTube personality who made the video describing how to curse someone?

✦ What if your symptoms are from an incidental crossing from someone you do not even know? Do you attack a stranger simply for getting angry?

You can hire a professional, use your own intuitive powers, use divination tools such as a pendulum or tarot readings, or trace energy patterns back to their source to try and determine who cursed you. However, in any of those cases, it is little better than a guess. Chances are, you could identify the wrong person. At best, you might not identify all the people who are culpable for the psychic attack.

Let It Go and Rebuild

I always recommend that my clients let go of the ambition to find out the identity of their attacker and instead use that energy to heal and rebuild their life. If there is a subsequent attack, then better protection and a stronger reaction are certainly needed. In that case, there are specific protection techniques later in this chapter that may be useful.

As mentioned in the discussion on Witch wars in chapter 1, living well is often the best revenge. The intention of someone who launches a full psychic attack is to bring the victim to their knees and harm them visibly and discernibly. Rarely does an aggressor seek a "behind closed doors" effect. A person who deliberately attacks someone wants to see the victim brought down in a public and obvious way.

When an attacker sees results of their work, they will likely continue it. For those who stoop to the level to psychically attack another person, there is pleasure in the downfall of their victim. They like disadvantaging the victim and creating hardship and will likely take credit for any misfortune that befalls their target. Seeing the victim's hardship makes the attack even more delicious, and the attacker feels like a puppet master pulling strings to get a reaction.

When a victim talks about being attacked and how horrible it was and all they endured, word is sure to travel to the aggressor, who will no doubt be delighted and gratified by the news. In posting all your woes on Facebook, trust me, the attacker will hear about it and receive an emotional payoff. If, however, the victim handles the attack discreetly, removes the influence, and grounds or returns the energy without making their circumstances public, the aggressor receives no reward for their efforts.

If the attack is managed outside of the public eye and there is no sign of the victim's disadvantages, the attacker will eventually grow bored. Like a toddler throwing a fit, they may escalate their efforts at first, but they will quickly tire out and some other shiny item will catch their attention. As difficult as it is, no reaction or minimal reaction is always the best approach, especially if you have conscientiously followed the instructions in this chapter to cleanse and protect your home and yourself.

People are often prone to drama and when they are in crisis, it is natural to want to solicit support and sympathy from others. Unfortunately, this results in excessive discussion of the attack, which gives it more power. The more that the attack is downplayed and calmly managed, the greater the chances are that it will taper off and the chances of a repeat attack are considerably reduced. While retribution seems attractive in the short term, overall it is ill-advised if your desired outcome is peace and a productive quality of life.

Revisiting Retribution

With all that taken into consideration, there are instances where an attacker has nothing but time on their hands and malice on their minds. Some cases may call for retribution, especially in the case of repeated attacks. As the modified Wiccan adage says, "Do no harm, but take no shit." There comes a time when enough is enough and the other cheek is getting worn out from being turned.

Since, as previously mentioned, you usually do not know exactly who sent the attack, the best management is to send the energy back to where it came from, wherever that may be. By returning the energy to sender, you ensure that no one innocent gets harmed or caught in the energetic crossfire.

Reversing Candles

A reversing candle, available at most botanicas and magic shops, is a great tool for sending energy back to its source. The reversing candles I make are constructed of rolled beeswax with Fast Action oil on an inner rolled layer of red wax and Reversing oil rolled into an outer layer of black wax. These are traditional Hoodoo oils easily available online or at botanicas or magic shops.

Burn the candle on a small, round mirror about three to four inches in diameter. Focus on rolling the energy that was sent to the victim into a tight ball of power and let the candle hurl it back to its sender. This way, they get no more and no less than what they sent to the victim. If there was no attack, then there is no sender to receive the energy and it is grounded.

I recommend starting the burn of the reversing candle while the cleansing is taking place and allowing it to burn to completion afterward. This captures the essence of the attack and automatically follows the original trail back to the attacker.

Mirror Box

Another form of nonaggressive retribution is to use a mirror box. A mirror box forces the aggressor to confront their actions, examine their motives, and reconsider their behavior. It is the ultimate "Go to your room and think about what you have done!" spell.

I make my own mirror boxes by finding small boxes I like and lining the inside of the box with adhesive-backed mirror tiles, cutting the tiles to fit the inside of the box until the entire box is covered with mirrors. I purchase tiny plastic babies like the ones used in New Orleans–style king cakes; the baby represents the sender of the attack. (You do not need to know the identity of the sender.) I then put the plastic baby inside the mirror box and close it. Holding my hands approximately two or three inches away from the box, I focus my full attention on the sender(s) confronting their behavior and having the effects of it reflected back onto them. You can keep multiple babies in one mirror box and still achieve great results.

I leave the baby in the box and several times a day, I shake the box and say out loud, "Wake up, baby! Look at what you have done!" The baby comes out of the box when and if the victim tells me they have received some form of apology or amends from the aggressor. If no apology or atonement comes, I leave the decision for how long the baby stays in the box up to the client. As you might guess, I have a very large mirror box.

Binding

When a subsequent attack occurs or advanced protection is otherwise warranted, you may want to energetically prohibit the attacker from inflicting further damage onto the victim. The best way to do this is through some sort of binding that restricts how the aggressor can access or influence the victim.

There are many different binding spells used for this type of work, including the Witch's jar outlined in chapter 4. Most binding spells involve the use of an effigy to represent the aggressor, such as a poppet, and other tools that symbolically restrict movement. My own preference is duct tape. One can use cords, sigils, or binding powders as well.

I choose an appropriate effigy, usually a poppet, and energetically dedicate it to the aggressor. I roll the poppet into a tight ball and wrap it securely in several layers of duct tape. Then I draw binding sigils on the tape and put the ball into a secure enclosure such as a jar or other tightly closed container. If I use a jar, I might also bring the Witch's jar effect into play and add restrictive or banishing powders and oils, glass, snake oil, or other items. I then use a substance like superglue or E6000 adhesive around the inner ring of the lid to permanently affix it to the jar. Finally, I bury the jar or place it in a secure location.

Since I am a devotee of Santa Muerte, the Saint of Death, I will sometimes give the jar to her, explain the situation, and ask her to manage the offending party. I trust that she will adjudicate the situation fairly, so I confidently leave it in her hands. As the Saint of Death, Santa Muerte does not instantly or necessarily invoke a curse of death onto the target. Instead, she acts as an impartial higher power and renders appropriate justice.

Freezing

Another way to restrict a person's ability to harm is to use a freezer spell. I use a plastic baby like the ones used in the mirror box spell and dedicate it to the aggressor. Then I fill a small, sealable container with water and place the baby and a slip of paper with the aggressor's name on it in the water. I sometimes include banishing herbs, powders, or oils. The container goes into a freezer, and as the water freezes around the effigy, their ability to harm is substantially reduced. When the water freezes solid, the aggressor is energetically immobilized.

When I work a freezer spell on behalf of a client, I use a small container because the intention is that it will remain in my freezer indefinitely. If you suspect you may have the need for multiple freezer spells, you can write a name, initials, or other identifier on the top of the container with a permanent marker.

Some of the spells in my freezer have been there for over a decade. If you decide to work a freezer spell, be sure to think long-term regarding the ongoing storage of the container. To date, I have only ever disposed of a freezer spell with the permission of the client who ordered it.

Although this is an effective form of binding, if the container thaws the spell will be lifted. This makes power outages particularly inconvenient in terms of freezer binding. You can, of course, refreeze the container and the effects will be the same as they were before the thawing. However, it is important to know that while the container is thawed, there is a window of opportunity for a repeat attack.

To read this chapter makes it sound as though the process of recovering from psychic attack is more daunting than the psychic attack itself, and that is a reasonable assessment. The difference has to do with results. Psychic attack continues to produce increasingly negative results for as long as it remains in the victim. The steps taken to manage psychic attack—including the cleansing and aftercare—all work together to help the victim recover and have a better quality of life.

CHAPTER FIFTEEN

STAYING CLEAN

Since these attacks occur far more often than the average person realizes, how can we keep ourselves energetically healthy? When you think of the human energetic system and all the contributing factors to its health and wellness, you become aware of how your own actions and emotions facilitate an attack. This does not mean you should blame yourself for someone else's inability to control themselves—far from it. What it *does* mean is that you must take a conscious, active role in making certain that your life and your energy are inhospitable to psychic attack.

The Best Defense

If you know that you are in a profession or lifestyle that puts you at high risk for psychic attack, it is essential that you practice exemplary energetic hygiene. You may have heard it said that "the best defense is a good offense." As discussed in chapter 6, a psychic attack needs a place to grab on to, and your weaknesses provide that. If you have toxic people in your life, that is where the attack will enter. If you feel insecure about your body, your relationships, how you spend your time, the way you manage your emotions, your addictions, and so on, the psychic attack will latch on to those weaknesses and use them as the framework of the attack.

Keeping your side of the street clean, so to speak, and living a life of integrity and confidence is the best way to avoid psychic attack. This ensures that you have few people in your life who might impact you with low-vibing, negative energy. If you are around people who frequently resort to unkind, debasing, and abusive behavior (even self-abusing behavior), then your likelihood of experiencing energetic contamination is much higher.

You create defensible energy around you by taking responsibility for your own spiritual health. This does not ensure that a psychic attack will never occur, but it does cause some of the less-aggressive ones to quickly lose their grip on you or fail to connect at all. Here are some suggestions for how to discourage psychic attack and streamline your life so that if you do sustain an attack, you can quickly identify it and take action before much damage occurs.

Have Regular Spiritual Cleansings

People often ask me how often they need an energetic cleansing, and it really depends on how at risk you are for contamination. It's a bit like a visit to the dentist; if you keep your teeth clean with regular brushing and flossing between professional cleanings, your dental hygienist will not have to work so hard at your annual cleaning. If you never brush or floss, your teeth are going to be a wreck when it is time for your cleaning, you will need more extensive work, and it will be more uncomfortable.

The same is true for spiritual cleaning. If you practice good energetic hygiene, you will not need frequent spiritual cleansings unless you have a high-risk lifestyle, such as working as a counselor, prison guard, social worker, teacher, or another profession where you often encounter intense negative energy from others.

For most people, cleansing two or three times a year is a good schedule to follow. Again, adjust this expectation accordingly if you are frequently in the line of fire as part of your everyday life. You can decide if you feel the self-cleansing techniques are sufficient or if a professional cleansing is required.

Keep Your Home Clean and Sacred

Make your home into your sacred space and sanctuary, whether that home is a mansion or a tiny apartment. Surround yourself with items that stimulate your higher self and raise your energy. Honor your home by keeping it uncluttered and clean. Include representations of earth, air, fire, water, and spirit throughout your home. Eliminate or reduce the presence of people in your home who drain your energy or are abusive.

Move Your Furniture

It sounds simple and superfluous, but I recommend rearranging the furniture in your home as soon as possible after your spiritual cleansing, within twenty-four hours if you can. Rearranging your furniture not only shifts your environment, but it quite literally changes the path you walk. It creates a physical representation of new energy and new approaches to your circumstances. After moving the furniture, you must engage more fully when you navigate your daily routines. You overcome behavior habits and muscle memory reactions that normally take you through your day. This causes the same adjustments mentally and spiritually as it does physically.

Control Your Emotions

Magic comes from emotion. Action and reaction come from emotion. When you effectively manage your emotions, the payoff is that suddenly you are in complete control of your actions, reactions, thoughts, and—by extension—your magical work.

As most people know, controlling your emotions is easier said than done, especially if you suffer from a chemical imbalance or are naturally volatile. People feel what they feel, and many people respond to strong emotions with explosive reactions or suppress those emotions until they fester. Worry, guilt, envy, fear, and frustration are all messy emotions that contaminate your interactions with other people and the energy that you put out into the world. The more that you put techniques to assuage those emotions into practice, the more empowered you become and the closer you get to your most sacred self.

This is not to say that negative emotions do not exist and that you should suppress any sign of them. Instead, you can experience the emotion without allowing it to control you. My favorite tool for doing this is to imagine water flowing over rocks. It coats the rock and it might even change the rock over time, but the rock is firm and strong. "Water over rocks, water over rocks" is a phrase I use to calm myself if I start to feel emotional turbulence building.

When you let your emotions control and define you, you are at the mercy of your own greatest weaknesses. Emotions are like the weather; they will change. Stay with one for a while, see what gifts it has for you, and wait until another emotion comes along.

Practice Radical and Aggressive Self-Care

Get plenty of sleep. Drink as much good, clean water as you can hold. Limit your use of alcohol and recreational drugs. Honor your body with a balanced, healthy diet of whole foods, shunning refined and manufactured foods, sugar, trans fats, and other unhealthy foods. Limit screen time and get fresh air and sunshine at least once a day. Take good care of your skin and teeth every day. Seek competent mental health support to work through old traumas and personal insecurities.

When a client comes to me, I know they are likely in distress and possibly under attack. My priority is to treat them with integrity, respect, and kindness. Why is it often so hard for us to treat ourselves with the same integrity, respect, and kindness? We are often quick to comfort our friends and loved ones and yet leave our own needs unattended, trying to fit a quick battery of self-care into what little time we have leftover in our hectic lives.

An untended, overextended, exasperated spirit is an easy place for psychic attack to land and take hold. The more you take time to care for yourself and tend to your needs, the more impervious to attacks—especially incidental attacks—you become. That does not mean you should not care for others, but that you should be diligent about identifying your own needs and making time to honor them.

Set Firm and Reasonable Boundaries

Many of us suffer from the need to please and deplete our resources by trying to be all things to all people, working hard to never rock the boat or upset anyone. As I used to tell my daughter when she was very little, "Sometimes, the answer is just 'no.'" You are enough. If you must prove your worthiness to someone through servitude to them or by performing tasks you will later resent, then they do not need to be in your life (or the dynamic needs to seriously adjust).

Emotions such as guilt, feelings of inadequacy, and martyrdom are great breeding grounds for psychic attack to nestle into and set up housekeeping. Know yourself well and understand what you can and cannot do without overextending your finances, physical energy, and time. Set the boundary and lovingly stand by it.

Meditate

The most spiritually significant act you can incorporate into your life is meditation. I hear so many people tell me they cannot do it and the moment they say the words, I know they do not know what meditation is. Meditation is not complete mental silence without thought or impression. It is stillness. It is listening. It is paying attention. It is passivity rather than activity.

Take a minimum of fifteen minutes a day to be alone with yourself, turning off all electronic devices and removing all potential distractions. Find a comfortable position and take several deep, cleansing breaths. Breathe in goodness and breathe out toxicity. Slow your normal breathing down while remaining in a comfortable respiratory state.

Let your thoughts fly around you, then feel them slow down. If one worry persists, tell it to wait and that you will be back to tend to it, then move it to the outer reaches of your thoughts.

Keep breathing. Track any unsolicited thoughts that come into your mind. Tell yourself to remember them. Listen to the sounds around you until you are part of the sounds around you.

Keep breathing. Manifest: "I am well. All is well with me. I am safe. All is safe with me. I am radiant. All is radiant with me."

Keep breathing.

There, you meditated. Over time, stretch this into twenty minutes, then thirty. Meditation shows you what *your* energy feels like, and this helps you to quickly and easily identify energy that comes to you from an outside source.

Purge Your External Life of Negativity

What people and situations drain your energy and zap your vitality? When you are stretched too thin by the patience you must show challenging individuals and the grace you must manifest under fire, it is easier to attract psychic attack and harder to recognize and fight it off when it occurs.

As I said in chapter 2, life happens. Things are rarely easy all the time. You will routinely have to deal with people who are hard to manage, and that will create anxiety and tension. Frustrating situations will happen. You are not required, however, to invite those people into your life. Don't let them take up valuable real estate rent-free. Do not allow abusive behaviors to continue. Distance yourself from the people who create hardship for you.

Take responsibility for your environment and the influences in it and work to create a healthier, more empowered day-to-day journey for yourself. It takes time and will likely not be done in a day, but the energy you invest into a life audit and purge is well worth the effort. When you purge your external life of negativity, your internal energy thrives.

Refuse to Say Your Attacker's Name

If you know the identity of your attacker, do not say their name once you are cleansed and free of their influence. Speaking of them gives them space in your new life, and they do not deserve that acknowledgment. Part of moving on from the experience involves putting the attack—and those associated with it—behind you. Refusing to speak the name of your attacker shows that they do not exist for you.

Remember that indifference is far stronger than anger or hatred. Relegate the attacker to the status of nonentity.

Carry a Protective Amulet with You

We discussed these at length in chapter 14. All protective amulets are as effective as the next. The amulet you carry should represent the power that *you* recognize as protective. It could be any of the previously mentioned stones, a hamsa, a Nazar, angel wings, a cross, a pentacle, or a saint medallion. Choose what feels right for you. The amulet serves as a comfort tool because it is a physical reminder of the protective energies that surround you.

Remember the Basic Points of Psychic Attack

Although we covered all of these in detail in previous chapters, it is good to reiterate:

1. Psychic attack usually comes from projected jealousy, a deliberate and active attack, or someone whose fear is so extreme that they create pervasive negative energy.

2. Psychic attack is invariably energy in (toxic energy received by the victim) or energy out (someone actively draining the victim's energy).

3. You heal psychic attack by breaking the energy cord between the victim and the source of the attack and then blocking any further connection.

4. Removing the psychic attack does not undo all the damage caused by the attack. It simply prevents further damage from occurring. The victim must still heal and rebuild their life.

5. Part of rebuilding involves course correcting so that the victim is not as vulnerable to attack.

6. Refuse to participate in energy wars. When they go low, go high. Your focus should be on healing.

7. Return the attacker's energy back to them, even if they are not identified. If you think about it, this creates an ethical safety net. A person only gets back what they sent, which establishes balance in a previously imbalanced dynamic.

Based on my experience and information gathered from my peers in the spiritual healing community, I believe that most people will experience some form of psychic attack in their lifetime, probably on multiple occasions. The ability to effectively manage it can mean the difference between continuing to suffer or finding relief.

Life is complicated and imperfect. *People* are complicated and imperfect. Part of that imperfection is that people do not understand what they might do until they are in the circumstances to do it. You might think you know how you would respond in certain situations, but until that experience happens, you cannot be sure. People often surprise themselves.

A woman from my local Pagan community who previously cast a sideways glance at some of the magic I practice on the behalf of other people phoned me recently and said that she needed a Shut Your Mouth candle and a mirror spell. I was surprised to hear her ask for this because she is not usually aggressive with her magic and is what could be referred to as a "love and light" kind of person. During our conversation, she said to me, "Katrina, I would never have imagined I would feel this way or even need to have this conversation." That moment—when fear, desperation, anger, and resignation all come together into one motivating force—is the spot most people are in when they reach out to me. I see my clients at their lowest moments. No one contacts me and says, "Katrina, things are going really well right now. I want to do some magic to send some of this good energy to other people." People contact me when they are in crisis, not when they want to actualize.

Whether people are desperate because they are under severe attack or because they have exhausted all practical problem-solving methods and need to transition to energetic solutions, they come to people who work in my field when they are in crisis. They come to us to curse others, to bind someone to keep them from harming others, to return the energy someone sent to them, and to clean out the damage caused by psychic attack. In any of those cases, they come to us as a last-ditch effort.

It would be easy to categorize those who deliberately launch a psychic attack as cruel and insensitive, and it would be just as easy to label someone who endures frequent attacks as careless or weak. It is never that simple! To engage in this kind of limited thinking is short-sighted and comes from a position of tremendous privilege.

There are times when the legal system fails people or when, for reasons of safety and security, they cannot stand up for themselves or take reasonable measures to protect themselves on a physical level. Life is often unfair, and the weight of a rigged game weighs heavily on a person. Occasionally, there are people in our lives who cause harm, not just to us but to the ones we love. If you walked up on someone inflicting grievous harm on a person you loved and had a weapon at hand that would stop the attack, would you use it? You probably would. Magic is a defensive weapon that can be quite effective.

I used to say that for every action, there is an equal and opposite reaction. Sometimes *I* am that equal and opposite reaction. People blithely talk about karma and "what goes around, comes around" without even a casual thought for the idea that maybe *people* are agents of karma. Perhaps *we* are part of that divine process that balances the scales. Two of the most chilling curses I have ever heard were "May you live in interesting times" and "May you be given all that you deserve."

Psychic attack should not be taken lightly. I do not psychically attack people for fun. As I said before, even on behalf of a paying client, the cause is either justified or not justified. Professionally, I turn away more attacks than I launch or otherwise redirect the client to a better course of action. I know how to heal a person who has experienced a psychic attack, and I heal far more often than I participate in any kind of attack.

Whew! It Was Just a Curse!

When I take clients through the process of the interview and the energetic cleansing and then send them out into the world with items of protection, there is often a part of them that is relieved to know that the problems they were experiencing came from a curse or an entity. They might have a moment of fear, revulsion, and confusion, but ultimately, hearing "It isn't your fault" is a profound blessing.

While that might be worth a sigh of relief, the truth is that what they experienced *is* often their fault—at least partially. A curse, hex, crossing, or even an unintentional infiltration needs a place to grab on to in order to do the most damage to a person. It seeks out weaknesses and finds the unguarded parts of people, the places where they are most vulnerable. If you are falling apart at the seams with a life that is poorly managed, psychic attacks—whether deliberate or incidental—can have a field day. That is how they manage to go undetected for so long in some cases. How can you discern an entity that is wreaking havoc on your personal relationships if your personal relationships are already struggling? How does a hex that drains away your prosperity stand out in your life if you are terrible at managing your money?

The very knowledge that there are entities, curses, hexes, and crossings out there that can create hardship in your life demands that you pay attention to the patterns of your joys and misfortunes. When you have your life in order, you can tell when something feels off. You can more easily manage the possibility of a psychic attack when you cannot find reasonable explanations for what you are experiencing.

The shadow side of the knowledge that these attacks are out there, seemingly spring-loaded to occur, is that some people will move in the opposite direction. Instead of concluding that they are under psychic attack *after* they rule out all other possible reasons for why their life went sideways, they jump to it immediately and ignore their own accountability in the challenges they experience.

As chapter 2 suggests, not all misfortune is an attack. One of the symptoms of a psychic attack is a series of unfortunate events that come one after the other. The trick is in identifying what is a psychic attack and what is a result of poor life choices. No one is perfect; we all have weaknesses. But some people incorporate feelings of shame around their weaknesses; they hang their head and placidly accept any negative outcomes. Others jump at the chance to use the idea of a psychic attack as the reason why nothing works out for them. As soon as they experience any kind of misfortune or negative results for their poor choices, they proclaim that they must be under attack and begin assembling the support they need to remove the curse or hex.

Psychic attack is not a fascinating toy to play with. It is not meant for exacting your revenge when you are too cowardly to face your problems. When you are in an untenable situation that can be managed in no other way, it is an option to consider. Psychic attack is a reminder that words and emotions have power and that you are accountable for the damage your words and emotions can cause. It is a reminder to keep your side of the street clean so that you can quickly discern when something is awry in your energy field. It is not an excuse, a joke, or a crutch to lean on to explain away the results of your own poor choices.

Take Back Your Power Eggs

Some Witches believe in the duality premise that if you are going to cure others, you must know how to curse. If you are going to heal, you must know how to hex. There is, of course, a big difference in knowing how to do something and in doing it all the time. Ultimately, you are the steward of your own power and you are accountable for where your energy goes.

When a person convinces themselves that misfortune must be from a curse and then tries to deconstruct the situation to figure out who cursed them so they can exact their revenge, they are giving their power away rather than taking hold of it. True power comes from identifying your flawed, vulnerable parts and working to shore them up. It comes from intimately knowing your own energy so that an infiltration is immediately identifiable. It comes from having the courage to admit who is and is not an appropriate investment of your time and attention. True power comes from feeling your authentic emotions without allowing them to control your reactions.

One of my mentors used to talk about a Native American legend regarding power eggs. He said that each of us comes into the world holding a limited number of power eggs. You give those power eggs away to each person who you allow to control you in some way. You give a power egg to the adult child that you coddle, and through your hovering, you keep them from learning to problem-solve and take pride in their own accomplishments. You give a power egg to the spouse who berates you and works to make you feel as if you are less than. You give a power egg to the boss who promotes less-qualified people over you and refuses to acknowledge your successes at work. You give a power egg to the sibling who bullied you as a child and now makes you feel like you are five years old and subjugated at every family gathering.

If you are not careful, you will run out of power eggs and have no control for yourself. You will give your entire power base over to others to hold. My mentor would shake his finger at me and say, "Know when to take back your power eggs."

Understanding the finer details of psychic attack gives you a basket where you can hold those power eggs. By knowing your energy, protecting your home, surrounding yourself with healthy relationships, and keeping your energetic system clean and healthy, you can recover from psychic attack and traumas of the past and prevent future disruptions in your ongoing journey toward your greatest good.

To Write to the Author

If you wish to contact the author or would like more information about this book, please write to the author in care of Llewellyn Worldwide Ltd. and we will forward your request. Both the author and publisher appreciate hearing from you and learning of your enjoyment of this book and how it has helped you. Llewellyn Worldwide Ltd. cannot guarantee that every letter written to the author can be answered, but all will be forwarded. Please write to:

Katrina Rasbold
℅ Llewellyn Worldwide
2143 Wooddale Drive
Woodbury, MN 55125-2989

Please enclose a self-addressed stamped envelope for reply,
or $1.00 to cover costs. If outside the U.S.A., enclose
an international postal reply coupon.

Many of Llewellyn's authors have websites with additional information and resources. For more information, please visit our website at http://www.llewellyn.com.